THE
UNEXPLAINED

A SOURCE BOOK

This is a Flame Tree Book
First published in 2003

01 03 05 04 02

1 3 5 7 9 10 8 6 4 2
Flame Tree Publishing
Crabtree Hall, Crabtree Lane, Fulham,
London, SW6 6TY, United Kingdom
www.flametreepublishing.com

Flame Tree is part of
The Foundry Creative Media Company Limited

Copyright © 2003 Flame Tree Publishing

ISBN 1 904041 41 8 trade edition
ISBN 1 904041 97 3 plc edition

A copy of the CIP data for this book is available from the British Library

Printed in China

THE UNEXPLAINED

A SOURCE BOOK

Karen Hurrell & Brenda Ralph Lewis

INTRODUCTION: Brendan Kilmartin

**FLAME TREE
PUBLISHING**

CONTENTS

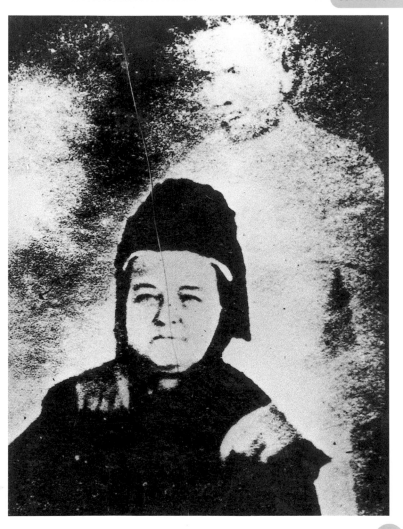

INTRODUCTION

I grew up in the presence of a phenomenon that today still poses un-answered questions. Stonehenge has been described as a 'wonder of the world'. To see huge stones of 60 tonnes and upwards, laid in a geometrically simple plan, was both bizarre and fascinating. It's this wonderment at unexplained phenomena that has held people's imaginations for centuries.

Paranormal and unexplained phenomena have been a part of social and religious life for many centuries, from painted inscriptions on cave walls apparently depicting visitors from other worlds, to prophets claiming to hold the future's secrets. As science has progressed, so have the explanations. Science, however, has not always been a fundamental part of people's lives, and because of this, many naturally occurring phenomena – which today we take for granted and can explain – were seen as either paranormal or supernatural.

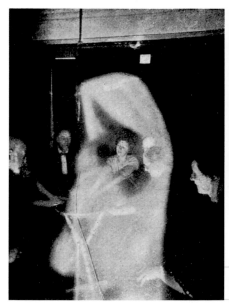

In the past, mythical creatures played a large part in people's cultures. Vampirism, for example, plagued villages for decades. The escaping gases and muscle spasms of a decaying body were seen as signs that the body lived on in death, and so the 'Vampire' legend was born. People's belief in the occult was so intense they believed their pets to be cursed. Many false beliefs, including witchcraft, were fuelled by a general lack of understanding about the world. During the Middle Ages, ignorance of the cause of diseases such as the plague led people to believe that something sinister was occurring, such as curses being placed on individuals or families who sickened or died. Women considered by the community to be 'eccentric' were blamed for outbreaks of disease and sudden deaths and branded as witches, before being burned at the stake in order to eliminate any trace of evil curses.

The paranormal has played a large role in religions throughout the world for centuries, and in numerous cases continues to do so. Although the Christian Church today would rather ignore unexplained phenomena, this has not always been the case. In the past, the Catholic Church helped individuals who believed they were possessed by demons. A visiting clergyman would carry out an exorcism to rid the person of their demons. This practice, however, is now very rare, and is generally frowned upon. The Turin Shroud, discovered in Italy in 1578, is a mystery that has been studied for centuries and still seems to defy explanation. According to those who believe the shroud to be genuine, the face depicted on this simple piece of woven cloth is that of Jesus Christ. The shroud has been subjected to numerous experiments and examinations, but remains as much a mystery today as it was when it was first discovered. The weeping Madonna is another mystery that remains unresolved. In 1954 in a church in Siracuse, Sicily, a statue of the Virgin

◄ *LEFT: Flash photograph taken during the Warrick-Deane series on 23 June 1924. In the foreground, a materialised form is just about to dematerialise.*

▶ *RIGHT: Death by 'preternatural combustlability'.*

Mary was said to have wept tears. So profound was the impact of this at the time that the Vatican actually authenticated the event. Numerous cases similar to this have been recorded all over the world, with some statues reported to be weeping blood. We can now offer scientific explanations of these occurrences, but people still believe that statues do actually weep.

Although we have a greater understanding of the world around us, not all unexplained phenomena can be easily explained away as natural occurrences. Because of this, the paranormal and supernatural play as big a role in our lives today as they did for our ancestors, albeit with a slightly different emphasis. People's fascination with the unexplained is unquenchable, and with so many mysteries remaining unsolved, this continues to be the case.

The media ensures that our appetite for the unexplained remains as strong as ever: never a week goes by without reports of crop circles appearing, or a strange beast being sighted, and films such as *ET* and *Close Encounters Of The Third Kind* tantalize us with the possibility of other life in the universe. Today, the prospect that life may exist on other planets is one of the most intriguing of all unexplained mysteries, to the extent that stories of alien life, UFO sightings and abductions take a central role in some people's lives.

Children today are subjected to every possible phenomena known to us, whatever their culture, whatever their race, and they grow up in a world that knows no bounds. They play with toys depicting creatures that are yet to be discovered, they watch cartoons about inter-planetary space travel, and they take school trips hoping to catch a glance of the Loch Ness Monster, a cuddly little creature in their eyes; the reality, I think, would be very different.

Such is the intense interest in any unexplained event that people will always hold a fascination for the supernatural. It's in our nature to be inquisitive, to want answers to things that defy explanation. Perhaps science will one day solve age-old riddles of sea monsters, lights in the sky and haunted houses, but until it does the desire we hold for this intriguing subject will remain.

The Unexplained is a definitive guide to every aspect of the supernatural world. Whether you have previous knowledge, or whether you are simply inquisitive, this book is sure to grab your attention and show you why people have been in awe of the unexplained for thousands of years, and why our interest in it seems to grow, unabated, as the years progress.

BRENDAN KILMARTIN
thesupernaturalworld.com
2003

GHOSTS AND GHOST-HUNTING

WHAT IS A GHOST?

The word 'ghost' conjures up an instant impression in most people's minds, and although there is little hard evidence of the existence of ghosts, they form part of the belief system of virtually every culture in the world. But what is a ghost? According to most contemporary definitions, a ghost is considered to be the spirit of a dead person, capable of making itself seen, felt or heard by the living. Frederic W. H. Myers, one of the founders of the Society for Psychical Research (SPR) in London in 1882, defined a ghost as a 'manifestation of persistent personal energy, or as an indication that some kind of force is being exercised after death which is in some way connected with a person previously known on Earth'.

Precise definitions as to whether ghosts can feel, or whether they have any awareness of their surroundings, varies between cultures. In some parts of the world people believe that ghosts are conscious entities, while others have concluded that they are automatic projections of consciousness with intellectual centres elsewhere. Modern researchers tend to agree that some ghosts have an awareness, and that they can be experienced by people unknown and unrelated to the deceased. The word ghost is widely used, but parapsychologists – those who study mental phenomena that are excluded from, or inexplicable by, conventional psychology – favour

LEFT: *Frederic W. H. Myers, one of the three prominent founding members of the Society for Psychical Research (SPR).*

the term 'apparition', although only a small percentage of cases involve visual images. Most ghostly encounters involve an entity making its presence known through smells, cold or hot air, moving objects and noises. The majority of sightings investigated have perfectly natural explanations. However, around two per cent of sightings have no explanation. Psychical researchers cannot dismiss the fact that ghosts, in one form or another, may exist.

◆ See Ghost Watchers p. 18; Who Sees Ghosts? p. 21

▶ RIGHT: A photograph by William Hope, a leading spirit photographer of the early twentieth century. As is typical of his work a 'spirit extra' can be seen.

GHOSTLY CONTACT

An overwhelming 82 per cent of apparitions appear in order to communicate something. A warning of imminent danger, comfort for the grieving, conveying information or simply demonstrating an emotional tie to the site are all common. Some apparitions are believed to be spirits of the dead, trapped by unfinished business on Earth. Apparitions that do not respond to communication have led scientists to believe that they are psychic recordings of an event.

TYPES OF GHOSTS

Ghosts or apparitions can be broadly categorised as follows:

- Crisis apparitions: this is the most common type. Many bereaved people claim to have seen an apparition of a relative when the relative was on the point of death. In 1917, for example, a British woman, Dorothy Spearman, claimed to see her half-brother. She later discovered that his plane had been shot down in Germany at the exact moment that he had appeared to her.

- *Doppelgänger*, or Double: many people claim to have seen their exact doubles appear as apparitions. Empress Catherine of Russia saw hers sitting on her throne and ordered her guards to shoot.

▶ RIGHT: *The ghost of Anne Boleyn has frequently been seen on Christmas Eve walking over the bridge to the grounds of Hever Castle.*

- Restless spirits: this type of ghost forms the basis of most sightings. Unsettled spirits supposedly continue to haunt their old homes until they are laid to rest. In 40 BC in Athens, the philosopher Athenodorus heard the sound of rattling chains and saw the ghost of an old man disappearing into the garden. When the garden was dug up the skeleton of a man in chains was discovered. When the bones were properly buried, the haunting ceased.

- Cyclic ghosts: these appear on the same day each month or year. Every 24 December, for example, the ghost of Anne Boleyn, second wife of Henry VIII, is alleged to appear at her childhood home, Hever Castle in Kent.

- Psychic recording ghosts: these spirits replay an event from their lifetime, and do not respond to human intervention. One of the best-known cases occurred in York in 1953, when Harry Martindale claimed to have seen a legion of Roman soldiers marching through the cellar of the Treasurer's House in which he was working.
- Poltergeists: these are noisy spirits or malevolent energy characterised by noises, moving objects and physical disturbances. Various theories have been suggested to explain their existence.
- Deathbed apparitions: the appearance of angelic beings, religious figures and dead loved ones is often reported by the dying shortly before death.
- Marian apparitions: visions or supernatural manifestations of the Virgin Mary.

See Crisis Apparitions p. 47; Dream Visions p. 48; Miracles p. 113; Poltergeists p. 51

CHARACTERISTICS OF GHOSTS

American sociologist and psychical researcher Hornell Hart noted the following major features of apparitions in a 1956 study:

- There are no significant differences between apparitions of the living and of the dead.
- Some apparitions seem real and solid (corporeal), with definable form, features and clothing (if human); other apparitions are luminous, transparent and ill-defined; others comprise streaks or patches of light.
- Apparitions appear and disappear suddenly, sometimes fading away.
- They move through objects and walls, or walk around them. Despite contemporary mythology, they can be reflected in mirrors and cast shadows.
- Some ghosts or apparitions are able to communicate verbally, while

others use gesticulation to make their message (if there is one) known.

- In many cases, witnesses claim that their hands pass through the apparition when they try to touch it.
- Many ghosts are accompanied by sounds, smells and a feeling of cold, and some have the ability to move real objects – making them appear much more tangible.

See Audible Ghosts p. 50; Olfactory Ghosts p. 50; Tactile Ghosts p.51

BELIEF IN GHOSTS

Ghosts or apparitions form part of the religion, mythology or folklore of almost every culture worldwide. The ancient Hebrews, Greeks and Romans believed that the souls of the dead could return to haunt the living. Romans called evil ghosts *lemures*; the spirits of virtuous people were known as *lares*.

Christian societies believe that the soul departs for heaven or hell. Thus, ghosts or the 'undead' are viewed as being unnatural and frightening. This is not so in other cultures. The Chinese, for example, believe in at least two aspects of the soul, which accounts for the fact that the dead can make their presence felt in more than one place.

In Asia, belief in ancestral ghosts is still strong, with rituals to honour and placate them. The Chinese believe that ancestral ghosts can be dangerous and are responsible for the luck and prosperity of individuals on Earth. These spirits intervene regularly in the affairs of the living to guide the course of human life.

▶ RIGHT: *The Chinese entertain and placate the spirits of their dead ancestors through prayer, the burning of joss sticks, and concerts and shows in their honour.*

According to a 2002 survey, 57 per cent of people in the UK believe that ghosts, phantoms and supernatural apparitions exist. According to these statistics, more people believe in ghosts than in God.

See Ghosts in Primitive Cultures p. 282; International Ghost Festivals and Beliefs p. 284

GHOSTS IN HISTORY

In the Dark Ages, people believed in demons, vampires and other frightening spectral creatures. By the Middle Ages, belief in ghosts was influenced by the Christian Church, which taught that ghosts were souls trapped in purgatory until they had been cleansed of their sins.

In seventeenth-century Europe, the dead were considered advisors to the living, used to see that justice was done. Ghosts became less popular in the eighteenth century, during the Romantic movement, but such

▲ ABOVE: A ghastly image from the imagination of the Dark Ages: a demon drags a child away having just paid his parents for his service.

beliefs experienced a renaissance in the nineteenth century with the advent of modern spiritualism, a system of religious beliefs centred on the presumption that communication with the dead is possible.

Spiritualistic practices, or *bhuta* worship, have a long history in India. Attempts to evoke the spirits of the dead are also recorded in ancient Near Eastern and Egyptian sources. In Assyria, evil spirits were called *utukku*. Many had no limbs, made terrifying wailing sounds and caused chaos. These ghosts were thought to appear because their burial rituals were incomplete or incorrect.

See Ghost Worship p. 283; Vampires p. 213

GHOST-WATCHERS

Systematic studies of ghosts began with the founding of the Society for Psychical Research (SPR) in London in 1882. Three of the SPR's founders – Edmund Gurney, Frederic Myers and Frank Podmore – questioned 57,000 people about apparitions of the living and published their findings in

Phantasms of the Living in 1886. In 1889, *the Census of Hallucinations* was produced under the direction of Henry Sidgwick, assisted by his wife Eleanor Sidgwick, Alice Johnson, Frederic Myers, A. T. Myers and Podmore. The census consisted of a single question: 'Have you ever, when believing yourself to be completely awake, had a vivid impression of seeing or being touched by a living being or inanimate object, or of hearing a voice; which impression, so far as you could discover, was not due to any external physical

◀ *LEFT: Members of the Birmingham Psychic Research Society inspect the haunted inn and home of Edward Westwood who refused to move back in while it was haunted.*

cause?' The SPR received 17,000 replies, of which 1684 (roughly 10 per cent) answered yes. There were 352 reported sightings of apparitions of the living and 163 reported sightings of the dead.

Other societies also began investigations of ghosts and other psychic phenomena, including the London Dialectical Society, formed in the late 1860s. When the SPR was formed in 1882, six research committees were established to investigate telepathy, mesmerism, hypnotism, clairvoyance, apparitions and hauntings, physical phenomena associated with mediums, and the collection and collation of data on these subjects.

In the 1940s, the SPR began to devote more attention to laboratory experiments and became active in the investigation of poltergeists and apparitions. Research articles continue to be published today in the *Journal and Proceedings*, while informal articles appear in the SPR's newsletter.

◪ *See* The GRS p. 19; Spiritualism p. 264

THE GRS
The Ghost Research Society (GRS) was founded in 1977 by Martin V. Riccardo, a Chicago hypnotherapist. The organisation was originally called the Ghost Trackers Club, and Dale Kaczmarek, a well-known psychical researcher, was named as its research director. The GRS researches, investigates and collects data on ghosts and related phenomena. The GRS holds one of the world's largest collections of spirit photographs and analyses them by computer. According to Kaczmarek, approximately 90 per cent of photographs have natural explanations. The GRS receives around 100 reports of ghosts and poltergeists each year, many of which take place in private residences. Most GRS members, including Kaczmarek, have seen enough evidence to conclude that ghosts do exist and that there is life after death.

◪ *See* Contacting the Dead p. 264

GHOST-HUNTERS

Investigators look for all possible natural causes, be they mechanical causes such as machinery, lights and road noises, or personal causes like tricks or effects caused by people. Investigators eliminate these causes by thoroughly evaluating a site, both day and night, taking into consideration historical research, geological conditions, construction activity at the time and press accounts of any hauntings.

Three basic techniques are used in investigation:
- The DESCRIPTION TECHNIQUE involves taking eyewitness accounts. Witnesses are interviewed separately, and their backgrounds, state of health and understanding of the paranormal are evaluated.
- The EXPERIMENTAL TECHNIQUE involves bringing in a medium or psychic who is asked to assess whether the eyewitness's story can be verified by his or her own impressions. A medium may be ushered around the house to point out places of activity (hot or cold areas of energy, for example), or a seance may be suggested.
- The DETECTION TECHNIQUE involves using electronic surveillance equipment (cameras, tape recorders, temperature sensors, Geiger counters, etc.), securing rooms to test for disturbance and setting up traps to detect footprints, for example.

See Ghosts Captured on Film p. 133; Mediums p. 266; Spiritual Activity p. 46

PRICE, HARRY

Harry Price was one of the first ghost-hunters in the UK. He was a British magician who used his knowledge of trickery to investigate hauntings and to decide whether or not they were hoaxes. After several years of investigative work, he came to the conclusion that ghosts did exist and during the 1930s he became the most famous ghost-hunter in the world.

He discovered several hoaxes committed by lonely people who manufactured ghosts to keep them company, and he was one of the first to use modern technology in his ghost investigations. Price's most successful and celebrated investigation took place at Borley Rectory, where he created a laboratory and conducted tests using 48 volunteers. Although his results were largely inconclusive, he wrote a book entitled *The Most Haunted House in England*, and claimed for years afterwards that he had experienced ghosts first-hand.

◻ *See* Borley Rectory p. 64; Ghost-Hunters p. 20

▶ *RIGHT: The famous ghost-hunter Harry Price alongside an unnamed spirit extra that appeared at a séance in 1932. Harry Price was the leader of the Crewe circle; a group of six spirit photographers who regularly held séances in a hall in Crewe.*

WHO SEES GHOSTS?

Studies show that only one person in six has the sensitivity required to see a ghost, a statistic that has led researchers to believe that a sort of sixth sense may be involved. However, spiritualists believe that everyone has the capacity to communicate with the dead after they have passed over to 'the other side'.

Ghost seers are part of folklore around the world, with many ancient beliefs surrounding the ability to see ghosts. For example, in Lancashire in the UK, it was once believed that children born during twilight hours had the ability to know which family members and acquaintances would die next. In parts of Europe, the day of birth was thought to predict the ability to see clairvoyantly. In Denmark, children born on a Sunday are reputedly able to see certain things, such as an impending death. In Scotland, children born on Christmas Day or Good Friday are believed to be able to see and control spirits.

Those who are able to channel emotion in different situations, such as actors, appear to be more likely to see or experience ghosts than others.

See Ghostly Contact p. 13; Spiritualism p. 264

SPIRITUAL CHILDREN

Children are often more sensitive to ghosts than adults, and hundreds of cases exist of children who claim to have seen dead relatives. Some experts believe that the natural animating energy of children is fresher than that of adults, which makes them more sensitive to changes in energy fields around them. Others suggest that children have an instinctive telepathy that allows them to read psychic conditions in a way that adults cannot. When a tragedy occurs, psychic conditions, or changes in energy, are created and can result in lasting impressions. Children and other sensitive individuals have an ability to read this energy (or the thoughts and emotions that caused it), which is then manifested as a haunting or a ghost.

See The Enfield Case p. 60; What is a Ghost? p. 12

◄ LEFT: Pilgrims at the site in Medjugorie, Croatia, where children claimed to see the Virgin Mary in 1990.

EXPLAINING THE UNEXPLAINED

A HISTORY OF THE UNEXPLAINED

One of the most profound differences between our modern-day culture and those of our forebears and more primitive cultures is the fact that we seek an explanation for everything. Technology and science have given us the wherewithal to assume that every mystery can be solved, and that there must be answers to every question. In the past, belief rather than technological know-how led to an acceptance that there are mysteries and parts of life that cannot be explained. For shamans, for example, out-of-body experiences, the power of the mind to heal and to communicate, and the possibility of life after death are all realities. They aim to neither dismiss them nor explain them. They do so not because they have studied these things, but because they are a part of life. They

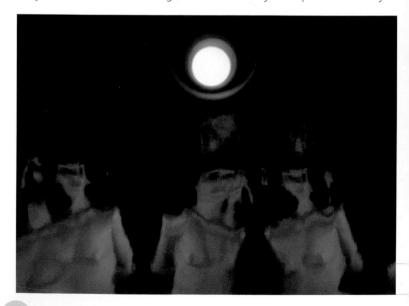

know which aspects of these mysteries they regard as having objective, non-personal reality and which are aspects of the spirit and mythology.

◆ *See* Ghosts in Primitive Cultures p. 282; The Shaman p. 293

MOODY, DR RAYMOND

A renowned scholar, Dr Raymond Moody is the leading authority on the Near-Death Experience. His landmark book, *Life After Life*, was published in 1975 and has sold some 14 million copies worldwide. Moody noted that people who had returned from the brink of death claimed they had seen a bright light. He collected a group of accounts and showed that this phenomenon was happening more and more in a world of medical miracles, where revival is much more prevalent than it used to be. He defined a common pattern for the cases, some of which exhibited many of the features he had described. Had he proved, with the approval of much of the mainstream scientific community, that there is life after death?

ANCIENT MYSTERIES

The number of 'mysteries' appears to be on the increase. UFOs have been spotted, cases of spontaneous human combustion are becoming more prevalent, we see (and more importantly, perhaps, believe in) ghosts, and we pour millions of pounds into investigating age-old mysteries, including pyramids, miracles, Stonehenge, lake monsters, fairies, and vanished people and vessels. Have the number of mysteries really increased, or have we just developed a fascination with the unexplained? Cases of unexplained phenomena have occurred across history, from the beginning of humankind. Cavemen scratched into the walls the stories that confounded them. Paintings of animals in European caves were

◀ LEFT: *A representation of the tunnel of light thought to be experienced by the human soul on the Astral Plane shortly after death.*

▲ *ABOVE: Fairies are among the phenomenon people have set out to both prove and disprove over the years. This is a scene from Shakespeare's play,* A Midsummer Night's Dream.

probably intended to have magical powers, and early peoples believed they were calling up spirits to help them. Classical Greeks documented details of curious cases. The difference is, perhaps, that in the past humans sought to learn from the unexplained rather than set out to discount it.

See The Nazca Lines p. 187; The UFO Age Dawns p. 230

KIRLIAN PHOTOGRAPHY

Kirlian photography, sometimes called electrophotography, uses high-voltage electricity to produce an image. The technique was perfected in 1939 by Soviet electrician Semyon Kirlian. In a typical procedure, the object being photographed is placed directly on an unexposed sheet of photographic film. In Kirlian photographs, objects appear to be surrounded by a glow or aura. In photographs of living objects this glow is quite pronounced, leading parapsychologists to claim that Kirlian photographs are evidence of the existence of 'psychic' energy.

DOES SCIENCE HOLD THE KEY?

Our collective fascination for mystery is one of the main reasons why our knowledge of the world around us, and the science of man and nature, has been extended. For example, our continued desire to solve the mysteries of space has pushed us towards an exploration of our solar system and beyond. But despite the huge technological advances, much still remains shrouded in mystery. Even today the mysteries of space, coincidence, paranormal phenomena and exceptions to what we consider to be the 'natural law' (the rules of life) remain elusive.

See Explaining the Paranormal p. 38

THE POWER OF THE MIND

Does the lack of hard evidence to prove paranormal phenomena make it impossible? Many scientists would say yes. Others, however, have used these mysteries as grounds for increasing our knowledge. For example, we are now learning that the human mind is much more powerful and capable than we could ever have imagined. Telepathy, teleportation, telekinesis, ESP (extrasensory perception) and prophecy are no longer the kingdom of fantasists. We study paranormal activity and ghosts; we have captured mysterious images on film. And although objects have been seen in the skies since ancient times and have been randomly interpreted as divine lessons, signs and tests, UFO sightings are on the increase and have spawned an industry of investigation. The Catholic Church views many miracles as signs from God and we have realised that the rich culture of belief in the unknown, which has been part of human life for over 50,000 years, has some gems of wisdom within it.

The following entries detail some of the theories that have been put forward to account for unexplained occurrences.

See Contacting the Dead p. 264; Mediums p.266

EARTH MAGNETISM

For centuries, people have sought explanations for mysterious phenomena. What might cause the appearance of poltergeists, the disappearance of human beings and objects, strange lights in the sky or visions on a hillside?

Just after World War II, Guy Underwood undertook a series of experiments. He began to explore prehistoric sites with a dowsing rod and soon discovered that every site had one or more centres or 'blind springs' from which streams ran. In these areas an electrical current seems to be present, often taking the form of a huge spiral. Stonehenge, for example, has masses of these currents in spirals and loops. Underwood believed that these electrical forces caused the Earth to hold the memory of an event, particularly if it was intense or highly emotional, allowing this event or emotion to remain in the atmosphere. This remains conjecture, but if true, the theory would explain many phenomena, such as the creepy feeling experienced upon entering a graveyard, a sacred place or a haunted house. It could also explain many hauntings and a wide range of natural phenomena such as crop circles.

Some years after Underwood's discoveries, British ethnologist T. C. Lethbridge enhanced the theory with his thoughts about magnetic fields, or

▶ *RIGHT: Stonehenge's spiritual power can be explained by Guy Underwood's electrical-current theory. The currents enable the emotions of an event to remain in the atmosphere.*

fields of force. He found that at sites where ghosts or other phenomena had been recorded, his dowsing pendulum started to swing, and when his hand rested on a rock, he felt a tingling sensation. The currents appeared to be very strong in these places.

See What is Paranormal Phenomena? p. 38

THE UNEXPLAINED

> ▶ RIGHT: *The resting place of many notables including Marx, Dickens and Rosetti, Highgate cemetery is a hugely atmospheric and evocative place to visit – its history hangs in the air.*

EARTHLIGHTS

During the 1970s, the investigator Paul Devereux began his research into the mysteries of the Earth, in particular those at prehistoric sites. He theorised that an energy is trapped within the body of the Earth and released into the atmosphere by an undetermined mechanism. It would focus at window areas and could provoke strange phenomena, such as poltergeist attacks, mysterious explosions and buzzing sounds, when unleashed.

He invented the term 'Earthlight' to explain how these energy emissions could create chemical reactions by exciting gases in the atmosphere, creating a glowing effect like plasma.

See Kirlian Photography p. 28

A FOURTH DIMENSION?

Around the turn of the twentieth century, theorists believed that they had come up with the answer to many of the unexplained phenomena

. . us. Some scientists came to believe that there must
. . . . imension, at right angles to the other three, and that the
. . . , we could not perceive it was not that it did not exist, but that
. . ve were limited by our minds. Russian philosopher P. D. Ouspensky
devoted a book to the subject. In *Tertium Organum*, he told the story of
scientist Johan van Manen, who described being able to visualise the
fourth dimension: 'I plainly saw before me a four-dimensional globe
and afterwards a four-dimensional cube'. Ouspensky argued that the
fourth dimension was the key to a proper understanding of the
universe, and was responsible for baffling mysteries of psychical

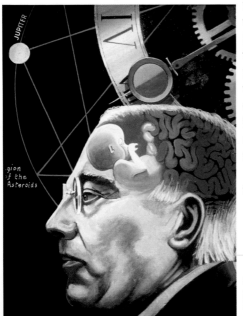

research, such as ghosts
walking through walls
(and poltergeists
throwing things),
prophecy, strange
vanishings and a variety
of other phenomena,
including teleportation
and perhaps even other-
worldly creatures.

◆ *See* Does Science Hold
the Key? p. 29

◀ *LEFT: A portrait of P. D.
Ouspensky, the Russian
philosopher and occultist who
believed in reincarnation.*

VORTEXES

The number of extraordinary disappearances on stretches of sea, such as the Bermuda Triangle and the Devil's Sea, prompted Ivan T. Sanderson, an avid collector of information on strange occurrences, to attempt to find a rational solution. He marked the Bermuda Triangle and the Devil's Sea on a map and observed that the two areas lie in roughly the same latitude and are approximately the same size. Other observations of similarly troublesome areas of sea led Sanderson to conclude that there are 12 zones lying on this latitude around the world. He suggested that the Bermuda Triangle is the most notorious because it is one of the busiest sea areas. He noted that these areas lie in parts of the ocean where warm and cold currents collide, causing 'nodal points' where surface and subsurface currents turn in different directions. He believed this created a magnetic vortex that draws ships under.

▲ ABOVE: The Sylvia, a Panamanian cargo ship 'lost' in the Bermuda triangle in 1975. It had 37 crew members on board.

Sanderson went on to conclude that some of these areas must exist on land.

Taking his theory further, it may be possible that there are spots on the Earth's surface where such fields are created by freak conditions, manifesting themselves as a kind of whirlpool in our space-time continuum. If so, objects passing too close could be absorbed and then spat out later, although they may be drawn in and never return in our normal space-time.

Sanderson's theory has been widely discounted, partly because it does not offer an explanation as to why some ships are simply abandoned. Perhaps, though, if crewmen were aware of a spiralling force beneath them, they might be tempted to abandon ship, then be sucked into the vortex. The ship could, theoretically, be spat back out, or only slightly submerged. The answer is that we simply don't know, but Sanderson's theory is worth considering.

◆ See The Bermuda Triangle p. 175; Ley Lines p. 186

BLESSED EARTH?

Some scientists have explored the idea that the Earth is alive, with the same type of life force or animating energy that humans have. If it sounds bizarre, consider the fact that acupuncture is now widely accepted in the Western world, despite the fact that we cannot scientifically prove the existence of meridians, or channels of energy that run throughout the body. Does the Earth have similar lines of energy? This theory would explain why parts of the Earth seem to be blessed while others are cursed. The Earth is now considered to be a connected system of characteristics and features. This theory is known as the Gaia Principle and it states that the many characteristics of the Earth, such as its magnetic fields, the biospheres of living creatures and plants, the atmosphere etc. are all interconnected. If this is the case, is it not possible that the living Earth has the power to create what we consider to be unexplained phenomena? Could this be the first step towards a scientific explanation?

◆ See Ley Lines p. 186

▶ RIGHT: Acupuncture is a traditional Chinese medical treatment involving the insertion of needles into the body to stimulate nerve impulses.

A NEW WORLD

Some of what we now term 'unexplained' will one day be accepted as completely normal. Perhaps the beliefs of those who struggle to develop an understanding of the unknown and the paranormal will eventually take us to the brink of a new world. We may not grasp today what we can do with the knowledge of why, for example, some people have an ability to communicate with others through the power of the mind, or how people suddenly combust or spontaneously heal, but by recognising that what we cannot explain is not necessarily trickery, superstition or simply madness, we can revolutionise our lives. This is not to say that all mysteries will have an explanation, or even that all of them are true. However, the one or two cases out of every thousand that are genuine can teach us a great deal about our world and what might lie outside it.

Unexplained phenomena are not new, nor have explanations been satisfactorily provided for age-old mysteries.

◆ *See* Explaining the Paranormal p. 38

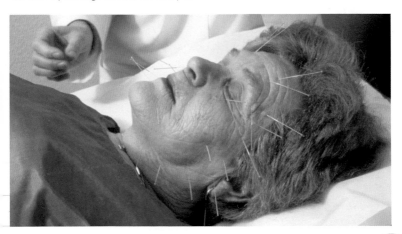

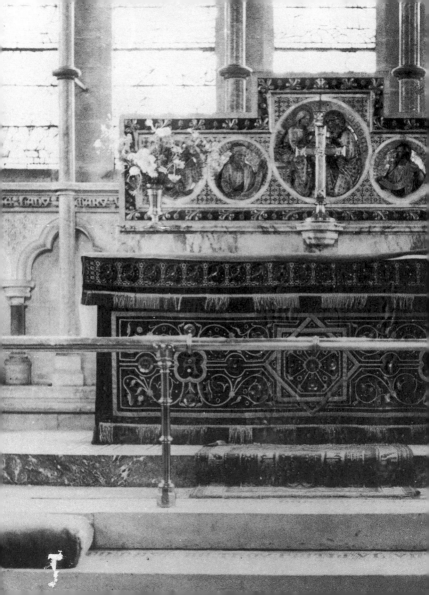

PARANORMAL PHENOMENA

WHAT IS PARANORMAL PHENOMENA?

The word 'paranormal' means 'beyond normal explanation'. Paranormal phenomena are events – sightings on Earth or in the sky or personal observations – that have no conclusive scientific or rational explanation behind them. For those who believe in the paranormal, there are always rival sceptics who disbelieve that any happening, however mysterious, can be paranormal. For sceptics, a scientific explanation can always be found, even if they themselves are unable to come up with them. Inevitably anyone who believes in the paranormal will always be confronted by scepticism. For instance, many people regard UFOs (unidentified flying objects) as spacecraft sent into Earth's orbit by extraterrestrial civilisations, however others hand have sought more rational explanations for them, such as weather balloons, lights emanating from the Earth, artificial satellites in orbit around the world or even secret military aircraft.

◄ *See* Ancient Mysteries p. 27;
Spiritual Activity p. 46

> ► *RIGHT: Theories and explanations abound as to what UFOs are, but they remain part of the paranormal: beyond normal explanation.*

EXPLAINING THE PARANORMAL

The traditional Christmas story tells of the Star of Bethlehem which, according to the Bible, led the Three Wise Men to the birthplace of Christ in Bethlehem, then remained still in the sky directly above the stable where he was born. Stars are not known to behave in this fashion, leading the event to be regarded by many as a miracle, by others as pure fiction and by some as a paranormal phenomenon. One scientific explanation has gone so far as to propose that the 'star' might have been the comet Hale-Bopp, which passes the Earth's orbit every 2,000 years, last appearing in 1997. Plausible as it sounds, the theory does fail to explain how a comet would hover in the sky.

Bethlehemum *Hierosolyma*

▶ *RIGHT: The star of Bethlehem; a miracle, pure fiction, a paranormal phenomenon or the comet Hale-Bopp?*

Similar disagreements surround the occurrence of other phenomena such as hauntings, poltergeists, ghosts and the recent inexplicable appearances of crop circles in fields. For every believer, non-believers have readily countered with rational or scientific theories. Other events deemed paranormal include: the sudden bouts of madness in dogs, sheep and other animals; mysterious mutilations of cattle; sightings of a strange creature known in the Himalayan mountains as the Abominable Snowman or Yeti and in the United States as Bigfoot, and the famous 'curse of the Mummy', which supposedly afflicted those connected with the opening of the tomb of the Pharaoh Tutankhamen in 1922 with death and disease.

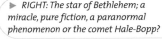 *See* The Curse of King Tutankhamen p. 105; Does Science Hold the Key? p.29

SPECTRAL OBJECTS

The idea that a house can be haunted by a spirit or ghost is generally accepted. Experts believe that energy can remain in an environment where a tragedy or traumatic event occurred, or where a previous resident had a forceful personality. What is more difficult to understand is how inanimate objects can have a life of their own.

There are many theories put forward about spectral objects, including poltergeist activity curses, but none provides a satisfactory answer. Some experts suggest that the energy of a human spirit pervades an object or a vehicle, imbuing it with the same qualities it would have had while that human was alive. In most cases, objects that are haunted have a history, having been present during a traumatic event.

◆ *See* Haunted Buildings p. 62

MOVING OBJECTS

Some experts claim that objects made of metal and wood (anything from the Earth) respond to powerful energies, such as the presence of a ghost or spirit, or even a negative energy left behind following a violent death or accident. When these objects respond to external energies, which can be imprinted on a location or on the item itself, they move or appear to be animate. When circumstances mimic the original distressing situation, the objects respond in kind. This is much the same theory as event re-enactment, whereby a profound energy is imprinted on an area (and all objects present), causing events to re-run. Frederic Myers believed that some form of consciousness survives death and is capable of telepathically projecting images, including those of material objects, to the living; these are then perceived as phantoms.

◆ *See* The Barbados Mystery p. 45

PHANTOM VEHICLES

Haunted vehicles are extremely common forms of paranormal activity; there are many reports of very life-like vehicles being seen travelling at top speed, sometimes without a driver. Many of these sightings take place on roads with a tragic history of fatal accidents or murders, but some do not appear to be linked to local incidents.

Lincoln's Train

After US president Abraham Lincoln was assassinated, a funeral train carried his body home to Springfield, Illinois, for burial. In April, every year since his death, a phantom funeral train travels along the tracks, on the route taken by the official funeral train. The phantom train never reaches its destination. Reports of the phantom train have appeared in many newspapers. New York's *Evening Times* reported one year: 'It passes noiselessly. If it is moonlight, clouds come over the moon as the phantom train goes by. After the pilot engine passes, the funeral train itself with flags and streamers rushes past. The track seems covered with a black carpet, and the coffin is seen in the centre of the

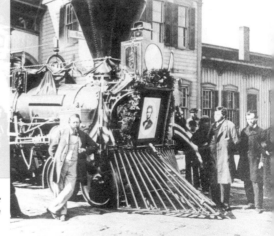

▶ RIGHT: The funeral train of Abraham Lincoln, which carried the president's coffin home to Illinois in 1865 and has been seen haunting the same route every year since.

41

car, while all about it in the air and on the train behind are vast numbers of blue-coated men ... if a real train were passing its noises would be hushed as if the phantom train rode over it. Clocks and watches always stop as the phantom train goes by, and when looked at are five to eight minutes behind.'

See Abraham Lincoln p. 81

A Runaway Bus

In 1934, a young man driving his car in Kensington, London, found himself on a collision course with a bus. The bus sped through intersections, with its headlights glaring. The young driver of the car swerved to avoid a collision, but collided with another car instead. He died in the accident. The bus, which was seen by other eyewitnesses, then disappeared. This same bus has been seen by many others over the years, and has been the cause of numerous accidents. One witness claimed that the bus was driverless.

See Phantom Hitchikers p. 86

Cemetery Traffic

At Bachelor's Grove Cemetery near Chicago, an extraordinary catalogue of vehicular paranormal activity has been reported. At dusk and during the night, phantom cars and trucks appear and disappear along or near the Midlothian Turnpike, which runs past the cemetery. Some drivers have reported being involved in accidents with the vehicles, hearing screeching tyres and the sounds of crushed metal and broken glass. Upon stopping and checking their vehicles, they have found no damage – and no sign of another vehicle. Experts have found no obvious cause for the haunting of this stretch of the road, other than its proximity to the cemetery.

See Animal Cemetery p. 223

STOPPED CLOCKS

There are many reports of clocks or watches stopping when their owners die. In Winnipeg, Canada, one celebrated story involves a grandfather clock. A man died of natural causes at the age of 72. His family were bemused to find that the clock had stopped at the exact moment of his death,

▲ *ABOVE: This pocket watch belonged to John Gill, one of the many who died when the Titanic sunk in 1912. It stopped at the exact time the ship sunk.*

and would not respond to any attempts to restart it. One year later, at the moment when his youngest daughter gave birth to a son, the clock started again and continued to keep perfect time. Lincoln's phantom funeral train is believed to be responsible for stopping clocks and watches in the places it passes through once a year.

See Lincoln's Train p. 41

THE HEXHAM HEADS

In 1972, 11-year-old Colin Robson found two small carved stone heads in Hexham, UK. He took them home, and a series of inexplicable and frightening events ensued. Showers of glass crashed down on to his sister's bed and shadowy, wolf-like figures were seen by all members of the family as well as by neighbours. The heads moved by themselves, and crockery in the house was smashed around them. The terrifying events became so extreme that the Robsons donated the heads to a museum and moved house. Expert Dr Anne Ross examined the heads, and then took them home to study them in more detail. When both she and her

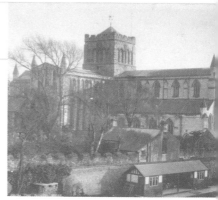

▶ RIGHT: Hexham, Northumberland, where the quartz carvings of heads were found; they brought terror and chaos to all who possessed them.

daughter saw a wolf-like man in the house, she disposed of the Hexham heads.

Dr Ross believed the stones to be Celtic and approximately 1,800 years old. One theory attributes their power to quartz, the material from which they were carved and one that has long been associated with the storage of energy. The mystery deepened when a local man claimed to have carved the heads in 1956. His assertion was questioned, but he did manage to carve identical heads as proof. Whatever the source, the heads seem to have caused chaos in the lives of those who possessed them.

◀▶ See The Curse of Ho-tei p. 104

MOVING COFFINS

It may not seem surprising that coffins are the focus of spiritual activity. Interestingly, however, the majority of coffin-related hauntings do not take place in cemeteries. Most cases of 'moving coffins' occur in sealed vaults, which, when opened, reveal the coffins in disarray. One explanation is that water seeps into or floods the vaults, causing the coffins to float and then warp. This cannot explain movements in hermetically sealed or water-tight vaults, however, and these remain a mystery.

◀▶ See Moving Objects p. 40

The Barbados Mystery

In Barbados in 1812, a strange sequence of
events occurred within a sealed tomb. A
family tomb was opened to bury Colonel
Thomas Chase, an affluent Englishman. The
tomb had been opened three times previously
to inter his wife and two daughters, and on
each of these occasions, nothing was found
to be amiss. However, when the tomb was
opened to bury the colonel, the coffins were
in disarray, as if they had been tossed in the
air and allowed to fall to the ground. Anxious
family members assumed that the tomb had
been vandalised (although there was no
exterior evidence of this), and the coffins were
duly rearranged and the tomb tightly sealed
once more. Over the following eight years,
whenever the tomb was opened, it was found
in disorder. Finally, in 1820, the governor of
Barbados ordered the tomb to be unsealed.
He found that sand laid on the floor of the
tomb was undisturbed, yet the coffins were
again in totally different positions around the
tomb. One of the coffins appeared to have
been thrown against the wall with such force
that a deep gash was left in the stone. This
prompted the family to remove all the coffins

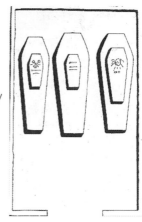

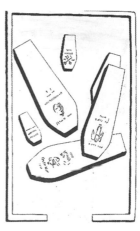

▲ ABOVE: The plan of the coffins in a Barbados vault, showing how they were placed
(top) and how they were found disturbed (bottom).

and bury them elsewhere, where they remain untouched. Paranormal scientists believe that poltergeists or restless spirits are responsible for coffins shifting. The majority of cases seem to occur when the dead died by their own hand, or were victims of a violent or unexpected death.

See Poltergeists p. 51

SPIRITUAL ACTIVITY

For every person who is sceptical of ghosts and hauntings, there are many who believe in them, and a science has grown up around them in an attempt to explain, or at least help define, their nature. The result is a catalogue of different types of ghosts and hauntings and a wealth of theories about their possible cause and purpose. Merely giving a scientific label to the paranormal does not, however, silence the critics.

What cannot be neatly explained by a world of science and technology is often discarded as being impossible or pure fantasy. Anyone who believes in ghosts is considered to have an over active imagination.

Some parts of the modern world, however, have accepted the existence of ghosts. In Norway, for example, the phantom hitchhiker – one of the most recurrent hauntings of modern times – is featured in the highway code. There are even warning signs showing a red triangle with a picture of a ghostly line on roads where these phantoms regularly appear.

By dismissing ghosts and the science of psychical studies out of hand, we are ignoring what is perhaps one of the most fascinating and least understood elements of the human spirit. Records of ghosts appear in police files, government agencies, family albums and in the folklore of almost every country around the world. If ghost stories leave you feeling sceptical, understanding how and why ghosts appear may change your perception and, possibly, your ability to see what may already be there.

◆ *See* Who Sees Ghosts? p.21

CRISIS APPARITIONS

A crisis apparition is a ghost or spirit that appears within 12 hours of a person's death, either before or after it has taken place. Theorists believe that these apparitions appear to communicate their death or their impending death to a loved one. Some indicate that they have been wounded or injured, others are simply reassuring, or request the assistance of a loved one. Crisis apparitions appear in both waking visions and during sleep in dreams.

◆ *See* Take My Ring p. 139

◀ *LEFT: The library of Combermore Abbey with the ghost of Lord Combermore sitting in his favourite chair while his funeral took place outside.*

Cases Of Dream Visions

In 1887, Englishwoman Lucy Dodson was lying in bed when she heard a voice call out her name. She quickly realised that it was the voice of her mother, who had died 16 years previously. She looked up to see her mother carrying two small children. The ghost placed the children in Lucy's arms and asked her to take care of them, because their mother had just died. Lucy promised to do so, and the ghost disappeared. The children remained in Lucy's bed and she fell asleep. In the morning they were gone. Two days later, Lucy was told that her sister-in-law had died, leaving two children. Lucy had not even been aware that her sister-in-law had a second child, which had been born just three weeks earlier. She later discovered that her mother's ghost had appeared to her just two hours after her sister-in-law's death.

Two weeks before World War I ended, Harold Owen was on a ship when his brother Wilfred, the famous war poet, appeared to him. Harold later wrote: 'He did not speak, only smiled his most gentle smile ... I felt terribly tired and I lay down; instantly I went into a deep, oblivious sleep. When I woke up, I knew with absolute certainty that Wilfred was dead.' It was later discovered that Wilfred had appeared to his brother within moments of his death.

In 1795, a Derbyshire woman, Mrs Howitt, was lying in her bed with the

▶ RIGHT: The famous war poet Wilfred Owen, who appeared in a vision to his brother, Harold just moments before his death.

bed curtains closed tightly around it. She heard someone enter the room and saw her brother Francis gently pull back the curtains. Mrs Howitt noted that he looked pale and concerned, and she asked him to come closer. Instead, to her surprise, he turned and left the room. She called her maid and asked her to search for him, but the maid claimed that he had not entered the house; nor, apparently, had he left. It later transpired that Francis had been murdered while on his way to the house. His ghost appeared to Mrs Howitt at the exact moment of his death.

See Clairvoyance p. 141

Ghost Soldiers

During the two World Wars cases of crisis apparitions were reported at the rate of between 250 and 400 a month. In some instances, apparitions of loved ones experiencing sudden stress or intense crisis were seen many miles from where they actually were. Often the figure appeared to be wounded and each witness would assume that they had seen the ghost of a loved one who had been killed. In fact, they would later discover that the person was not harmed, but that at the time of the haunting was in a situation that strongly suggested they might suffer physical injury.

See Crisis Apparitions p. 47

▶ RIGHT: Many soldiers reported seeing apparitions, particularly of wounded comrades, during the First and Second World Wars.

AUDIBLE GHOSTS

Audible ghosts are those that are heard but never seen. The best example of this type of ghost is the banshee, which wails or cries, but is heard only by close family members. Many reports involve people hearing the voices of their loved ones, either in their sleep or when awake, but having no other tangible clue that they are present.

◆ *See* Characteristics of Ghosts p. 15

OLFACTORY GHOSTS

Olfactory ghosts are those that can be smelled but not seen. In the late nineteenth century, Empress Eugenie of France lost her son when the British Army invaded Zululand in 1879. The Prince Imperial's body was brought back to England, and a cairn of stones was left to mark the spot where he had fallen. A year later the Empress went to visit the battlefield and was distressed to find that it had become so overgrown that she could not find the cairn. Suddenly she lifted her nose to the air and shouted: 'I smell violets; they were always his favourite flower.' She literally followed her nose directly to the stones without hesitation.

◆ *See* Characteristics of Ghosts p. 15

▶ *RIGHT: Empress Eugenie of France, who smelt violets at the scene of her son's death; they were his favourite flowers.*

TACTILE GHOSTS

Tactile ghosts, or ghosts that touch without being seen, are very common. In 1993, a fire started in the home of the Duggin family. The parents managed to escape with three of their four children, but their youngest, eight-year-old Michelle, was trapped in her room. The family watched helpless as flames spread up to the window, their daughter's hands stretching pleadingly out to the glass. Suddenly something appeared at the window and Michelle was thrust, head first, through the glass, falling to the ground below. Amazingly unhurt, she claimed that her grandfather, who had been dead for many years, had lifted her up and pushed her through the window. Although some experts were sceptical, it was decided that no child could have propelled herself through a window with such force.

See Characteristics of Ghosts p. 15

▶ *RIGHT: Poltergeists make their presence known in various ways. Here the Stringer family of Peckham clear up after a visit from their pyromaniac spirit.*

POLTERGEISTS

Poltergeists, or angry, disruptive spirits, are some of the most frightening forms of paranormal activity, and although various theories for their existence have been put forward, many cases remain inexplicable. The word 'poltergeist' is derived from German and literally translates as 'noisy spirit', although many cases are far more malevolent than the name suggests.

Poltergeist hauntings sometimes involve violent activity, such as physical attacks, outbreaks of fire, levitation, missiles of rocks and stones, electrical disturbances and even oozing blood. Poltergeists often make their presence known in a household by disrupting normal activity, creating loud noises and sometimes violently assaulting family members.

Witnesses do not have to be sensitive to experience their presence or see their activity. One such example was the case of a QC. He was sceptical of spiritual activity until he stayed at Shelley's Hotel in East Sussex in 1978 to deal with a case at Lewes Crown Court. In the night, his bed levitated three inches above the ground. The terrified barrister fled immediately, adamant that spiritual activity was at the root of the event. Around the world, literally hundreds of cases have been logged by policemen and women and a great deal of poltergeist activity has been captured on film.

Most poltergeist activity is reasonably short-lived, lasting for a few days or months. There are, however, cases that appear to go on indefinitely, until the occupants of the building move or changes are made that distract the ghost from its work.

◻ See The Enfield Case p. 60; Types of Ghosts p. 14

POLTERGEISTS OF THE SEA

Harry Price, the famous psychic investigator, suggested in 1945 that poltergeist activity could have been responsible for the strange abandonment of the ship *Mary Celeste*. Poltergeists are not unknown on board ship, although they are more rare than on dry

▲ ABOVE: *Benjamin Spooner Briggs, captain of the* Mary Celeste. *Could the ship that sailed itself actually have been manned by a poltergeist?*

land. A ship bound for Newcastle had been the subject of poltergeist
activity, causing the crew to abandon her. The French ship *Rosalie* had
been found abandoned in 1840, as was the American vessel *Carol
Deering*, which was deserted when she was discovered on the high seas
in 1922.

See The *Mary Celeste* p. 173

ARE POLTERGEISTS GHOSTS?

Until the nineteenth century, poltergeist activities were blamed on the
devil, demons, witches and evil spirits that manifested themselves as
physical energy within a household. With the advent of spiritualism,
this view changed, and it was believed that poltergeist activities were
the result of physical mediums that allowed themselves to become
temporarily possessed by spirits of the dead. This interpretation was
widely accepted for many years, although it soon became obvious that
'possessed' individuals could not single-handedly create the chaos that
accompanied most poltergeist episodes.

See Spiritualism p. 264; Types of Ghosts p. 14

THE POWER OF THE UNCONSCIOUS

From the nineteenth century, poltergeists were believed to be an
involuntary type of psychokinesis on the part of someone living. In other
words, unconscious thoughts were responsible for the disturbance.
Sexual or pubertal tension in older children and young adults was later
the attributed cause of poltergeist activities, particularly since most
cases appear to centre around one member of a household, normally
a young woman or girl. While sexual tension could be a cause in some
cases, it does not explain all. In the 1940s and 1950s, experts asserted
that poltergeists were the projections of repressed emotions, such as

hostility, anger or distress. In fact, research in the 1960s seemed to confirm this theory.

William G. Roll, project director of the Psychical Research Foundation in Durham, North Carolina, USA, provided written reports of 116 poltergeist disturbances across four centuries. From these reports, he found that poltergeist activities repeatedly occurred when a particular person was present, indicating that the disturbances were likely to be expressions of unconscious disharmony. He found that many of these central figures felt

▲ *ABOVE: Douglas Drew, the poltergeist boy investigated by the famous ghost-hunter, Harry Price.*

deep anger or stress, and that many suffered from physical or mental imbalances, exhibiting hysteria, anxiety reactions, phobias, manias, obsessions and even schizophrenia. This led him to conclude that their mental problems were manifested physically, by a type of telepathy, to the objects around them.

But this theory does not explain all cases of poltergeist activity. Ian Stevenson, a psychiatrist and parapsychologist who works with children who have recollections of past lives, is concerned that the possibility that poltergeists are spirits of the dead may have been overlooked. The fact that exorcism works to remove many poltergeists from their situations is evidence that emotional factors of individual people or other 'agents' cannot be considered to be the whole cause.

◆ *See* Extra-Sensory Perception p. 138; Spiritual Children p. 23

THE ROSENHEIM CASE

In Rosenheim, Germany, in 1966, a team of investigators was called into a lawyer's office after engineers failed to find the cause for a series of electrical disturbances. Thc investigating team, headed by Dr Hans Bender, identified 19-year-old Annemarie Schneider as the focus of the problem. They noticed that the trouble started at 7.30 each morning, exactly the time of her arrival at work. Lamps swung as she walked past, telephones were spontaneously dialled at lightning speed, a heavy oak cabinet was moved (it took two policeman to return it to its former position), drawers shot out of desks, light bulbs exploded and pictures crashed to the floor. When Annemarie took her Christmas holiday, the activity ceased, only to begin again on her return. Annemarie's employers finally gave up and asked her to leave, after which the poltergeist disappeared. However, the strange effects seemed to follow Annemarie from job to job, despite her protests that she could not possibly be at fault. Investigators concluded that she 'seemed to instigate psychokinesis in response to emotional problems', but confirmed that there was no wilful or malicious intent involved.

See Eleonore Zugun p. 59

LEFT: Annemarie Schneider was discovered to be the cause of the poltergeist activity in her office; when she left the disturbances stopped.

FAMOUS POLTERGEIST CASES

COX, ESTHER

Esther Cox, from Nova Scotia in Canada, was an ordinary 18-year-old when poltergeist activity changed her life in 1878. One night she woke up and screamed, declaring that there was a mouse in her bed. Rustling sounds were heard in a box that was rising and falling in the air, but it proved to be empty. The following night Esther once again woke in terror. She claimed she was dying and her body swelled to almost twice its normal size. Her family heard the sound of thunder, although the sky was cloudless. Esther recovered from the swelling but strange activities such as bedding flying about the room continued, becoming increasingly violent.

Esther's family called the family physician, Dr Carritte. While he was examining her, the bolster upon which she was resting rose and hit him on the head. A metallic scratching sound then occurred behind him and he saw, written on the wall, the words: 'Esther Cox! You are mine to kill!' The episodes went on for months, ceasing only when Esther left the property. When fire broke out in the family barn, Esther was blamed and imprisoned

for four years, after which the poltergeist activity stopped altogether. Her family, the doctor and many local witnesses became convinced the poltergeist was the work of an evil ghost who had decided to torment her.

Experts believe that Esther was the unwitting focus of psychokinetic energy, which caused the phenomenon. Whether she had repressed anger or other emotions, or sexual feelings that she could not communicate, there is no doubt that all haunting ceased when she left the premises.

◆ *See* Psychokinesis p. 145

THE BELL WITCH

The Bell Witch is one of the best-known cases of poltergeist haunting. The witch set in motion a series of events that ended in death. In 1817, John and Lucy Bell lived with their children on a farm in Tennessee in the USA. One of the children, Elizabeth, became the focus of malicious activity. In the beginning, scraping sounds and other noises were heard, but soon her bedclothes and furniture began to be thrown around the room. She was subjected to physical attacks, which included being pinched, slapped, bruised and stuck with pins. Her family first thought she had assaulted herself, but as the attacks became more intense, and the spirit began to speak, it became clear that external factors were at work. The spirit claimed to be 'a Spirit from everywhere, Heaven, Hell, the Earth ...' and said that she was Kate Batts' witch. Kate Batts was a local woman who had once fallen out with Bell and had threatened retribution. She was still alive, but denied any knowledge of the haunting. From then on, the spirit was popularly known as Kate.

The activities continued even when Elizabeth left the property and went to stay with a neighbour. When Elizabeth became engaged to a

◀ *LEFT: The house at Amherst, Nova Scotia, scene of the poltergeist case that centred around Esther Cox.*

local man, the poltergeist began revealing her intimate secrets, and the marriage never took place. The poltergeist continued to plague the family for more than two years, and John Bell became increasingly ill. The poltergeist took credit for his condition and promised that Bell would be tormented until his death. On 20 December 1820, John Bell died. A strange bottle was found in the medicine cabinet, and when the contents were administered to the family cat, it suffered convulsions and died. The poltergeist declared that she had poisoned Bell while he was sleeping, and she shrieked in triumph. The poltergeist left for seven years and then returned, wreaking the same havoc. The Bell family never learned why they had been singled out for such an attack.

Theorists explain the Bell Witch legends by claiming that Elizabeth may have been the cause. She was a young girl living in a repressed Baptist household, and may have carried some sort of resentment towards her father that manifested itself in this tragic manner. However, there is no evidence that she was unhappy before the haunting, and the poltergeist did travel all over Robertson County, causing trouble and meddling in other people's affairs. Some experts believe that the pent-up anger of the real Kate Batts may have taken on a life of its own.

◑ *See* Curses and Jinxes p. 103; The Power of the Mind p. 29; Psychokinesis p. 145

SANDRINGHAM

Sandringham House in Norfolk, one of the British royal family's residences, is haunted by a poltergeist who, on Christmas Eve, throws Christmas cards on the floor of the servants' quarters on the

second floor, pulls blankets off the beds and breathes on the maids' necks. One footman refused to sleep there after he saw something that resembled 'a large paper sack breathing in and out like a grotesque lung'. While staying at Sandringham, Prince Christopher of Greece, an uncle of Prince Philip, once saw the head and shoulders of a strange woman reflected in a mirror. Next morning he saw a portrait of the same woman, Dorothy Walpole, who died in 1726. Her ghost was also seen by King George IV at Raynham Hall in Norfolk.

See Haunted Buildings p. 62

ZUGUN, ELEONORE

In 1926, a 12-year-old Romanian girl named Eleonore Zugun began to suffer attacks from a poltergeist. She experienced bites, scratches and strange swellings on her arms, face and hands. British ghost-hunter Harry Price witnessed the marks, which appeared even as he observed her. Teeth marks appeared on her skin, and saliva was found in the wound. Subsequent examinations showed that the saliva did not belong to Eleonore.

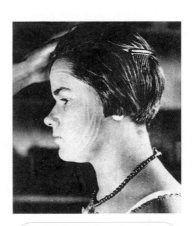

▲ *ABOVE: Scratch marks on the face of 12-year-old Eleonore Zugun, who was attacked by a poltergeist.*

See Demonic Possession p. 128

◄ *LEFT: Sandringham House in Norfolk, a home not only to the British royal family but to poltergeists and ghosts.*

THE ENFIELD CASE

One evening in late August, 1977, Mrs Peggy Harper, a divorcee in her mid-forties, had put two of her four children to bed. They lived in a house in Enfield, North London. Late at night, Janet, aged 11 and her brother Pete, aged 10, complained that their beds were 'jolting up and down and going all funny'. As soon as Mrs Harper got to the room the movements stopped.

The following night the children complained of a shuffling sound, and said the chair had moved across the room. Mrs Harper removed the chair and turned off the light. She heard the sound again, but when she turned on the light, it stopped. Next, loud knocks could be heard on the wall of the house, and a heavy chest of drawers moved across the floor. Mrs Harper pushed it back, but it moved out again. She grabbed her children and ran next door. The neighbours searched the house, but there was no sign of anything amiss. The knocks continued, so they called the police, who also witnessed a chair moving across the floor and heard the noises. The events continued for three days but the police, a medium and the local vicar were unable to help. The *Daily Mirror* newspaper witnessed some of the activity and featured photographs of many them, including one of Janet floating in mid-air while asleep. Maurice Grosse from the SPR was called in to help.

◆ *See* The Real Exorcist p. 130

▲ ABOVE: *Investigator Maurice Grosse from the SPR with some items from the Enfield Case.*

The Violence Continues

The Harpers became media celebrities, but the phenomena continued and even the press themselves suffered. There was interference with electrical systems in the house, electrical faults and mechanical equipment failure. As soon as camera flashes were recharged they were quickly drained of power, an infra-red sensitive television camera was brought in to monitor the bedroom remotely, but as soon as it began filming the tape would jam. The same thing happened to the BBC radio reporters' tapes.

▶ *RIGHT: Items burned by the Enfield poltergeist, which tormented the Harper family for two years and made them media celebrities.*

The knocking on walls and floors became an almost nightly occurrence. Furniture slid across the floor and was thrown down the stairs, drawers were wrenched out of dressing tables. Toys and other objects would fly across the room, bedclothes would be pulled off, water was found in mysterious puddles on the floors, small fires broke out and were inexplicably extinguished, curtains blew and twisted in the wind when all the windows and doors were closed, and Janet claimed to have been picked up and flung about her room by an unseen entity (witnessed by neighbours passing by and looking up into the girls' bedroom).

A male voice began to emanate from Janet's throat, and she was admitted to hospital for psychiatric tests, all of which proved normal. The activity ceased when Janet was in hospital, but started again when she returned. The voice claimed to have several identities and often spoke in obscene language.

◀ *See* Demonic Possession p. 128

Explanation for the Enfield Case

After two years the events subsided and the Harper family resumed their normal lives. There was never any satisfactory explanation for the haunting, although some experts believe that the combination of Janet entering puberty and her mother entering menopause may have caused external turmoil. Janet's parents had also recently been divorced, which may have led to increased emotional instability, although psychiatrists failed to find anything wrong with her. A Dutch medium, Dono Gemlig-Meyling, declared that the house seemed to be full of spirits from the local graveyard.

See The Bell Witch p. 57

HAUNTED BUILDINGS

The word 'haunt' comes from the same root as 'home', and a haunted location is normally the former home of the deceased, or the place where he or she died. Often, though, favourite places of the deceased or the home of someone who has caused his or her untimely death may be haunted by the deceased's ghost.

A building is considered to be haunted when there are, on a repeated basis, strange and inexplicable sounds, smells, sensations and visions (apparitions) caused by a ghost or spirit associated with the premises. Hauntings can occur for whole centuries or just days, and may be cyclical, occurring at the same time each day, year or group of years. Hauntings do not necessarily involve apparitions; other clues can suggest that an unsettled spirit is about. Tapping, crying, unusual smells (flowers, rotting flesh and perfume are common), inexplicable breezes and pockets of cold, the feeling of being touched and violent crashing and smashing can all take place.

A haunting may not be experienced by everyone present, and even those who are 'sensitive' can feel different degrees of haunting. Some ghosts exhibit angry or fearful emotions, while others seem benign and even helpful. Some hauntings involve animals and objects, or poltergeists.

See Moving Objects p. 40; Poltergeists p. 51

▲ *ABOVE: The beautiful but haunted castle of Eileen Donan in Scotland, which featured in the film* The Highlander.

WHAT CAUSES HAUNTINGS?

Most suspected hauntings have natural and easily traced causes, but certain cases defy explanation. Frederic Myers of the SPR believed that most hauntings are fragmentary and meaningless, involving traces of energy left behind by people after their death. Depending on the psychic sensitivity of the witness, this energy can be manifested in a variety of ways. Eleanor Sidgwick, also of the SPR, believed that houses and objects absorb the vibrations of their owners, and these 'psychic impressions' can include the actions, feelings and thoughts of its previous occupant.

Hauntings may be stopped by many different methods, including exorcism and laying the body of the ghost to rest, but in some cases, the haunting continues.

See What is a Ghost? p. 12

HAUNTED HOUSES

BORLEY RECTORY

Borley Rectory, located near the River Stour in Essex, was built in 1863 by the Reverend Henry Bull, and was destroyed by fire in February 1939. The ground it was built on had a reputation for being haunted, with many strange phenomena reported in the area before the rectory was built.

The house was said to host several ghosts, including that of its first vicar, Henry Bull. Other spirits included a phantom nun and a ghostly coach that could be heard rattling up the drive. Many residents complained of poltergeists; one vicar was reputedly hit on the head with a hairbrush. The occupants who allegedly experienced the most paranormal activity were the Reverend Lionel Foyster and his wife Marianne, who moved into Borley Rectory in 1930 and left five years later. During their stay, over 2,000 alleged paranormal events took place.

◪ See Harry Price p. 20

▶ *RIGHT: In 1944, during the demolition of Borley Rectory, a photographer for* Life *magazine witnessed a brick launch itself four feet into the air, where it remained suspended.*

The Most Haunted House in England?

The rectory, in its day known as the most haunted house in England, is most famous for the ghost-hunting investigations instigated by Harry Price, who claimed that the hauntings included strange whispers, a woman's voice that moaned and then exclaimed, 'Don't, Carlos, don't!', unexplained footsteps and the phantom nun who had been seen by almost all residents. His investigations led him to believe that the hauntings had been occurring for some 50 years. Strange activities recorded included the banging of doors, footsteps, voices, spontaneous combustion of portions of the house, wall writings, touchings, choir singing, music, strange lights, odours, mysterious smoke in the garden, rappings and even communication with the equivalent of a Ouija board.

Price himself heard bells ringing and witnessed strange poltergeist activity, such as objects raining down stairwells.

Price held a séance and he and others claimed to hear tapping in response to questions asked. The spirit identified himself as Henry Bull. The investigating team received further messages from spirits, who revealed that

▲ ABOVE: Among the supernatural activities reported at Borley Rectory was wall writing. A BBC engineer watched in horror as these words were spell out on the wall.

the premises were also haunted by the mysterious nun, who was said to have been murdered and buried in the cellar. One message claimed that the hauntings would end when the rectory burned to the ground, at which time the cause of the haunting would be revealed. When the rectory did burn down in 1939, in a fire caused by Captain W. H. Gregson, who lived there at the time, a woman's skull was found buried in the cellar.

See Harry Price p. 20; Séances p. 274

▶ RIGHT: Bones found under the ruins of Borley Rectory, which was built on the site of an ancient monastery.

WINCHESTER HOUSE

Sarah Winchester, the last surviving member of the affluent Winchester family, moved into a farmhouse in San Jose, California, in 1884. She believed that she was haunted by all those who had been killed by Winchester rifles. She received messages from her dead relatives encouraging her to add more and more rooms to the house. They warned her that a curse would be enacted the moment she stopped building. Sarah continued to build for 36 years, using a crew hired to work seven days a week. Eventually Winchester House spread over six acres, with 160 rooms, 47 fireplaces, 2,000 doors and dozens of secret rooms and corridors. Every night at midnight, dressed in robes, she entertained her ghost guests in the Blue Room, summoning them with a tolling bell. There she hosted dinner parties, setting 13 places, one for herself and 12 for ghosts, and served them meals cooked by chefs from Europe. When she died in 1922, she bequeathed her house to a niece, and requested that the ghosts continue to be cared for. Winchester House is now a tourist attraction.

See Borley Rectory p. 64

▶ RIGHT: With 160 rooms to explore and dinner parties held in their honour every night, the ghosts of Winchester house in California, USA, must have led a life of luxury!

BELMEZ DE LA MORALEDA

Known as the 'house of faces', Belmez de la Moraleda in Spain had a concrete kitchen floor in which mysterious faces appeared. The first face appeared in 1971. It was removed and the floor laid with fresh cement. However, other faces immediately took its place and at one point there were nine faces in the concrete. The house had been built over a graveyard and ghost experts concluded that the faces were made by poltergeists. More recently, the house has become a place of pilgrimage to those who believe that the faces are portraits of saints.

See Miracles p. 113

AMITYVILLE

A house in Amityville, Long Island, was once the most famous haunted house in the United States. In 1974, Ronald De Feo killed six members of his family there. In 1975, the Lutz family moved in but left after only a month. They claimed they had been driven out by phantom footsteps, horrible smells, clouds of flies in the sewing room and the children's playrooms, window panes that broke simultaneously, extreme cold and heat, personality changes, levitations, strange scratches and ghostly hands.

George Lutz, the father of three children, grew a beard and began to closely resemble De Feo. His wife Kathy suffered strange scratches to her body, and her brother and his bride mysteriously lost $1500 in cash in the house. Father Ralph Pecararo, the local priest who blessed the house after the Lutzes moved in, suffered illness, anxiety and pain that caused him to be transferred to another parish. He claims to have heard a voice ordering him to get out when he sprinkled holy water.

In 1977, *The Amityville Horror* was written by Jay Anson, and published

as a non-fiction title. The book, avidly publicised by the Lutzes, became a best-seller, and several films and book sequels followed.

Anson's book contained a number of discrepancies, which brought the case to the attention of the Psychical Research Foundation. On examination, they concluded that the incidents were not

◀ *LEFT: The house in Amityville, Long Island, made famous by the book and films based around the supernatural activity witnessed by the Lutz family.*

paranormal, claiming that the evidence was subjective. It emerged that the Lutzes had financial difficulties and had concocted at least some of the story to make money. Kathy Lutz's story of the scratches was analysed on a Psychological Stress Evaluator, however, and the results suggested that events had happened as she believed them. Although several phenomena were fabricated, it is possible that some haunting did occur there – not surprising, given the violent events that had previously taken place in the house.

⟡ *See* Explaining the Paranormal p. 38;
Films from the 1970s p. 302

SAWSTON HALL

The ghosts of Queen Mary I
and a lady in grey are said to
haunt this sixteenth-century
house in Cambridgeshire, UK. In
1553, Mary, the daughter of Henry VIII
and Catherine of Aragon, was involved in a
struggle for the throne of England. Edward VI, who was dying of
tuberculosis, was persuaded by the Duke of Northumberland to give the
crown to his daughter-in-law, Lady Jane Grey, who was Henry VIII's
grandniece. The duke attempted to imprison Mary, but she fled, taking
refuge for the night with a family named Huddlestone at their home,
Sawston Hall. Mary escaped the following day disguised as a milkmaid.
When the duke's men arrived, they burned the house to the ground.
Mary was duly crowned queen; Lady Jane Grey's reign had lasted only
nine days and she was later beheaded.

▲ ABOVE: *The beheading of Lady Jane Grey in 1553. Her ghost is said to haunt Sawston
Hall in Cambridgeshire.*

Mary later rebuilt Sawston Hall to thank the Huddlestones, and to this day her ghost may be seen gliding through the house and the gardens. The Lady in Grey appears in the Tapestry Room, where she knocks three times at the door and then floats across the room. It is believed that Mary once slept in this room, now also known as Mary's Room. Those who have spent the night there report being disturbed by rapping sounds, phantoms and the sound of someone fumbling with the latch.

See The Tower of London p. 74

HAUNTED CHURCHES

BATTLE ABBEY

Battle Abbey was constructed by William the Conqueror on the site of his victory at the Battle of Hastings in 1066. According to legend, a phantom fountain appears on the altar to commemorate the bloodshed. The Normans called the site of the battle Senelac, meaning 'lake of blood', and witnesses claim that the ground oozes blood when it rains.

Almost 500 years after the abbey was built, in 1538, King Henry VIII gave it to Sir Anthony Browne. At the celebratory feast, a monk laid a curse on Sir Anthony, claiming that possession of Church property was heresy. Some 200 years later, Sir Anthony's inherited property, Mondray Hall, burned down and a week later the last male heir in his family drowned.

A phantom has subsequently been seen at Monk's Wall at Battle Abbey, believed to be the ghost of the monk who laid the curse. The current owners of the abbey believe it to be haunted by the Duchess of Cleveland, who resided at the abbey for some time.

The high iron content of the soil around Battle Abbey is believed to cause the effect of sweating blood, and may even cause sporadic fountains if there has been a great deal of rain. However, numerous unrelated eyewitnesses claim to have seen apparitions on the site, and these cannot be explained, but experts agree that the high number of tragic, violent deaths there could be at the root of the sightings.

See Curses and Jinxes p. 103

CANTERBURY CATHEDRAL

This twelfth-century cathedral in Kent, where Thomas Becket (Archbishop of Canterbury 1161–70) was murdered, is a famous pilgrimage site. However, it is the ghost of another archbishop, Simon Sudbury, that allegedly walks the cathedral to this day. Sudbury was murdered by Wat Tyler, leader of the Peasants' Revolt, in 1381. Sudbury, a pale man with a long, grey beard, haunts the tower that bears his name, and at least 100 sightings have been documented over the past century.

A passage in the cathedral known as the Dark Entry is haunted by Nell Cook, who was a servant of a canon of the cathedral. On discovering her employer was having an affair, Nell was so angry that she poisoned the canon and his lover. As punishment for her crime, Nell was buried alive beneath the Dark Entry. Her spirit is believed to haunt the passageway on dark Friday evenings. According to legend, anyone who is unfortunate enough to see the ghost of Nell Cook will die soon after.

The cathedral is also said to be haunted by a monk who can be seen walking in the cloisters with a thoughtful expression on his face.

See Vengeful Ghosts p. 77

▲ *ABOVE: Steeped in legend and history, Canterbury Cathedral's ghosts include Nell Cook who was buried alive in the Dark Entry of the cathedral.*

WOBURN ABBEY

Woburn Abbey in Bedfordshire was originally a Cistercian abbey and was rebuilt in the middle of the eighteenth century. It has been the home of the dukes of Bedford for nearly 300 years and is reputedly haunted by a number of ghostly forms.

According to *Haunted Mansions of the World*, the most recent haunting to take place in the abbey is thought to be the ghost of a young man who was half strangled and then drowned in the lake. Although he cannot be seen, doors open and close for him as he walks through rooms. Witnesses claim that the door handle turns and then opens, as if a person was coming through. In the time it would take for a person to cross the room, the door at the other end opens and closes again for this invisible figure.

The ghost of a monk is also said to haunt the abbey and has been seen most often in the crypt, where monks were buried. He may be the abbot of Woburn, who was hanged when he opposed Henry VIII's marriage to Anne Boleyn.

The summerhouse is said to be haunted by the present duke's grandmother, who died in a plane crash. Although she has not been seen, witnesses claim to experience an overwhelming feeling of sadness in the summerhouse, which was her favourite place.

See The Tower of London p. 74

HAUNTED HOTELS

THE CROWN HOTEL

The Crown Hotel in Poole, Dorset, is reputedly haunted by a number of ghosts. Most activity supposedly takes place in the old stable block. Some workmen witnessed one of the stable doors swing open of its own accord, despite being bolted. More horrifying are the reports of witnesses who claim to have heard the sound of children's screams. Local legend has it that a former landlord kept his two deformed children locked in the stable block and later killed them. The stables were later converted into a nightclub, and during the 1960s were standing empty when the sound of someone playing the piano was heard coming from them.

Other ghostly activities in the hotel include the sound of something (a body?) being dragged across the upper floor, and a fluorescent mist that forms in the shape of a child's head.

◀ *LEFT: As with many haunted houses, Woburn Abbey in Bedfordshire is plagued by spirits who suffered during their time there.*

THE RAFFLES HOTEL

The Raffles Hotel is one of the oldest hotels in Singapore. It was built in 1897 on the site of a girls' boarding school. The hotel was renovated in the 1980s, and until then more than 100 witnesses independently claimed to have heard a girl's voice singing an English nursery rhyme. It was widely believed that the voice belonged to a long-dead pupil of the school.

See Audible Ghosts p. 50

◀ LEFT: The interior of the Raffles Hotel in Singapore, where many people heard the singing ghost.

DRYBURGH ABBEY HOTEL

This hotel in St Boswells, Scotland, was built in about 1845. When the adjacent abbey was still in use, one of the monks had an affair with the young lady of the house, Lady Grisell Baille. The abbot ordered the monk to be killed. Lady Baille, hearing of the monk's death, drowned herself in the river. She became the Grey Lady and has been seen walking across the chain bridge and in an outbuilding. She makes her presence felt when change is afoot at the hotel.

See Woburn Abbey p. 72

OTHER HAUNTED BUILDINGS

THE TOWER OF LONDON

A great many ghosts of historical significance are said to haunt the Tower of London, including Henry VI, Thomas Becket, Anne Boleyn, Lady

Jane Grey and Sir Walter Raleigh. The ghosts of King Edward V and Prince Richard, brothers who died mysteriously in the Tower as children in 1483, have been seen.

One of the most gruesome ghost stories of all time is linked with the Tower of London, and concerns the sad fate of the Countess of Salisbury. She was sentenced to death in 1541 due to alleged criminal activities (it is now widely believed that she was innocent). Sent struggling to the scaffold, she broke free, but was pursued until captured and hacked to death by the axe-man. Her execution ceremony has been seen, re-enacted by spirits on Tower Green, greatly disturbing the many who have witnessed it.

Anne Boleyn, beheaded on the orders of her husband Henry VIII, has also been seen here, often in the White Tower. A headless figure, she is surrounded by an eerie light. Lady Jane Grey was executed in 1554 at the age of 16 at the Tower of London, after watching her husband's decapitated body being carried away from the block. She haunts the Tower on the anniversary of this terrible event. Sir Walter Raleigh's ghost is said to haunt the Queen's House, near the cell in which he was incarcerated.

Other hauntings at the Tower include the sounds of a phantom patrol marching past, terrible screams and cries coming from the torture chambers and bizarre smoke-like apparitions floating in the air around the battlements.

▲ ABOVE: One of the many unfortunates to be executed there, Sir Walter Raleigh is also amongst those said to haunt the Tower of London.

According to many psychical researchers, the high number of brutal deaths at the Tower account for the wealth of paranormal activity at the site. There is no doubt that legend has inspired many sightings, but researchers claim that a significant number of hauntings in a variety of forms, not only visual, have been independently and identically reported.

◑ *See* Hampton Court Palace p. 78; Sir Walter Raleigh p. 82

THE THEATRE ROYAL, DRURY LANE

This theatre, in the heart of London's West End, is believed to be one of the most haunted sites in the world, hosting a variety of thespian ghosts.

Most famous of these apparitions is the Man in Grey, who appears, only during the day, in the theatre auditorium. He is dressed in elaborate costume and has been linked to a man murdered in the theatre some 200 years ago, whose skeleton was found in a sealed room backstage with a dagger still wedged in the ribcage. Many actors have seen him

while rehearsing. He is a benign spirit and a sighting has now come to represent a good omen, as the plays in which the ghost has appeared during rehearsals have gone on to be great successes. While the long-standing legend may have encouraged false sightings, investigations

◀ LEFT: The Theatre Royal, Drury Lane, is believed to be haunted by several benign ghosts. Some have come to be seen as good omens.

can find no natural explanation. The ghost is so popular that offers to exorcise him have been firmly declined by the theatre's management.

Another apparition, believed to be the spirit of the comedian Dan Leno, has been spotted in the dressing room that Leno inhabited in his acting days.

FAMOUS PHANTOMS

The ghosts of famous people appear to be particularly restless. It is believed that a forceful personality is more likely to remain on Earth after death, causing his or her spirit, or 'energy', to haunt the places they frequented during their life. Individual spirits can appear as 'intelligent' ghosts, with the ability to communicate, and it is their high energy that makes them more likely to be seen by witnesses. Apparitions often re-enact key events in the lives of well-known individuals where they once lived or worked.

It has been suggested that places of tragedy hold an energy that is effectively 'burned' into time and place, allowing an event to be re-enacted over and over, with or without the presence of a spirit.

See What Causes Hauntings? p. 63

VENGEFUL GHOSTS

Many famous phantoms return to avenge a wrongful death or to take care of unfinished business, but there are also cases of ghosts who return to protect the living and pass on valuable information. In particular, hauntings by former monarchs and prime ministers seem to follow this pattern. Having undertaken a demanding and high-profile role while living, these ghosts seem determined to continue in that manner after death, and it is their high energy or strong personalities that allow them to do so. The ghosts seen at Hampton Court, thought to be those of Henry VIII, his wives and others connected to him, are an example of this.

A possible explanation is that Henry focused all his love, hate, rage and fears on the great halls of the palace and the people surrounding it. There is certainly some truth in the view that witnesses are actively looking for a famous ghost, particularly when previous sightings have been made, and therefore seeing what they want to see or creating it in their own minds. Many, but by no means all, sightings can be put down to hallucinations or thought transference.

◌ *See* The Tower of London p. 74

◁ *LEFT: Unlike many ghosts, that of Henry VIII has no wrongful death to avenge – so why does he continue to haunt Hampton Court?*

ROYAL PHANTOMS

HAMPTON COURT PALACE

Ghosts of King Henry VIII's wives have been seen in several parts of the UK. Visitors to Hampton Court Palace in London have spotted an apparition that resembles Jane Seymour, who died shortly after childbirth. Her ghost, carrying a lighted candle, has often been seen on the anniversary of her son's birth. Another of Henry's wives, Catherine Howard, was imprisoned for adultery in the Palace, but escaped and ran to the chapel to find Henry and beg his forgiveness. Henry, deep in prayer, ignored her and she was recaptured and dragged away screaming. She was subsequently executed, and to this

◀ LEFT: Despite being a popular tourist attraction and a great day out, Hampton Court Palace has a strong negative energy due to the many traumatic events in its history.

day her screams are said to echo around Hampton Court. Several years ago, when the Gallery was open to the public, an artist sketching a picture repeatedly saw a ringed hand in front of his work. He drew what he saw and the jewel in the ring was later identified as belonging to Catherine Howard.

King Henry himself was one of the first to see the ghost of his second wife, Anne Boleyn, who was beheaded on his orders. Sightings of Anne Boleyn vary, with witnesses claiming to see her both with and without her head; in some sightings she is carrying her own head. Those who have seen Anne Boleyn in the Palace describe her as walking slowly, looking either distressed or angry. Many witnesses describe a strong sensation of rage, most likely Anne's grief, anger, dread and fear of dying.

▶ RIGHT: The screams of Catherine Howard have apparently been heard in the corridors of Hampton Court Palace, but some believe this is a ploy to attract the paying public.

79

The sheer number of tragic events connected to Hampton Court make it an ideal site for hauntings. Because the same sightings have been recorded by unrelated individuals, many of whom had no prior knowledge of other incidents, it is believed that a strong negative energy remains in the Palace. Although some sightings have been discounted, efforts to explain many more have been largely unsuccessful.

See What Causes Hauntings? p. 63; Windsor Castle p. 80

KENSINGTON PALACE

Kensington Palace has three ghosts in residence. Most frequently observed is the ghost of King George II, seen on the roof staring at the weathervane and asking 'Why don't they come?' The King died on 25 October 1760 at the palace, waiting for news from his homeland of Hanover in Germany.

See Famous Phantoms p. 77

WINDSOR CASTLE

Windsor Castle is reputed to house at least 25 ghosts, four of them monarchs. Princess Margaret once saw the ghost of Elizabeth I, as did a guard officer, who followed the former queen into the library, where she suddenly disappeared.

The same library is a favoured haunt of Charles I, who has been seen several times standing by a table. Many people have seen George III in various rooms, muttering his favourite phrase of 'What, what?'.

Two guards saw Henry VIII walk through a wall on the castle's battlements in the mid-1970s. They later learned that there used to be a door where the ghost disappeared.

RIGHT: On the day of Napoleon Bonaparte's death, his mother experienced a crisis apparition.

FAMOUS MEN

BONAPARTE, NAPOLEON

In 1821, Napoleon Bonaparte died in exile on the island of St Helena in the Atlantic. On the day of his death, a stranger with his face covered by a scarf arrived at the home of Napoleon's mother and told her that the emperor had died that day, then hurried away. Madame Bonaparte asked her

servant which way he had gone when he left, and was told that no one had left the house. Official news of her son's death did not reach Madame Bonaparte for more than 10 weeks.

◆ See Crisis Apparitions p. 47

LINCOLN, ABRAHAM

US President Abraham Lincoln was assassinated in 1865 and his ghost has been seen by many inhabitants and staff of the White House in Washington. Soon after his death, photographer William Mumler took a photograph of a woman – unbeknown to him, Lincoln's wife. When it was developed, a spirit, thought to be the ghost of Abraham Lincoln, could be seen behind her with his hands on her shoulders. A later US president, Harry Truman, said that the White House maids had seen Lincoln's ghost. Truman himself heard knocking sounds, which he believed to be Lincoln walking outside his office. Other guests claim to have seen him, appearing in the halls or putting on his boots. Jacqueline Kennedy said she had felt Lincoln's presence many times, and took great comfort in it. Many speculate that Lincoln's spirit stays on in the White House because of the trauma he endured while in office. Others feel Lincoln appears when America is in a time of crisis.

◆ *See* Ghosts Captured on Film p. 133

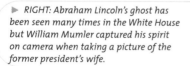

▶ *RIGHT: Abraham Lincoln's ghost has been seen many times in the White House but William Mumler captured his spirit on camera when taking a picture of the former president's wife.*

RALEIGH, SIR WALTER

Sir Walter Raleigh was a favourite of Elizabeth I, but he fell out of favour when James I succeeded in 1603, after which Raleigh was imprisoned in the Tower of London for 13 years. In 1616 he persuaded the king to allow him to search for gold in South America. When this expedition failed, he was sent back to the Tower and executed in 1618. His ghost is said to haunt the Queen's House and Raleigh's Walk, the battlements where he once strolled. In 1983 a Yeoman of the Guard heard a door handle rattling in Byward Tower. At first he thought it was the wind, but on investigation he saw a solid figure staring back at him. He was convinced that it was Sir Walter Raleigh.

◆ See The Tower of London p. 74

TURPIN, DICK

The ghost of Dick Turpin, one of Britain's most famous highwaymen, is believed to haunt Hounslow Heath and large stretches of the route between London and Scotland. A brutal criminal, he was eventually caught and hanged in 1739 for stealing cattle.

Hundreds of sightings of Dick Turpin's ghost have been reported, mainly on motorways across the UK. On the A1, nicknamed the Dick Turpin, a spectral horseman frequently appears to unsuspecting drivers. He is believed to haunt the area between Hinckley and Nuneaton in the Midlands, and has been seen as a cloaked figure near the village of Woughton-on-the-Green. Historical records show that he once used the village as a hideaway. On the A11 between London and Norwich, his ghost gallops down a hill on a black horse with a shrieking woman holding on to his waist. He did in fact waylay a wealthy widow in the area and torture her until she revealed where her jewellery was hidden. He then tied her to his horse and dragged her to death.

A number of accounts are given by tourists unfamiliar with Dick Turpin, and many scenarios match local records. Some witnesses claim not to have actually seen an apparition, but on lonely stretches of the motorway, have felt a distinct and unnerving presence.

◆ See Phantom Hitchhikers p. 86

FAMOUS WOMEN

BORDEN, LIZZIE

In a landmark case in the US, Elizabeth Borden was cleared of murdering her father Andrew and stepmother Abby with an axe. On the day of the murders the only people at home were Lizzie, Andrew, Abby and a maid, who was outside washing windows. Lizzie also claimed to be outside at the time. Abby was killed in the guest bedroom and Andrew was killed in the sitting room. Since then, the family home in Fall River, Massachu-setts, has been the focus of much spiritual activity. Cold spots are felt in many

of the rooms, and people who work in the house say they hear voices, the opening and closing of doors, and unexplained footsteps. Abby's ghost has climbed into guests' beds and has been seen dusting and making the beds in other rooms. Arguments and crying have been heard between two female voices.

MARIE ANTOINETTE

The ghosts of French queen Marie Antoinette and her contemporaries are reputed to haunt the Petit Trianon at Versailles. These hauntings became an important and controversial case for psychical researchers in 1901. In 1982, the Society for Psychical Research finally conceded that the experiences fit a pattern of 'aimless haunting', not linked to any traumatic or violent events. They suggested that the area acquired its emotional power because the inhabitants sensed that their era was drawing to a close.

◆ See What Causes Hauntings? p. 63

MONROE, MARILYN

Screen star Marilyn Monroe was found dead in her Hollywood home in 1962. Despite the mysterious circumstances surrounding her death and speculation that she was murdered, American healer and psychic photographer John Myers claims that Monroe's spirit told him that her death had been an accident. Her ghost has been seen in her garden by neighbours and, usually on the anniversary of her death, hovering near her tomb in Westwood Memorial Cemetery. Several people have reported seeing Marilyn Monroe's image reflected in a mirror that once hung in a room she frequented in Hollywood's Roosevelt Hotel.

◀ LEFT: The funeral of Marilyn Monroe on 10 August 1962. Exactly how and when she died has prompted great debate and numerous theories.

UNEXPLAINED HAUNTINGS

PHANTOM HITCHHIKERS

One of the more frequent ghost sightings worldwide is the phantom hitchhiker, or passengers who appear without being picked up. These hitchhikers are often associated with tragic events that occurred on a particular stretch of road, although the romance of travel, and the emotion of partings and meetings, is believed to inspire some ghosts to appear.

The most common scenario is a distressed young woman, coincidentally en route to the same place as the driver. When the drivers reach their destination they inevitably find she has vanished. In some cases she has left something behind, and the seat is damp. Sometimes drivers arrive at an address given by the woman only to find that the incident has occurred before, and that the girl or woman had died years earlier, often killed or murdered in the place where she had been picked up.

In 1978 a motorcyclist in South Africa gave a lift to a girl who subsequently disappeared while they were riding. He knew the exact moment when she left because the change in weight caused his bike to slew. The passenger was later identified as Maria Roux, who had died 10 years earlier.

◆ *See* Spiritual Activity p. 46

BLUEBELL HILL

The area around Bluebell Hill in Kent, UK, has recurring episodes of phantom hitchhikers. In 1992, a man named Sharpe described how a girl suddenly appeared in front of his car. He hit her, and she looked

---

▶ RIGHT: *The view from Bluebell Hill, near Maidstone, Kent. Bluebell Hill is the scene of one of the most common ghost sightings: the phantom hitchhiker.*

right at him at the moment of impact. He stopped the car and searched for the body, but could find nothing. He called the police, who found no sign either. Some years earlier, another driver had a similar experience, but he found the body and covered it with a blanket before going to find help. When he returned with the police, the body was gone, but the blanket lay in place with no bloodstains or any sign of tracks away from the site.

▲ *ABOVE: A newspaper cutting on the mysterious disappearance of the passenger liner* Waratah.

STRANGE VANISHINGS

The phenomenon of unexplained disappearances is recorded in the earliest written works. Indeed, several examples of strange vanishings are mentioned by the Greek poet Homer in his epic poem *Iliad*, which was composed in the eighth century BC. The Bible's Old Testament contains further examples, including the miraculous departures from the world of the patriarch Enoch and the prophet Elijah.

Many of these early disappearances can be considered allegorical, or the stuff of legends. More inexplicable are the vanishings that occurred in the twentieth century, when science and technology appear to have answers to many questions about unexplained phenomena. In most cases there are, eventually, explanations, but in a minority of cases, the disappearances defy logical explanation – such as the passenger liner *Waratah*, which was last seen off the coast of Africa in 1909. No wreckage or flotsam was ever found and her fate is unknown to this day.

All over the world, individuals or groups of people have vanished and never been seen again. Sometimes ships are found floating intact upon the seas, but with no sign of captain or crew; sometimes aircraft with all their passengers vanish without trace of wreckage. Whether they occurred on land, at sea or in the air, these disappearances show that even in the scientific age there is still much in our world that eludes explanation.

See Marine Mysteries p. 172; Why do Disappearances Occur? p. 96

◄ *LEFT: Unexplained disappearances are not a new phenomenon, eighth-century BC poet Homer included them in his epic poem* Iliad.

MISSING CHILDREN

THE VAUGHAN CHILDREN

This is one of the most peculiar disappearances on record, and to this day the case has never been satisfactorily resolved. In June 1906, the three children of a railway brakeman named Vaughan – his son aged 10 and his two daughters aged five and three – went to play in a large pasture field known as Forty Acres, a mile outside Gloucester They played there regularly and had never come to any harm. On the day in question, the children did not return home for their tea and Mrs Vaughan went to look for them. There was no sign of them anywhere, and she instantly raised the alarm. A large search party consisting of policemen and volunteers was organised and for three days and nights, every inch of Forty Acres was searched. One of the search-party members, who later wrote about the case in his book *Mysteries Solved and Unsolved*, was Harold T. Wilkins. He said: 'We paid particular attention to the north-east corner of the field, where the pasture was bordered by tall, old elms, a thick hedge of thorn and bramble, and a deep ditch, separating it from a cornfield. Every inch was probed with sticks, and not a stone left unturned in the ditch. Had a dead dog been dumped there, he would certainly have been found. Not a trace of the missing children was found.'

After three days, the search party was called off. It was decided that the missing children had been taken from the area and might never be seen alive again. And then, at 6 a.m. on the fourth day, a farm worker walking to work along the edge of the cornfield happened to look over the hedge and saw the three Vaughan children lying asleep in the ditch. The children were clean and didn't seem hungry, and they were amazed to hear that people had been looking for them. All they could remember was going to sleep in the ditch. For the rest of their lives, they claimed that they did not know what had happened for those three missing days. They all thought they had been to sleep for just a short time in the ditch and woken up later to the furore that had surrounded their disappearance.

◇ *See* The Green Children p. 235

MISSING MEN

BATHURST, BENJAMIN

Bathurst was the third son of a bishop and a well-known and highly regarded diplomat. Early in 1809 he was sent to Vienna on a secret mission to the court of the Emperor Francis at a time of critical importance in the Napoleonic Wars. He was instrumental in mobilising the Austrian army against Napoleon, and as a result Bathurst believed that Napoleon was intent on revenge. He travelled as a merchant under the assumed name of Koch, and on 25 November he arrived at Perleberg, midway between Berlin and Hamburg, at a post-house. While the horses were being changed, he ordered some refreshment, and after his meal visited the local garrison. There he sought an interview with the commander Captain Klitzing, and informed him that he feared for his life. He asked for full protection and two soldiers remained with him until 7 o'clock that evening. He decided to travel on by night, which he believed would be safer, and arranged for the horses to be ready at nine. He stood outside the inn, watching his luggage being replaced in the carriage, and then stepped around to the head of the horses. He was never seen again. Without a word, a cry or any alarm, he had been spirited away.

Full searches went on for over a year, and the only sign of Bathurst was a pair of trousers found on 16 December in the local wood. The trousers were soaked with water and contained two bullet holes. One of the pockets revealed a note in Bathurst's handwriting, which stated that he feared danger from the Count d'Entraigues, a French double agent. Despite generous rewards being offered, no further clues came to light.

◆ See Why do Disappearances Occur? p. 96

▲ ABOVE: Benjamin Bathurst, who mysteriously disappeared while carrying dispatches from Vienna.

MILLER, GLENN

The famous bandleader Glenn Miller disappeared on 15 December 1944. Along with other famous entertainers, Miller joined the USAAF entertainers during the war and formed his famous American Air Force Band with the intention of entertaining the troops. In June 1944, they travelled to Britain to broadcast to the invasion forces. Regular BBC broadcasts were made and Miller planned a Christmas concert in Paris, which had been recaptured by the Allies in August 1944. The band was due to be flown out from England in three USAAF transport aircraft, but bad weather delayed departure. Miller decided to go on ahead, and got a lift in a light aircraft – a 600 horsepower Norseman, on a non-operational flight to Bordeaux. On the morning of 15 December, the Norseman, piloted by Flying Officer John Morgan, took off from Abbots Ripton and made for the RAF airfield near Bedford to pick up Miller and his friend, Lt Colonel Norman Baessell, who had arranged the flight. The Norseman departed on the second leg of its journey at 1.55 p.m. and was never heard of again. The band followed on 18 December and were surprised that Miller was not there to meet them.

The plane and its occupants were the subject of an intensive search, and despite rumours of crash landings, no wreckage was ever found, nor did communications with Paris and Britain ever show any problems while the plane was in the air.

↭ See Marine Mysteries p. 172

▶ RIGHT: A C64 Norseman, the plane Glenn Miller took from Bedford on 15 December 1944. The plane never reached its destination and the reason remains a mystery.

MISSING WOMEN

EARHART, AMELIA

Amelia Mary Earhart was the first woman to make a solo flight over the Atlantic Ocean. In July 1937, as she attempted the first round-the-world flight via the equator with navigator Frederick J. Noonan, her plane mysteriously disappeared after take-off from New Guinea. A massive search for Earhart and Noonan failed, and their fate became the subject of unending speculation. One theory is that their plane went down on the Pacific island of Nikumaroro, 800 km (500 miles) to the south of Howland Island, where she was to have landed. This theory was given more

▲ ABOVE: The disappearance of Amelia Earhart's plane made headline news in 1937; despite a two-week search Earhart's body was never found.

credibility in 1989 when an International Group for Historic Aviation Recovery announced that an expedition to the island had unearthed several artefacts, including a cigarette lighter and a pre-war aircraft battery. There was, however, no other sign of the wreckage, and certainly no bodies. Some theorists believe that Amelia had been on a spying mission aimed at taking aerial photographs of Japanese military installations in the Marshall Islands and that she had been taken prisoner by the Japanese. Some weight was given to this theory in 1944 when Marshall islanders told the invading American Marines of two American flyers, a man and a woman, who had been taken by the Japanese seven years previously. A photograph of Amelia was later found on the body of a dead Japanese soldier in Okinawa.

A contemporary female pioneer of the air, Jacqueline Cochronie, who claimed to possess psychic powers, suggested shortly after Amelia went missing that she and a badly injured Noonan were alive and afloat on the ditched aircraft for some time after the crash. Despite a four-million-dollar search lasting for two weeks, no sign of the craft or Earhart was found.

◆ *See* The Bermuda Triangle p. 175

MISSING REGIMENTS

THE NORFOLK REGIMENT

In 1915, the second year of World War I, troops of the Royal Sandringham Company were part of a British, Australian and New Zealand coalition force that landed at Gallipoli on the Dardanelles in Turkey to attack the Turkish forces. The company comprised servants, gardeners and grooms from the British royal family estate at Sandringham, Norfolk. On 12 August, the entire company vanished completely in full view of three soldiers of a New Zealand field company.

The soldiers witnessed the company climb up a hillside near Suvla Bay and vanish from sight into low-lying cloud that was hovering over the slope. The last of the Royal Sandringhams had just entered the cloud when it suddenly began to rise off the hill. The British soldiers should have been clearly visible, but they were nowhere to be seen.

In 1999, a film entitled *All the King's Men* was made which suggested that the Royal Sandringhams had been quickly killed and buried by the Turks. This, though, was something the Turks persistently denied. After the end of the war in 1918, the British government presumed the Sandringhams were prisoners and demanded their return. The Turks replied that they knew nothing about the soldiers, and had made no contact with them. Since then, no explanation for their disappearance has come to light.

◆ *See* Ghost Soldiers p. 49

◀ *LEFT: British troops land on Suvla Bay during the Dardanelles campaign. The entire Royal Sandringham Company mysteriously vanished on the nearby hillside.*

THE CHINESE ARMY

In 1937, China and Japan had been at war for six months, and Japan was about to undertake one of the most horrific massacres in history – the 'rape of Nanking'. But events leading up to the massacre hold the secret of one of the most bizarre disappearances in history. South of the city, Chinese Colonel Li Fu Sien decided to make a last-ditch stand in the low hills. Three thousand reinforcements were ordered and the colonel set them up in a 3.2-km (2-mile) line close to an important bridge across the Yangtse River. They had a great deal of heavy artillery and were set to fight to the death. The colonel returned to his headquarters behind the line and waited for the Japanese to attack. At dawn he was awakened by an aide, who told him that they were unable to contact the soldiers at the line. They immediately set off to investigate and found that the positions were deserted. The guns were in position, but the men had vanished. There was no sign of fighting or trouble. The sentries on the bridge testified that no-one had crossed the bridge in the night. When the war was over, the Japanese had no record of the 3,000 missing men. They were never found.

See The *Mary Celeste* p. 173

WHY DO DISAPPEARANCES OCCUR?

J. W. Dunne was a British aviation pioneer in the early twentieth century, and enormously well regarded. In his famous book, *An Experiment with Time* (1927), Dunne described how he often had dreams about major disasters, only to find them later documented in the newspapers. He began to keep a dream diary, in which he maintained a highly detailed summary of each night's dream experiences.

▶ RIGHT: Chinese soldiers in Nanking. During the war with Japan 3,000 Chinese soldiers disappeared from their front-line post with no explanation; no bodies were ever found.

▲ ABOVE: According to Dunne, time is like a piano keyboard and when we dream time is not linear; we can move between the past and the future with ease.

He began to examine the dreams for possible evidence of future events, not just disasters or other major occurrences, but happenings of any magnitude. At the same time he kept a list of past events that appeared in the same dreams. After several months, he made a startling discovery, which was confirmed as time passed. He found that his dreams contained approximately the same number of past and future events.

He came to believe, based on this research, that in sleep we escape the linear, one-directional time that we think of as reality while awake. He compared time to a piano keyboard. When we're awake, we're sitting at the keyboard striking one note at a time, in sequence, from left to right. We cannot normally strike keys to the left ('the past') of the one in front of us, nor keys to the right ('the future'). But when we sleep, we are freed from the rigorous linearily.

Dunne's theory has been strongly criticised by many scientists, but it does offer an explanation for some of the strange disappearances that occur. Perhaps these people have jumped forward or backward in time? Time is like a record, and our human consciousness is like the record player's needle. Occasionally the needle can skip a groove, or even several grooves. Dunne's theory also offers an explanation for the strange glimpses of the future that provide such a challenge to parapsychologists.

See A Fourth Dimension? p. 31

DISAPPEARANCES AT BENNINGTON

In 2000, an unusual festival was held at Bennington, Vermont, in the north-eastern United States: the inhabitants celebrated the fiftieth anniversary of the last unexplained disappearance to take place in the town, on 28 October 1950. That day, Frieda Langer went hiking near Glastenbury Mountain in the wilderness around Bennington. Frieda was walking along a wooded track when she suddenly disappeared without trace. Several extensive searches were made of the area, but nothing was found until seven months later. In May 1951, it was discovered that Frieda's body had reappeared on the same wooden track. She was wearing the same clothes and there was no sign that her corpse had decomposed. Subsequently, it proved impossible to find a cause of death.

Most other disappearances from Bennington remained complete mysteries. No bodies or evidence were ever found to explain them. On 1 December 1946, an 18-year-old student, Paula Welden, vanished while she was taking a walk. On 1 December 1949, a man named Tetford disappeared from his seat in a bus in front of 14 other passengers: his belongings remained in the luggage rack above. On 12 October 1950, eight-year old Paul Jepson vanished while playing outside his parents' house and was never seen again.

The native American Indians offered explanations for the multiple disappearances that took place at Bennington. Some believed the area surrounding the town was haunted by evil spirits or that an enchanted stone was buried somewhere nearby and swallowed anything and anyone that came close to it. Others thought that the north, east, south and west winds met at Bennington, making it susceptible to paranormal activity.

See Native American Traditions p. 292; Vortexes p. 33

THE DISAPPEARANCE OF DAVID LANG

An American farmer, David Lang, vanished in full view of his wife, Emma, his two children, George and Sarah, and a visiting friend. Lang was never seen again and the mystery of his disappearance has never been solved. The incident occurred on 23 September 1880 on the family farm near Gallatin, Tennessee. George and Sarah Lang were playing outside the farmhouse when their father set off across the nearby field. Just then, a family friend, Judge August Peck arrived at the farm in a horse and buggy. Lang saw the Judge and waved to him in greeting. Then, just as he did so, he disappeared.

His wife and children and the Judge hurried to the spot, but they found no sign of him. They believed, at first, that Lang had fallen down a hole in the ground, but there was no such hole. The field in which Lang had been walking was searched, but nothing was found. Mrs Lang went into shock and was left bedridden for weeks. Then, some months later, George and Sarah Lang noticed that the grass around the place where their father had disappeared had turned yellow and rotten.

Sarah called to her father, and later claimed that she heard him faintly calling her for help, but then his voice faded away. After that, no one saw or heard David Lang ever again.

THE VANISHING VILLAGE

An Eskimo fishing village of around 2,000 inhabitants, situated on the shores of Lake Anjikuni in the far north of Canada, was the scene of a mass disappearance late in 1930. In November of that year, Joe Labelle, a fur trapper, arrived at the village and found it completely empty. There was no one in the huts or storehouses. No tracks of footprints led away from the village.

That same night, Labelle noticed a fire flickering in the distance, but, sensing an evil atmosphere, he was very much on his guard as he approached it. Moonlight revealed a pot of stew on the fire: the stew was blackened as if it had been left to cook too long. Thoroughly shaken, Labelle hurried to the nearest telegraph office and contacted the Royal Canadian Mounted Police. When the 'Mounties' arrived, they were just as baffled as Labelle to find that 2,000 people had mysteriously disappeared, leaving no sign of where they had gone.

Even so, there were some weird discoveries. The villagers' sleigh dogs, which had starved to death, were found buried under a snowdrift 3.6 metres (12 feet) high. At night, a strange pulsating blue glow lit up the horizon, then faded away. And most chilling of all, the graves in the village cemetery were empty. The Eskimos, both living and dead, had vanished.

▶ RIGHT: In 1930 the 2,000 inhabitants of an Eskimo village in north Canada disappeared; even the graves in the cemetery were empty.

VANISHING AT STONEHENGE

The circle of standing stones at Stonehenge on Salisbury Plain in the UK were erected many thousands of years ago, in prehistoric times, and is thought by some to be a structure connected with the practice of the ancient pagan religions that once prevailed in England. In recent years, Stonehenge has become the focus of gatherings to celebrate the summer solstice. In August 1971, a group of hippies pitched their tents in the centre of the circle and prepared to spend the night. At 2 a.m., however, there was a violent thunderstorm. The rain came lashing down and big bolts of lightning crashed to Earth and illuminated the night sky: some of them supposedly even struck the stones. During the storm, Stonehenge was lit up by an eerie blue glow which was so intense that two onlookers – a policeman and a farmer – had to look away. They heard terrible screams coming from the hippies' tents, but when the storm had passed and the two witnesses rushed to the campsite, they found not a soul. All that remained were smoking tent pegs and the remains of a campfire.

Since 1971, the public has been banned from entering the circle of stones at Stonehenge during the solstice. The hippies or their remains have never been found, nor has anyone been able to explain their disappearance.

See Ball Lightning p. 165; Stonehenge p. 185

CURSES AND JINXES

There is no question that some people – or even animals and vehicles –
attract more than their share of tragedy. These cases are immediately
considered to be the victim of a curse, a hex or a jinx. In other words, people
are all too willing to believe that fate, religion or even the occult can control
events on Earth. But how much can be attributed to bad luck or coincidence?
And how many events occur because the people involved believe in curses?

TRAGIC AURAS

Some experts believe that tragedy can
create a 'negative thought field', which
predisposed people tune into. If a tragic
event has occurred, a sort of tragic aura is

left behind. When people are frightened, nervous or even simply sensitive,
they can be affected by this aura in a negative way.

Similarly, when individuals who have been cursed as the result of
non-Western or primitive rituals die, it is believed to be because of the
victim's belief in the power of the curse.

Dr Herbert Basedow described the agony of an Australian aboriginal
he watched being cursed by a bone. The man stared with fear, his cheeks
lost their colour and his whole face became distorted. His body started
to shake and he died. On another similar occasion, a more powerful
magician was able to lift the curse, after which the subject made a
full and immediate recovery.

See Aboriginal Belief in Ghosts p. 297

▲ ABOVE: An Australian aboriginal pointing bone, used to place curses.

◄ LEFT: Stonehenge is lit up here by the comet Hale-Bopp but in 1971 a eerie blue glow was
reported to have illuminated the stone circle.

THE CURSE OF HO-TEI

In 1928, a middle-aged English couple, the Lamberts, purchased an ivory statue of the Japanese god of good luck, Ho-tei, from a shop in Kobe, Japan. The Lamberts were on a cruise, and when they returned to their ship, Marie Lambert

stowed the statuette in her luggage en route to Manila. Two days later, she began to suffer from an excruciating toothache. She was prescribed painkillers, but they did little good. Mr and Mrs Lambert then came down with an unpleasant fever, with severe aching in the joints. Finally she managed to get to a dentist, but during treatment the drill slipped and drove through the nerve of her tooth, causing terrible pain.

The Lamberts next went to Australia, and the figurine was transferred to Mr Lambert's luggage. The following day, he too experienced an agonising toothache. He visited several dentists and even had a tooth extracted, but whenever he was in the cabin, the pain started again. The Lamberts finally worked out what was happening when they offered the gift to Mr Lambert's mother in the US. She was delighted, but when her teeth started to ache a few hours later, she handed back the gift claming that it was 'bad medicine'.

Once back in the UK, Mr Lambert took the statue to a Japanese art shop, where the manager offered to buy it. He explained that the Ho-tei was a temple god, and in the East, statues of such gods are sometimes given 'souls' in the form of small medallions hidden inside them. He arranged for an old man in Japanese national costume to place the statue in a shrine, and light incense. This appeared to appease the statue and Lambert

◀ LEFT: Some experts believed that the elephant-tusk ivory that was used to carve the statue of Ho-tei was the cause of it's owners' toothache.

assumed that the god of luck had been taking revenge on disbelievers who had removed him from his temple. Other experts suggested that the painful removal of the tusk from the elephant may have induced a form of psychic disturbance that manifested itself as severe toothache.

◆ See Japanese Ghosts p. 290; Shinto Offerings p. 291

THE CURSE OF KING TUTANKHAMEN

The Valley of the Kings is one of the world's most impressive burial grounds; it lies in a desert valley in Egypt, near the modern city of Luxor. For 500 years, the valley was a royal cemetery, where some of the most famous pharaohs of ancient Egypt were buried, surrounded by treasures, in tombs cut out of the valley cliffs.

Sponsored by a wealthy British aristocrat, Lord Carnarvon, a young archaeologist, Howard Carter, set out on a mission that would change our knowledge of Egyptian history. Since his first visit to Egypt at the age of 16, Carter had always believed that there was at least one tomb still hidden in

▶ RIGHT: Tutankhamen's funeral mask is made of solid gold and inlaid with semi-precious stones and glass paste.

the Valley of the Kings, an area that had been exhausted by excavations and grave-robbers for many years.

After years of searching, the tomb was discovered on 26 November 1922, when one of Carter's team noticed the top step of a staircase which led down to a sealed door. Beyond the door, as Carter and his team would discover, lay magnificent treasures untouched since the young pharaoh had been buried there more than 3,300 years before. Carter's greatest moment came on 17 February 1923, when he opened the burial chamber in which the pharaoh's sarcophagus lay. Sadly, Lord Caernarvon did not

live long to enjoy his triumph. A mosquito bite he received proved fatal as it turned septic. Lord Caernarvon, who had been in poor health for some time, could not fight off the infection and developed pneumonia, dying on 5 April 1923. Strangely, a power failure occurred in Cairo an hour after his death. Power cuts were by no means uncommon occurrences in the Egyptian capital, but this one added to the belief that all who were present at the opening of the tomb were cursed.

Other individuals connected with either Lord Caernarvon or the excavations also began to die. Far away, in London, Caernarvon's dog, a fox

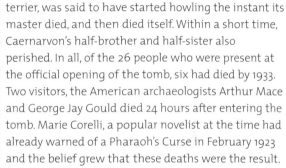

terrier, was said to have started howling the instant its master died, and then died itself. Within a short time, Caernarvon's half-brother and half-sister also perished. In all, of the 26 people who were present at the official opening of the tomb, six had died by 1933. Two visitors, the American archaeologists Arthur Mace and George Jay Gould died 24 hours after entering the tomb. Marie Corelli, a popular novelist at the time had already warned of a Pharaoh's Curse in February 1923 and the belief grew that these deaths were the result.

Others thought to have succumbed to the curse included the radiologist Archibald Reid, who prepared Tutankhamen's remains for X-ray, and Carter's personal secretary, Richard Bethel. The press took up the story of Tutankhamen's Curse, and embellished the facts: there were reports, for example, that a curse was inscribed in hieroglyphics on the seal to the

◀ *LEFT: Howard Carter and members of the team that discovered Tutankhamen's tomb believed to curse all who entered it.*

tomb entrance though, in fact, no such inscription was ever found. Nevertheless, belief in the Pharaoh's Curse persisted and 50 years later, in 1972, there were press reports that ascribed to it the death of an Egyptian archaeologist who was preparing some of the Tutankhamen exhibits for display on a world tour.

In 1934, when belief in the Curse had reached near-hysterical proportions, the American Egyptologist Herbert Winlock published statistics in an attempt to explode the myth. He revealed that of the 26 people present when Tutankhamen's burial chamber was opened, 20 were still alive, all of whom who had seen the pharaoh's sarcophagus opened and of whom had witnessed the unwrapping of the mummy. Howard Carter himself died just before his 65th birthday in 1939. Dr. D.E. Derry, who conducted the autopsy on Tutankhamen's corpse lived until 1969. Alan Gardiner, who studied the inscriptions on the tomb, survived until 1963. Lady Evelyn Herbert, Lord Caernarvon's daughter and one of the first to enter the tomb, died at nearly 80 in 1980.

One of the firmest believers in the existence of the Pharaoh's Curse was Sir Arthur Conan Doyle, the spiritualist and novelist famed for his creation of the detective character Sherlock Holmes. Sir Conan Doyle, a trained physician, did however believe that Lord Caernarvon had died after breathing in germs placed by priests inside Tutankhamen's tomb to deter grave-robbers. As modern research shows, he may not have been far off the truth, and these 'germs' were able to survive for over 3,000 years as spores, according to research conducted in 1998 by Dr Sylvain Gandon of the Laboratoire d'Ecologie in Paris. 'The death of Lord Caernarvon could potentially be explained by infection with a highly virulent and very long-lived pathogen' commented Dr. Gandon.

See The Curse of Princess Amen-Ra p. 113; The Pyramids of Ancient Egypt p. 191

THE *SCHARNHORST* DISASTER

Few sailors doubt that there are ships that have been jinxed, and one of the best-known examples is the German battleship *Scharnhorst*, which was launched in October 1936. When only half completed, the ship rolled on to its side, killing 60 workmen. Hitler and Goering arrived for the eventual launch only to discover that the ship had somehow launched itself the previous night, destroying several barges.

In her first major engagement – the attack on the Danzig in 1939 – the *Scharnhorst*'s guns exploded, killing nine men, and the air-supply system broke down, causing the deaths of 12 of the gunners. A year later, during the bombardment of Oslo, the ship was damaged and towed away. In the

▲ ABOVE: The Scharnhorst *was involved in so many accidents that people began to conclude that it was jinxed.*

dark, she collided with the ocean liner *Bremen*, which settled into the river mud and was bombed by the British. After being repaired, the *Scharnhorst* was sent to the Arctic in 1943, but she was bombarded by several British cruisers. She was chased and finally hit, sinking to the bottom with most of her crew. Yet the curse apparently continued. Weeks later, two survivors from the damned ship were found washed up on the shore of a beach. They were both dead, having been killed by an emergency oil heater that had exploded when they tried to light it for warmth.

In his book on sea mysteries, *Invisible Horizons*, Vincent Gaddis writes:

'There are happy, gay ships, and there are others so impregnated with evil that they must be destroyed by fire.' Eventually, the *Scharnhorst* was brought to the surface and burned.

See Marine Mysteries p. 172

RIGHT: The captain of the Scharnhorst *inspecting his crew before the ill-fated voyage to the Antarctic.*

GRAVEYARD SHIPS

THE *HINEMOA*

The *Hinemoa* was a British vessel, launched in 1892. The sailors on board the ship knew that the ballast had been taken from a graveyard, and were wary of sailing her. During the voyage, four sailors died of typhoid. The ship's first captain went insane and the second ended up in prison. The third died of alcoholism, the fourth in mysterious circumstances in his cabin and the fifth committed suicide. The reason? The crew were unanimous: the combination of the graveyard ballast, and the bones of the four dead crew members, had jinxed the ship.

THE *GREAT EASTERN*

The *Great Eastern* was another much-maligned and unlucky ship. As they did in the case of the *Hinemoa*, the crewmen believed that the bones of dead men were at the root of the ship's disasters. It was built by the famous Victorian engineer Brunel. He collapsed with a heart attack on her deck, and died soon after. A riveter and his boy assistant vanished without trace during the

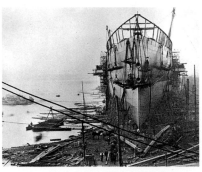

▲ *ABOVE: The unlucky ship* Great Eastern, *suffered a spate of disasters believed to be caused by a curse.*

ship's construction, and on its maiden voyage, a steam-escape valve was left closed, causing an explosion that scalded five men to death. Its subsequent misfortunes became legendary – including explosions, collisions, accidents at sea and a spate of deaths among the crewmen. Finally, after 15 years, she was brought back to Milford Haven in South Wales, where she rusted and blocked the shipping lane. Breaking her up proved almost impossible and the wrecker's iron ball was invented in order to do so. Inside the double hull, the demolition experts discovered the skeletons of the riveter and his boy. Seamen believed the cause of the curse had been found.

◆ *See* Phantom Vehicles p. 41

THE *FLYING DUTCHMAN*

The *Flying Dutchman* is probably the most celebrated ghost ship, dating from the seventeenth century when Captain Hendrik van der Decken, rounding the Cape of Good Hope, encountered such unfavourable weather that he had difficulty progressing. He refused the pleas of passengers and crew to seek a port until the storm abated, and stubbornly fought to round the Cape. He swore that he would round the 'damned' Cape if it took until Doomsday.

The ship was lost with only one or two survivors, and legend has it that a supernatural force condemned the captain and his crew to sail the seas forever. Sightings of the *Flying Dutchman* in the area in which it sank have been reported over the years by many experienced and reliable sailors. This is a phantom that has some official recognition: records of sightings are preserved in the files of the British Admiralty. Among the alleged sightings are those that took place in 1823, 1835, 1881, 1890, 1893, 1905, 1911, 1916, 1923, 1939 and 1942. Among the witnesses are King George V, when he was a naval cadet, together with 12 other witnesses including his brother the Duke of Clarence, then heir to the throne. Seeing the ship is believed to be an omen of disaster; during World War II Admiral Karl Doenitz, Hitler's commander-in-chief of U-boats, reported sighting the *Flying Dutchman*: 'Certain of my U-boat crews claimed they saw the *Flying Dutchman* or some other so-called phantom ship on their tours of duty east of Suez. When they returned to their base, the men said they preferred facing the combined strength of Allied warships in the North Atlantic than know the terror a second time of being confronted by a phantom vessel.'

◀ *See* Marine Mysteries p. 172

▶ RIGHT: *Visions of the Virgin Mary are some of the most commonly-experienced phenomena – often appearing to whole crowds of people at a time.*

THE CURSE OF PRINCESS AMEN-RA

In 1868, the story of the mummy of an ancient Egyptian princess became headline news. Four young Englishmen bought the mummy of the princess. Soon after, one of them walked into the desert and vanished. Another of the buyers had his arm shot off, while a third had his bank fail and the last one became insolvent. The next owner of the mummy had three of his family injured in an accident and his house caught fire. The mummy was then given to the British Museum, where things continued to go wrong. Among an alleged catalogue of horrors were the deaths of porters and exhibits that were thrown about at night. The British Museum offered to sell the mummy to anyone who would buy it. According to legend, she was placed on the *Titanic* in 1912. Perhaps the mummy's curse caused the ship to strike an iceberg on her maiden voyage?

 See The *Titanic* p. 180

MIRACLES

No other form of apparition or vision has such an emotionally overwhelming effect as the sighting of the Virgin Mary, the mother of Jesus. Some of these visions are accompanied by other events, such as weeping, bleeding or even moving statues.

Visions of the Virgin Mary are widely attested to by individuals and whole communities around the world. While one or only a small group of people may witness the actual vision, pilgrims and other witnesses experience all types of paranormal phenomena, such as burning bushes, heavenly music and visions of a spinning sun. The tears of a weeping statue, the waters from a holy spring, or the directed spiritual energy of a healer have been known to produce miracles. People's lives have been saved and dramatically changed by contact with these phenomena. But how much of this really lies in the power of the mind?

Some theorists allege that it is the power of collective faith that triggers these miracles. Others believe that people see what they want to see, and that their intense concentration is responsible for physical changes, both in their bodies and to their environment. But what of the fact that many witnesses are children, or unwilling and unwitting visionaries? How can we explain what happened at Fatima, where tens of thousands of people saw something miraculous happen?

Miracles happen both to those who believe and those who do not. They illustrate another part of the human body and mind, and the world around us, that we may never be able to understand.

See The Fatima Miracle p. 116; The Weeping Madonna p. 119

THE MADONNA OF MEDJUGORJE

Late in the afternoon of 24 June 1981, six children – four girls and two boys, some together and some alone – witnessed a vision of the Virgin Mary on a rural hillside. She told the children she would return the next day, and every day thereafter.

This amazing story took place in the tiny village of Medjugorje, in Bosnia-Herzegovina. Medjugorje is now a major centre of pilgrimage, attracting millions of visitors from around the world. Within three days of the first encounter, 15,000 people congregated on the hill to see the Virgin. A bright light shone over the village before the apparition, and the word 'Mir', or 'Peace', was once emblazoned in the sky in red. Strange

▲ ABOVE: *The site in Medjugorie, Croatia, where six children saw the Virgin Mary and thousands of pilgrims have visited since.*

lights regularly played across the giant cross that was erected on the next hill in 1983.

For more than five years, the visions occurred, although only the original six children could see the Virgin herself. The children appeared to go into a kind of trance during visits, and medical checks showed them to be immune to stimuli and even pain during these periods. The trances seemed genuine and the children returned with detailed messages and prophecies. By 1985, the children had experienced more than 2,000 visions between them, and the Virgin told them it would be her last appearance on Earth.

Scientists have not been able to find an explanation for this manifestation of the Madonna. Even the most advanced research techniques of psychologists and neurologists have proved inadequate to throw light on the phenomenon.

A Dutch professor of theological psychology, Dr J. Weima, concluded, after submitting the group to regular and thorough physical and psychological examinations, that was no question of deceit or derangement. Dr Weima affirmed that something very unusual was being perceived that others could not see, but as to exactly what happened, he concluded: 'Science, as it is at present, has not yet found an explanation.'

See Trances p. 278

THE FATIMA MIRACLE

On 13 May 1917, two nine-year-olds and a seven-year-old saw a 'brilliant lady in white' while working in a field in the rural area of Fatima in Portugal.

The woman was described as being radiant, and she appeared from a beam of light that flashed from the sky. She said that she had come from heaven and asked the children to return on the 13th day of each month.

The local residents were astonished by the suggestion that an angel had appeared to the three children, and

▶ RIGHT: The three children of the 1917 Fatima miracle. From left: Jacinta, Francisco and Lucia.

word soon spread. On the 13th of each month a crowd gathered to watch and although only the original three witnesses ever saw the 'angel' again, many believed that they had been visited by the Virgin Mary. More than 20,000 people had turned up to witness the miracle by September. According to witnesses a 'luminous globe' travelled across the sky from east to west. On 13 October, the children saw a vision at noon precisely, and some 70,000 came to watch. One of the girls announced that she had seen the Holy Family in the sky, and the crowd looked up to see the sun 'whirling and dancing in the sky'. Many onlookers claimed that a hole was punched through the rain cloud at noon, and a spinning disk (the Sun) poured down blinding radiance and great heat on the ground before swirling back up again. The visions stopped after October and never recurred.

No photographs of the miracle exist, but there were literally thousands of witnesses. Prophecies had also been given to the children, one for the imminent Russian Revolution, one for World War II and a third that was long held in the Vatican in a sealed envelope, the contents of which were revealed in 2000. One of the interpretations of this third vision was a prophecy of the attempted assassination of the pope in 1981.

See Extra-Sensory Perception p. 138

THE ICON OF CALCUTTA

According to a 1998 BBC news report, thousands of visitors have flocked to see a 'bleeding Christ' statue in Calcutta. A lawyer who lives in the compound of a church in the city said she saw blood coming from wounds of the Christ figure on a 45-cm (18-in) cross at her home. 'I went to clean it and noticed it was bleeding from where Christ was nailed and where the crown of thorns was,' said Ajanta Rovena Chatterjee. More than 10,000 people have since prayed at the icon.

SOUTH AMERICAN MIRACLE

In November 1992 in the working-class La Cisterna district in the south of Santiago, Chile, a small blue-and-white porcelain statue belonging to Olga Rodriguez, a housewife, began to weep blood. Doctors attached to the police Criminal Investigation Department confirmed that the mysterious red liquid which flowed from the eyes of the statue of the Virgin Mary was human blood. Dr Inelia Chacon, working on the project, confirmed that three samples of the liquid examined in a laboratory were shown to be blood. According to the *Guardian* newspaper: 'The Santiago coroner's office pronounced the substance is type O-4 human blood. The statue weeps regularly, particularly in the presence of children.'

◆ *See* The Weeping Madonna p. 119

▶ *RIGHT: This statue of the Virgin Mary, from a private home in Canada, is reported to have bled and wept in 1986.*

THE VIRGIN OF GUADELOUPE

In the garden shrine of Pablo Covarrubias stands a statue of the Virgin of Guadeloupe, brought from the Basilica in Mexico City. Since 1998, the Virgin has regularly wept real tears that are then harvested in little cotton balls and distributed to the faithful. According to Pablo, many supernatural healings have been documented, and on one very windy day, an apparition of Mary appeared in the sky above the shrine.

THE WEEPING MADONNA

In a back room of the Post Office in the tiny southern Ireland village of Grangecon, County Wicklow, the post mistress Mary Murray keeps her statue of the Virgin Mary. The painted statue stands about 30 cm (12 in) high and is housed in a sealed glass case. BBC2's *Everyman* programme of 18 December 1994 told how the statue had been found to be 'crying blood'. The statue, with its blood-stained cheeks, was clearly shown to viewers. At 3 p.m. every day, the glass case with its holy contents is taken, to the accompaniment of Hail Marys, to be placed beside the outdoor shrine of the Madonna nearby.

CHICAGO, 1997

Hundreds of Christians regularly visit the home of Salim Najjar in North Hirschberg, Chicago, where an image of the Madonna has appeared in a window and a small picture of an icon produces tears. An Orthodox Christian bishop officially proclaimed these events to be 'an extension of the miracle of Our Lady of Cicero' – an icon at the St George Church in Cicero that began weeping.

Salim Najjar said that when the image of the Madonna appeared on his front window, the amazed family, who attend the St George Church, taped a small reproduction of the weeping icon to the window. To their astonishment the small picture began giving off oily tears.

See The Icon of Calcutta p. 117

THE CARDINAL AND THE VIRGIN MARY

Blurred images on two photographs taken during the requiem mass for England's Cardinal Basil Hume could be the Virgin Mary, claims one of the photographers. The two photographs were taken at exactly the same time during the service in September 1999. Terence Wynn, a photographer for the

Northern Cross newspaper, took his photograph from the television. He said the same image appeared on another photograph taken at exactly the same time – and also from television – by a priest in Hartlepool. Mr Wynn believes the translucent image resembles the statue of the Immaculate Conception, Our Lady of Lourdes, which is in the grotto at Lourdes.

➲ *See* Ghosts Captured on Film p. 133; Lourdes and St Bernadette p. 120

LOURDES AND ST BERNADETTE

In 1858, in the grotto of Massabielle, near Lourdes in southern France, the Virgin Mary appeared 18 times to Bernadette Soubirous, a young peasant girl. Mary revealed herself as the 'Immaculate Conception'. Bernadette described her as 'a girl in white no bigger than myself'. The vision spoke to Bernadette and asked that a chapel be built at the site of the visitation. She also told the girl to drink from a fountain in the grotto. There was no fountain in evidence, and Bernadette scrabbled in the mud, to the amusement of onlookers, in an attempt to dig for a stream. The following day, there was a clear stream running where Bernadette had been digging, and the water from the stream immediately restored sight to a blind man.

The water from this spring still flows and it has been shown to have a remarkable healing power, though it contains no curative property that scientists can identify. Lourdes has become the most famous modern shrine of the Virgin Mary.

After enduring a period of painful publicity, Bernadette entered a convent at Nevers, France, where she remained until her death. She was canonised in 1933.

In 1962, the results of a four-year enquiry by the Catholic Church into events at Lourdes were published. The Bishops' Commission concluded: 'We have also sought the opinion of scientists and we are finally convinced that the Appearance is supernatural and divine, and that consequently, She whom Bernadette has seen is the Most Blessed Virgin Herself. Our conviction is based, not merely upon the testimony of Bernadette herself, but more especially upon the events which have taken place and which can only be explained by divine intervention.'

◆ See The Madonna of Medjugorje p. 114

◀ LEFT: *While gathering firewood, Bernadette Soubirous sees the Virgin Mary in the grotto.*

STIGMATA

Stigmata are unexplained wounds on the body that bear a resemblance to the wounds of Christ when he was crucified on the cross. The people who suffer from stigmata are often nuns, priests or people with strong religious beliefs. Stigmata do not always appear in the same way. One stigmatic, for example, might only have the wounds that would have been made by the crown of thorns, while another might experience only a lance-wound in the side, or the wounds in the wrists or palms of the hands, or in the feet. The wounds from which stigmatics suffer are almost always identical to the wounds shown on the statues of Jesus to which they pray: if the statue has nails in the palms, blood will flow from the sufferer's palms.

◆ See Padre Pio p. 122

Visible and Invisible Stigmata

Physical wounds are called visible stigmata. Other ecstatics (people who are subject to mystical experiences) might only experience the suffering, without any outward marks – this phenomenon is known as invisible stigmata. Many experts consider stigmata to be one of the most baffling and intriguing of medical and scientific mysteries. The most common theory about stigmata is that the sufferers have caused it themselves by the power of their own mind and the strength of their beliefs. Science has yet to explain the phenomenon. Religious theorists argue that this is the power of faith.

St Francis of Assisi

St Francis of Assisi had stigmata of a character that has never been seen since. In the wounds of his feet and hands were excrescences of flesh representing nails – those on one side having round back heads, those on the other having rather long points, which bent back and grasped the skin. Many of his brethren were witness to the wounds, and a number of contemporary historians have confirmed their existence.

▶ *RIGHT: A painting showing St Francis of Assisi receiving the stigmata.*

Padre Pio

In September 1918, a 31-year-old Capuchin monk, Padre Pio, saw a mysterious person whose 'hands, feet and side were dripping blood'. He said: 'The sight terrified me and what I felt at that moment is indescribable. I thought I should die, and really would have died if the Lord had not intervened and strengthened my heart which was about to burst out of my chest. The vision disappeared and I became aware that my hands, feet and side were

dripping blood. Imagine the agony I experienced and continued to experience almost every day. The heart wound bleeds continually, especially from Thursday evening until Saturday.'

Although he found the wounds 'embarrassing', and prayed for the visible marks to be removed, he did not ask for relief from the pain. He believed that the wounds, which stayed with him for 50 years, gave him the strength to fend off attacks by the devil.

Many were suspicious of Padre Pio and his miraculous wounds. The Vatican even bugged the padre's confessional and opened his post. He was also banned from saying Mass for many years. But the present pope, who travelled from Poland to visit Padre Pio in 1947, accepted him back into the Church's fold and honoured him with the title 'The Venerable'. Beatification – an honour that

123

usually leads to sainthood – requires evidence that the candidate has been responsible for working miracles. In 1991, a woman who had been hospitalised for a burst lymph vessel made a rapid recovery after praying for the padre's intervention. After investigating the case at length, the Vatican declared the cure to be authentic and 'extraordinary' – evidence enough to put Padre Pio on the path to sainthood.

▶ RIGHT: Father Pio Forgione (Padre Pio) received stigmata in 1918 that were eventually corroborated by the Vatican.

THE TURIN SHROUD

The Shroud of Turin is a centuries-old linen cloth that bears the image of a crucified man – a man that millions believe to be Jesus of Nazareth. The shroud has been the object of much detailed study and intense research. Many experts have concluded that it was the cloth that wrapped the crucified body of Christ, although the controversy is still intense.

The shroud, widely believed to be Christ's burial cloth, bears a faded image of a bearded man and what appear to be bloodstains that coincide with Christ's crucifixion wounds. The 4-m (13-ft) long linen cloth has been kept in the city of Turin, Italy, since 1578. American biochemist Dr Alan Adler established in 1988 that the shroud image was indeed that of a person, and the blood came from violently inflicted wounds. He said blood flowing from wounds has a different chemistry to blood that flows in veins. But he said he couldn't prove whether the image on the shroud was Christ's. 'We know for sure it's human blood and it came from a man who died a traumatic death,' Adler said in a 1998 interview. 'There's no laboratory test for "Christ-ness".'

Some experts suggest that the shroud is a medieval fake. However, its mystery continues to puzzle scientists. No one is sure how the startling image of Christ was produced, but an experiment in 1999 managed to create a replica of the shroud image by covering a human subject with aloe and myrrh. To the believers, the cloth is a miracle and a sign of Christ's divinity that no amount of scientific tests can explain. One investigator suggested that it was created by 'a sudden radiance of Our Lord's body at the moment of resurrection'.

◀ See Stigmata p. 121

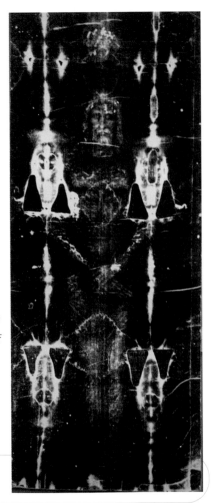

▶ RIGHT: The replica of the Turin Shroud created by covering a human subject with aloe and myrrh.

MILK-DRINKING STATUES

The spiritual, mysterious nature of faith has also produced miracles in religions other than Roman Catholicism. In 1995, for example, milk-drinking statues of the Hindu gods were reported all over the world. The miracles began in Delhi, the Indian capital, on Thursday, 21 September, after a Hindu dreamed that Lord Ganesh, the elephant-headed god of wisdom wanted a drink of milk. The man rushed to the nearest temple, and persuaded the priest there to let him feed a bowl of milk to a stone statue of Ganesh. The two men watched in amazement as the milk vanished.

Before long, the news had spread across India like wildfire. Millions of Hindus queued up at temples all over the country, carrying offerings of milk to feed to the statues of the gods – and not only Ganesh, but Shiva, Parvati and Nandi as well. New Delhi ran out of milk as worshippers snapped up its stock of around one million litres. Declared 'the supernatural event of the twentieth century' by the *Hindu Times*, but dismissed as 'mass hysteria' and delusion by sceptical scientists, the milk-drinking incidents occurred among Hindu communities throughout the world – in the USA, Canada, the Caribbean, Asia, Africa, the Middle East, Australia and New Zealand. In Malaysia, a metal image of Ganesh attached to the dashboard of a car was said to have absorbed six teaspoons of milk. In New York, a Hindu woman reported how the milk 'was sucked up, like someone was drinking it through a straw.'

Within 24 hours, the milk-drinking 'miracles' were over, but according to Hindu priests and astrologers, the point had been made: the 'miracle' was auspicious, portending some benefit to humankind.

◻ *See* The Weeping Madonna p. 119

◀ *LEFT: Milk is given to Nandi, the vehicle of Hindu deity Shiva, at the Vishnu temple in Southall, London, in 1995.*

SECRETS OF THE FRUIT AND VEGETABLES

In 1996 and 1997, Muslims experienced a strange sequence of events involving the name of God – Allah – which was found on or inside various fruit and vegetables. On 20 January 1996, in Senegal, the name appeared on a watermelon. Next to it, the Arabic word *hamdoulillah*, 'Praise be to God', could be seen. Thirteen months later, on 20 February 1997, a fruit and vegetable wholesaler in London was slicing an aubergine when he saw that the seeds spelled out Allah in Arabic script.

After this, similar instances occurred in Britain at Huddersfield and Bradford. The incident at Bradford involved not Allah, but the Hindu symbol for God. It, too, was found on slices of aubergine. The miraculous vegetable went on display in a local Hindu temple. At Huddersfield, a Muslim schoolgirl cut a tomato in half and found two messages reading 'There is only one God' and 'Mohammed is the messenger'. Other, similar, events occurred in the United States where the name of Allah appeared on the side of a fish, in the Netherlands where the name appeared on eggs and beans and in India, where 'Allah' and 'Mohammed' appeared on a potato.

Though widely regarded by worshippers as miracles and messages from God, the authorities at the Huddersfield mosque, for one, were cautious: 'We don't consider it a miracle, but it is certainly a blessing!' said a spokesman.

DEMONIC POSSESSION

A belief in possession by demons can be found all over the world, and in almost every religion. Symptoms and signs many believe to demonstrate demonic possession in an individual include hearing strange voices, suffering blackouts or fainting fits, suddenly going into a trance, acting irrationally or, in extreme cases, violent behaviour and acts of suicide.

As the medical profession is at pains to point out though, the potential for many people to mistake mental illness for 'demonic possession' are great, a possibility recognised by church authorities, who instruct their priests to enquire into the mental health of people requesting exorcisms before conducting any ceremonies. Belief in demonic possession is at its greatest in countries like Indonesia, the Philippines, India and other generally poor Third World countries. In such places medical care, including diagnostic expertise, is not of the highest standard and it is conceivably easier, and more convincing, to attribute unusual behaviour to demonic possession rather than a mental problem.

See Ghosts in Primitive Cultures p. 282

▶ *RIGHT: Onlookers watch what is considered to be a 'fit of demoniac fury' involving the twisting of body members.*

EVIL SPIRITS IN HISTORY

Belief in demons is arguably older than civilisation itself. In ancient Canaan and Babylonia, and later, in ancient Israel, people believed in evil spirits called *Dybbuks* which were supposed to live in dark places. Arguments and discord or fighting in wars attracted them and gave them the energy they needed for their main purpose: to take temporary possession of humans and cause them to do evil or make mischief. Fortunately for humans, the Dybbuks hated music and much religious Jewish music took the form of chants designed to ask God to driving them away.

See Ghosts in History p. 17

129

THE REAL EXORCIST

The theme of demonic possession has provided film makers with many opportunities to create suspense in cinema and thrill audiences with frightening special effects. One of the most famous of these films, *The Exorcist*, was made in 1973 and was apparently based on a series of real-life events that occurred in the United States. The story goes that on the evening of 15 January 1949, strange scratching and dripping sounds were heard by a young boy called John Hoffman (an alias) and his mother. These noises soon ceased, but on 25 January, they were replaced by the sounds of footsteps and drumbeats. No explanation could be found for any of these noises.

About four weeks later, towards the end of February 1949, something took possession of young John. Red marks forming words started to appear on his skin. John's parents became desperate after doctors could find nothing wrong with him and took him to Catholic priests in the hope that they could cure him with prayers and holy water. The results were disastrous. The priests simply infuriated whatever was possessing John. At their third attempt, after two crucifixes had been placed under John's pillow, one crucifix was hurled across his bedroom and the other moved to the foot of the bed which shook violently.

Next, when formal exorcism was tried, marks appeared on John's skin making the word 'Hell' and tracing the image of Satan. John himself became increasingly distressed and suffered violent seizures while yelling fearful curses. Several ceremonies of exorcism were performed, with John uttering the words 'I am always with him' and reacting in increasingly violent fashion.

Finally, the priest, Father Lawrence, tried a different method. On the night of 18 April, he made John wear a chain of religious medals and hold a crucifix as the exorcism was performed. The result was dramatic. Father Lawrence ordered the demon to declare itself and John suffered a tremendous spasm: it was so great that five men were required to hold him down. Suddenly, at 11 o'clock the same night, John shouted: 'Satan! I am St. Michael! I command you, Satan, to leave his body now!' The demon, it seems, immediately obeyed. John calmed down and returned to his normal self, but afterwards remembered nothing about the seven weeks when he was possessed by a demon.

See Esther Cox p. 56; Films from the 1970s p. 302

◄ LEFT: Max Von Sydow as Father Merrind in The Exorcist. The film was apparently based on real-life events.

LIVING GHOSTS

Not all ghosts are of dead people. A wide belief is held of living ghosts, people still alive who have appeared as ghosts to those they know or love many miles away. This phenomenon, known as crisis apparition, is believed to be a cry for help being sent in psychic form in situations of distress or danger. Often, the person involved is unaware that they are sending this message. Sometimes the message comes in the form of words, which can be heard from great distances. During World War II, in December 1943, a British soldier was under heavy enemy shellfire in North Africa. He prayed to God to save him so that he could see his wife again. At the exact moment he was praying, his ghost appeared floating above the bed in which his wife, Mrs Violet Almond, had been sleeping.

It is also possible for someone far away to perceive danger about to happen to a friend and to warn them by means of a crisis apparition. For example, Helene Crone saw the apparition of a friend which told her to go and check up on her child. She did so at once to find that the child had opened a drawer full of sharp knives.

Violet Almond and Helene Crone seem to have been particularly receptive to crisis apparitions, since both saw them in their entirety. However, people who are less attuned to the phenomenon tend to see the apparition as a light, a mist or a part-ghost. Most photographs showing evidence of crisis apparitions are of this latter kind.

 See Crisis Apparitions p. 47

GHOSTS CAPTURED ON FILM

Ghostly images that cannot be seen by the naked eye can sometimes be caught on film. Many ghost photographs have nevertheless been declared as misidentifications, with the 'ghost' being anything from the camera strap, overexposure, dirt or moisture, to condensation from the photographer's breath. However, Lewis and Sharon Gerew, leaders of the Philadelphia Ghost Hunters Alliance, claim that they regularly take photographs of ghosts that cannot be seen with the naked eye. They now have a collection of snapshots showing shafts of light that resemble reflections, raindrops, smoke or overexposed film, despite the fact that Gerew strictly controls the investigation scenes; perhaps these are supernatural images?

See Ghost-Hunters p. 20

▲ ABOVE: A spirit caught on camera? This picture was taken by the Rev. Kenneth Lord, the vicar of Newby church in Yorkshire.

THE FIRST 'GHOSTLY' PICTURE

Taken by William Mumler, a Boston engraver, the first ghost picture appeared to show a ghostly figure behind the live sitter but was actually a fake. The cause was an accidental double exposure. Since then, the ability of the camera to produce trick imagery has meant that most ghost pictures are dismissed as fakes. However, some notable exceptions have occurred.

See Clever Hoaxers p. 276

THE PHANTOM AT THE CEMETERY

In 1959, Mrs Mabel Chimney visited the cemetery where her mother was buried and took a photograph of her grave. Her husband was waiting for her in the car and Mrs Chimney took a picture of him as well. There was no one else in the car, but when the picture was developed, Mrs Chimney's dead mother was clearly visible, sitting in the back seat. The picture has since been declared authentic, one of the very few ghost photographs to be recognised as genuine.

RAYNHAM HALL

One of the most important spirit photographs was taken at Raynham Hall in Norfolk, UK. The ghostly figure is known as the Brown Lady, named for the brown flowing dress she wears as she descends the staircase. She is thought to be the ghost of Dorothy Walpole, sister to eighteenth-century English prime minister Robert

Walpole. She was said to have been held prisoner at Raynham by her angry husband, following an affair. Those who have seen her ghost describe an illuminated, gaunt face, with dark hollows instead of eyes. She appears to be benign, walking peacefully through the premises. The photograph was taken in 1936 by Captain Provand, a photographer for *Country Life* magazine. The image has been examined by numerous experts who found no evidence of forgery.

See Haunted Buildings p. 62

PHOTOGRAPHS OF THE DEAD

Sometime in the summer of 1976, two visitors to Hastings Castle took photographs of each other and then asked another tourist to take one of them together. When the photographs were printed, the third picture had what appeared to be an additional figure, a woman in a nun's habit, which can be seen standing behind the couple. Photography experts have been unable to find any natural explanation for the image. Local residents had reported the appearance of a ghostly nun in a brown habit, seen digging a few feet from the entrance to an old dungeon.

In September 1993, the treasurer of a Conservative club in the north of England saw a figure outside the door of the club on his security monitor. He immediately investigated, but could find no evidence of anyone having been there. He returned to his office and saw the same figure still on the monitor. The apparition was recorded on film for several minutes, and made another appearance just a month later. Experts assessing the film could find no explanation.

See The Cardinal and the Virgin Mary p. 119

◀ *LEFT: The Raynham Hall ghost, known as 'The Brown Lady' and thought to be the spirit of Dorothy Walpole.*

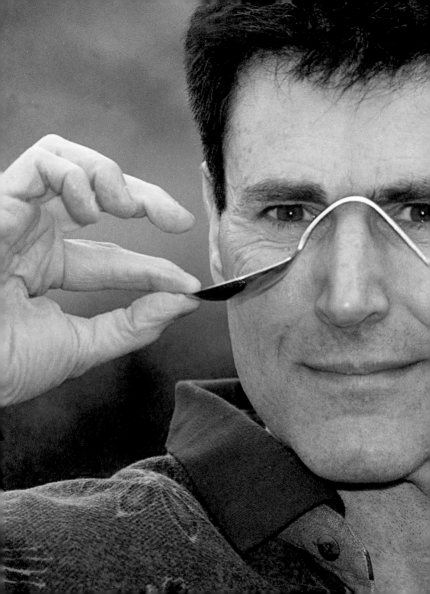

THE POWER OF THE MIND

EXTRA-SENSORY PERCEPTION

Extra-sensory perception (ESP) means the perception of objects, thoughts, or events without the use of the known human senses. Such perceptions, collectively called psi phenomena, are grouped in four main categories: telepathy, or mind-to-mind communication; clairvoyance, or the awareness of remote objects, persons, or events; precognition, or the knowledge of events lying in the future; and retrocognition, or the knowledge of past events in the absence of access to information about those events. Other forms of ESP include psychokinesis, the power to bend or shape objects through the influence of the mind.

All the major world religions have had their prophets or prophecies, many predicting dire consequences for ungodly behaviour. This was a speciality of the Old Testament prophets, although the passage of time inevitably encompassed a downturn in fortunes that validated their forecasts.

◀ LEFT: The prophet and priest Samuel, who warned of divine punishment after the Jews defied God.

The prophet Samuel, for example, warned of frightful punishment in the future after the Jews defied God to acquire a king. Eventually, the Romans conquered Israel and threw the Jews out, although in reality some 12 centuries elapsed between these two events. Since those ancient times, however, ESP has been treated less in spiritual and more in scientific terms.

Scientists have argued against paranormal researchers for decades about the possibility of ESP, and many tests have failed to prove that it exists. However, the files of the Society for Psychical Research in London are full of uncanny cases and the police have been known to use psychics in some of their investigations.

See Clairvoyance p. 141; The Power of the Unconscious p. 53; Precognition p. 143; Psychokinesis p. 143; Retrocognition p. 142

TAKE MY RING

On 9 September 1848, on the field of battle, a soldier was severely wounded and thought to be dying. He requested that his ring be removed and sent to his wife. His wife, who lay sleeping some 240 km (150 miles) away, woke up and had a vision of her husband being carried off the field. She heard his voice saying, 'Take this ring off my finger and send it to my wife.' The ring and the news of his death reached her several days later.

See Living Ghosts p. 132

GELLER, URI

Uri Geller became famous in the 1970s for his ability to bend metal by concentrating on it. Spoons, forks and keys allegedly continued to bend after he had left the room. Geller first became aware of these powers of psychokinesis (known as PK) when he was just four years old. On many occasions he has been able to read material in sealed envelopes, and to 'see' while blindfolded. His skills have been dismissed as trickery by some, but no one has been able to provide a rational explanation.

◆ *See* Psychokinesis p. 145

▶ RIGHT: Uri Geller, the parapsychologist from Israel who became a household name due to his skill at bending cutlery.

THE CINCINNATI PREMONITION

One of the best-documented cases of premonition occurred in 1979 in Cincinnati, Ohio. An office manager named David Booth had a vivid dream for 10 nights running, in which he 'saw' an American Airlines jet crashing into flames in an area full of buildings. Booth recognised that he was having a premonition, and contacted American Airlines, a psychiatrist and the Federal Aviation Authority. Finally, he was taken seriously and the FAA tried to link his dream with a particular type of aircraft. Then, on 26 May, a day after the last vision, an American Airlines DC10 took off from Chicago's O'Hare Airport. Seconds after it cleared the runway, an engine fell off and the plane crashed in a massive fireball at the edge of the airport and near to buildings on the site. Everyone on board was killed instantly. After the accident, the Civil Aviation Authority confirmed that many details of the crash had matched Booth's dreams. Booth never understood why he was given advance notice of this event when he, and everyone else, was powerless to change it.

◆ *See* Nostradamus p. 260

VISIONS OF ABERFAN

On 21 October 1966, a huge spoil heap of coal slurry collapsed and buried a school in the mining town of Aberfan, South Wales. More than 140 people, including 128 schoolchildren, were killed. During the weeks that followed, it became clear that many people had foreseen the tragedy. Thirty-five cases were recorded by British psychiatrist J. C. Barker.

One of the children killed in the slide had told her mother that she had had an odd dream: 'I dreamt I went to school,' she had explained, 'and there was no school there. Something black had come down all over it.' Two hours later she was killed in the tragedy. Her mother was comforted by the fact that the day before the disaster, her daughter had suddenly started talking about death, and explained that she wasn't afraid to die.

▶ RIGHT: The funeral of the 144 people who died in the coal slide in Aberfan, Wales in 1966.

CLAIRVOYANCE

The term clairvoyance, which comes from two French words meaning 'clear' and 'to see', means the ability to perceive future events or those that occur beyond the normal reach of eyesight. More commonly termed 'extra-sensory perception' (ESP), this ability has been claimed throughout the ages by astrologers, the seers of Ancient Greece and Rome, by Biblical prophets, by people who claim to be telepaths, by spiritualists and, in more recent times, by 'remote viewers'. A variation is clairaudience, which is the ability to hear sounds or messages from far away. Both clairvoyance and clairaudience are said to occur while practitioners are in a normal state of consciousness, but can also be induced with the aid of drugs, fasting or scrying. Scrying involves staring with great concentration at a shiny-surface object until a vision emerges. Gypsy fortune-tellers gazing into their crystal balls is an example of scrying.

During the Cold War (1945–90) 'remote viewers', otherwise known as psychic spies, were employed by both superpowers. Their task was to extend their consciousness to observe events or acquire secret information located thousands of miles away. The value of this type of observation was that it could be done in relative safety and free from discovery. In the twenty-first century, remote viewers are reportedly still being used by the Pentagon to discover facts or predict future events, particularly in the United States' war against terrorists like Osama bin Laden and his terrorist group Al-Qaeda. It is even believed that remote viewers, who target the minds of terrorists and then draw their plans on paper, forecasted and sketched the attack on the World Trade Center in New York on 11 September 2001: the relevant drawing showed two tall towers with an aircraft heading straight for one of the upper floors.

⬥ See Extra-Sensory Perception p. 138

PRECOGNITION

The famous nineteenth-century clairvoyant Daniel Douglas Home who was born in Scotland, first displayed his amazing gifts in his teens. While in his aunt's house, furniture began to move and strange noises were heard. His aunt, believing her nephew to be possessed, called in the exorcists. They, however, told her that God had granted the boy special gifts, including the ability to levitate. Home could also make tables lift close to the ceiling, and make musical instruments materialise and begin playing by themselves.

Another clairvoyant, the Brazilian Jose Pedro de Freitas, known as Arigo, first realised his gift when he cured a dying woman of a tumour that was killing her. As her last rites were being read, Arigo grabbed a kitchen knife and cut the tumour out. The woman was said to have

▲ ABOVE: Daniel Douglas Home demonstrates his gift of levitation. He could also levitate furniture.

made a complete recovery and Arigo subsequently became a famous psychic surgeon. He claimed that he was working with the spirit of a German doctor named Adolphus Fritz who had died during World War I. In 1956 Arigo was was arrested for illegally practising medicine. However, after Arigo was sentenced to eight months in prison, the president of

◀ LEFT: A medium practising the art of scrying by gazing into a crystal ball.

Brazil intervened and saved him by issuing a pardon. Arigo's cures seemed miraculous and in one case he was witnessed cutting into the cornea of a patient's eye with a pair of nail scissors; within seconds he had removed a cataract. Arigo then said a prayer and wiped the woman's eye with a piece of cotton on which a few drops of liquid had miraculously appeared. The patient felt no pain during the entire operation and was said to have been completely cured.

◆ *See Daniel Douglas Home p. 260; Retrocognition p. 144*

◄ *LEFT: The psychic surgeon Arigo on trial in 1964. He was imprisoned for practising medicine illegally.*

RETROCOGNITION

The term retrocognition means the opposite of precognition and is the paranomal knowledge of previously unknown events from the past.

One recorded instance took place in 1938 and involved a woman named Marguerite Vassar. She was walking towards the water pump outside her California farmhouse when she saw a terrified woman run towards the riverside path where two men were carrying the body of a young girl who had drowned. Marguerite followed them into the farmhouse, where the girl was laid on the bed. Suddenly, the vision faded and Marguerite found herself outside the farmhouse once again. Later, Marguerite learned that the daughter of a family who had once lived at the farmhouse had drowned in the river around 1904.

The famous clairvoyant, Edgar Cayce, claimed that in the past, the Sahara desert had once been fertile land. In 1986, the shuttle imaging radar from the space shuttle proved him right, with a picture of a previously unknown river running beneath the Sahara desert.

See Precognition p. 143

PSYCHOKINESIS

The term psychokinesis comes from the Ancient Greek words for 'life', *psyche,* and *kinein*, which means 'to move'. Similar to telekinesis, but greater in scope, psychokinesis, or PK, is a technique in which mind operates over matter through unseen means. Under psychokinesis can be grouped such phenomena as miracle healings, mysterious lights, the weaving of magic spells and curses, weather-controlling rituals and the use of the Evil Eye. Also known as the envious eye, the belief in the Evil Eye – that a person can unknowingly cause harm to another by merely looking at them with envy – is an ancient one. It is mentioned in the Bible and became a commonly held belief in the Middle East, around the Mediterranean and throughout Europe. During the Middle Ages, the Eye was thought to induce sickness or death, to cause a variety of ills, including the drying up of milk in nursing mothers, the withering of fruit in orchards and impotence in men. To ward off the Eye, amulets and the reciting of protective sayings or verses were often used.

See Shamanic Healing p. 147

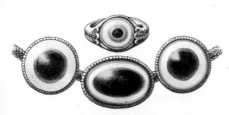

◀ LEFT: Some agates resemble an eye when they are cut, and are therefore worn as a protection against the Evil Eye.

WITCHES

Before the advent of modern scientific medicine, when numerous diseases and conditions, now preventable, had no cure, it was easy to presume that an evil force was abroad spreading infections and causing epidemics, suffering and death. In medieval Europe, witches were frequently blamed for the use of the Evil Eye or otherwise causing evil by means. The burning at the stake of innocent women denounced as evil witches for simply being eccentric were widespread.

◆ *See* Evil Spirits in History p. 129

WITCH DOCTORS

Outside Europe, the attitude towards psychokinesis and its practitioners was different. In Africa and pre-Hispanic America in particular, tribes and past civilisations relied heavily on witch doctors, medicine men and shamans to cure their ills, help defend against enemies, bring rain, produce thunder and drive the Moon from the face of the Sun during a total eclipse. As a truly impressive example of psychokinesis, it was even believed that certain sorcerers could curse and kill enemies from a distance through the use of magic.

See The Shaman p. 293

SHAMANIC HEALING

In more recent times, many psychokinetic abilities have been revealed as mere sleight-of-hand magic tricks or illusions. Even so, the need for the spiritual healing in which the ancient shamans and witch doctors specialised has persisted into the twenty-first century as the pace of modern life drains physical and mental energies. As a result, there has been an upsurge of interest, particularly in the United States, in spiritual shamanic healing. One such healer, the Native American Rosalee Sirgany, uses her contacts with Indian Spirit Guides and Masters to calm and cure her patients. Another, Clay Miller, who is based at Sedona in the Arizona desert, takes his patients on a 'soul journey' in order to soothe their troubled psyches.

Today people such as Sirgany and Miller have given psychokinesis a gentler image, offering alternative healing methods to people who have lost faith in conventional medicine and have returned to more ancient,

◄ LEFT: Witches being burned at Derneburg in 1555.

more spiritual means of finding a cure for their mental or physical ills. The Center for the New Age at Sedona, for instance, contains a community of psychics, astrologers, aromatherapists, numerologists and masseuses, as well as spiritual retreats.

◆ See Psychokinesis p. 145; Spiritual Healing p. 148

SPIRITUAL HEALING

Spiritual healers focus their attention on the highest source of peace and love in the universe that they can imagine, whatever their spiritual beliefs. This is called 'attunement to the universal source' and is similar to meditation. It is a state of heightened awareness: being totally present and at the same time having an attitude of detachment.

Spiritual healers consciously direct this experience of union with the universal source through themselves to the patient. This is called channelling. This type of healing, where a patient is present, is sometimes called 'laying on of hands', although the hands are mainly held a short distance from the body. At the end of a healing session, healers will consciously break the connection they have made with the patient and resume their normal everyday conscious state of being.

◆ See Spiritualism p. 264

HEALING IN JAPAN

In September 1994 the Japanese conducted a healing experiment. Carol Everett, a healer from Devon in the UK, was flown to Tokyo's Denki University to participate in tests with Professor Yoshio Machi. She was hooked up to a series of monitors which would chart changes in her body and mind during the healing process. She was introduced to a girl she had never met before, and correctly diagnosed a lump on one of the woman's ovaries. Carol then began a healing process to remove the

▶ *RIGHT: The celebrated healer Matthew Manning. While a teenager he demonstrated his ability to use psychokinesis.*

tumour, which was about 2 cm across. During the healing, changes were noted in the healer's brain activity, and at the same time, the image of the patient on the scanner altered radically. The heat intensity of the tumour cooled and the spot reduced until, after seven minutes, it disappeared completely. Carol came out of her trancelike state, and the imaging equipment confirmed that she was right. A month later, the girl's doctor confirmed that the tumour was completely gone.

One of the most famous New Age healers is Matthew Manning, whose psychokinetic ability was confirmed in a series of experiments in Toronto, Canada, after he seemed to be the focus of poltergeist activity. At the age of 19, he became a world-class celebrity through a seeming ability to use psychokinesis to disrupt electrical systems, cause machines stop working and produce automatic writing in languages unknown to him. His abilities as a healer emerged in 1977 when he demonstrated at a scientific experiment at San Antonio, Texas, that he could influence cervical cancer cells and cure the afflicted. Subsequently, Manning embarked on a career as a healer, encouraging his patients to use their own positive energy to achieve health and well-being.

◆ *See* Matthew Manning p. 268; Precognition p.143

TELEKINESIS

The ability to make objects move, levitate or change their form purely by means of thought is referred to as telekinesis. Probably the best-known demonstrations of telekinesis have been provided by the Israeli paranormalist Uri Geller, who uses mind-power to bend spoons and keys or stop watches. Telekinesis is not always applied deliberately. It is suspected that young people around the age of puberty can cause poltergeist activity, in which objects appear to be moved around by some mischievous unseen spirit. This is not the result of conscious effort, it just happens, seemingly on its own. Poltergeist activity is often violent and destructive but the ability seems to fade away when puberty is over.

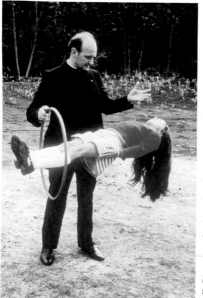

Telekinesis can also occur when emotions run high. For example, in 1997 in the USA, a couple had a fierce argument in the kitchen of their home while the husband was preparing omelettes for supper. Suddenly, there was a sharp cracking sound and a china bowl containing the eggs split into three neat sections. At the same time a bite-sized chunk fell off a china plate which contained

◀ *LEFT: Father Quevedo performs levitation, a form of telekinesis in which the mind alone makes objects move.*

the cheese for the omelettes. Neither the bowl nor the plate had been touched. It is possible that sound waves could have been disrupted by the argument, so causing 'sonic' cracks in the china. However, another theory suggests that neural emissions from the quarrelling couple produced telekinetic effects by joining up with Zero Point Fluctuation (ZPF), or the background radiation of free space.

◆ *See Uri Geller p. 139*

REINCARNATION AND PAST LIVES

Reincarnation involves the idea that the spirit of a person leaves the body at death and is reborn into someone else. In Hinduism and Buddhism, it is believed that the spirit passes either to a higher or lower form of life, depending on the righteousness of the life just left, while Christians believe that Jesus was reincarnated after he died on the cross. Is reincarnation just a religious belief or actual fact?

◆ *See Inherited Memory p. 154*

▶ *RIGHT: An Indian belief asserts that if a live black cat is thrown into a fire, a reincarnated soul is liberated.*

MARY SUTTON

In 1993 a woman from Northamptonshire, Jenny Cockell, claimed that from an early age she was beset by dreams of a woman in a cottage, with a large family and an abusive husband. Jenny was haunted by these dreams, despite growing up and having her own family. She was convinced that the woman lived in Ireland, and was able to draw maps of the town and the household from memory. Feeling that unfinished business was the cause of the dreams, she travelled to Ireland and located the village. She discovered that the long-dead woman of her dreams had lived in a cottage outside Dublin. Her name was Mary Sutton and after her death at an early age, her children had been separated and sent off to foster homes. They'd never seen one another again. Jenny decided that it was her responsibility to resolve this and tracked down several of the surviving children. She organised a reunion in the house they had all shared. The children were astonished by the intimate details of their childhood that this woman could provide, particularly since Jenny was years younger than Mary Sutton. Was this reincarnation? Or was Jenny Cockell haunted by an unhappy ghost?

THE DALAI LAMA

Dalai Lama is the title of the religious leader of Tibetan Buddhism, who was also, until 1959, temporal ruler of Tibet. Each Dalai Lama is believed to be the reincarnation of his predecessor. When one dies, the new incarnation is sought among newly born boys; the child is identified by his ability to pick out possessions of the former Dalai Lama from a group of similar objects.

THE POLLOCK TWINS

In 1957, two sisters aged 6 and 11, and the only children of the Pollock family from Hexham in Northumberland, were tragically killed in a car accident by a woman who had decided to take her own life.

Their father, John Pollock, was a strong believer in reincarnation and when his wife announced she was pregnant some months later, he prophesied that she would bear twin girls who would be their daughters reincarnated.

The family doctor detected only one foetus in the womb and Florence Pollock refused to believe her husband. However, on 4 October 1958, twin girls were delivered. One of the twins had a faint white mark on her forehead that matched a scar on the head of one of the dead daughters. The other twin

▲ ABOVE: Some evidence suggests that the Pollock twins might be reincarnations of their older sisters, who had been killed in a road accident.

had an identical birthmark to the other dead daughter. The strange coincidences did not stop there. The children recognised the school that their sisters had attended, knew uncanny facts about the dead girls' childhoods, and could correctly name their older siblings' dolls (and knew which one had belonged to each). More frightening still, they were often found together, one cradling the other, and talking about blood pouring from her mouth, just as it had during the accident. Once, when a car started up that was facing them at the same angle as the car which killed their older sisters, they screamed and clutched each other in terror.

The incidents ceased when the twins reached five years of age, and they had no recollection of them. The case has never been satisfactorily explained.

RAVI SHANKAR

In 1953, a two-year old Indian boy named Ravi Shankar (not the famous sitar-player) told his parents that he had lived in a previous life, as Munna, the son of a barber. According to Ravi, two men, a barber and a washerman had enticed Munna into an orchard near the Chintamini

Temple where they beheaded him with a razor and buried him in sand. The two men, though suspected, were never prosecuted due to lack of witnesses.

Ravi was born six months after the murder, in July 1951, bearing a mark similar to a scar from a knife wound across his neck. Ravi would often tremble when he saw a barber or a washerman, and once became terrified at the sight of a stranger who turned out to be the suspected washerman. In 1955, Sri Jageshwar Prasad, the father of the murdered six-year old Munna, went to see Ravi, then aged four, after hearing of him. Upon seeing him Ravi instantly recognised him as his one-time father, even identifying the watch Prasad was wearing as an old gift to Munna. In addition he recounted correctly that Munna had taken some guavas to eat just before he was killed. By the time he was 18, Ravi's memories of his previous life had all but gone, though he still felt uneasy whenever he went near the Chintamini Temple, where Munna had met his death.

EXPLANATIONS OF REINCARNATION

Most accounts of reincarnation come from India and other parts of Asia where belief in the phenomenon is part of the Hindu and Buddhist religions. Stories from Western culture, where neither Christianity nor Judaism officially acknowledge reincarnation, appear to be less frequent and recorded cases are less vivid and complete. This difference has given rise to the theory that accepted widespread belief in itself in Asian countries give rise to incidences of reincarnation.

Inherited Memory

A rival reincarnation theory concerns inherited memory, or 'genetic programming'. This works by passing on tastes, preferences, instincts, talents and other skills and knowledge or memories through the genes.

Physical characteristics, like birthmarks, can be passed on in the same way. In 1995, a man belonging to the Tlingit tribe in Alaska showed his niece two operation scars on his body, one at the corner of his right eye and the other on his back. He forecast that he would return after death and that she would know him by these marks. Some 18 months after the man died, his niece gave birth to a son who had exactly the same marks on his body as his great-uncle's operation scars.

A third theory marries inherited memory to Charles Darwin's theory of evolution and treats reincarnation as a form of the 'survival of the fittest'. Some people possess social skills that allow the creation of supportive lifestyles. These lifestyles favour the rearing of children so that the more socially adept are more likely to survive. Recently, it has been discovered that magnetic processes present in the brain shortly before death make tiny 'splashes' in the Earth's magnetic field. These 'splashes' contain information about the dying person's consciousness. Information suitable for reincarnation is 'tagged' for repetition. The unsuitable is also marked, but as a factor to be avoided.

◆ *See* The Pollock Twins p. 152

▶ *RIGHT: Charles Darwin*

OUT-OF-BODY EXPERIENCES/ASTRAL PROJECTIONS

Although quite different from each other, out-of-body experiences and astral projections are often classed together. The out-of-body experience, or OBE, is supposed to occur when a person is awake. By comparison, astral projection requires the individual to enter a dreaming state. An out-of-body experience has been compared to a near-death experience, and the person's consciousness detaches from its physical body to take

on an external perspective of hovering above it. Astral projection is more dramatic, taking the person on a journey in which anything is possible – flying, performing great physical feats and visiting faraway places.

Astral projection stems from an occult belief that reality is divided into seven planes and that we have a different body for each. The astral plane is a dreamlike world and during astral projection our astral body leaves the other six planes. Scientific investigations into astral projection have shown that the body responds to whatever is taking place in a dream.

Spiritualists believe that in OBEs, the soul temporarily leaves the body, or in cases of imminent death, transports it to another body for reincarnation. In 2002, doctors in a Swiss neurology clinic reported artificially producing, by accident, an OBE in a patient being treated for epilepsy when the angular gyrus in the right cortex of her brain was stimulated by an electrode. From this, it was deduced that OBEs could result from disconnection or misfiring in imparting information to the brain. The Swiss medical team also discovered that when patients were about to suffer a seizure, they registered floating above their own bodies, seeing flashing lights or cartoon characters, or experiencing *déja vu* ('already seen') or its opposite, *jamais vu* ('never seen').

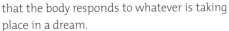 *See* Extra-Sensory Perception p. 138

◄ *LEFT: The projection of the astral body.*

NATURAL PHENOMENA AND THE ANCIENT WORLD

FREAK WEATHER OCCURRENCES

THE SIBERIAN FIREBALL

Just after 7 a.m. on 30 June 1908, a huge fireball struck the snow-swept tundra of Siberia, incinerating all life over a 65-km (40-mile) area.

In seconds, the sparsely inhabited Tunguska River valley was destroyed. Farmer Sergei Semenov was one of the few witnesses whose recollections of the disaster were recorded. He was some 80 km (50 miles) from the centre of the blast when it happened. He wrote: 'There appeared a great flash. There was so much heat, my shirt was almost burnt off my back. I saw a huge ball of fire that covered an enormous part of the sky. Afterwards it became very dark. It shook the whole house and moved it from its foundations.' Another was thrown more than 6 m (19 ft) by the shockwave and reported 'the sky ... split in two and high above the forest, the whole northern part of the sky appeared covered with fire... There was a bang in the sky and a mighty crash. The earth trembled.' Tunguska forest remained on fire for many weeks. For two months afterwards, clouds glowed a strange silver at night: dubbed 'White Night', the effects were global.

Russian investigators were astonished by the sight. Herds of reindeer were literally roasted where they stood grazing. Some 40,000 trees were destroyed, an area of around 320 km (199 miles) radius was laid to waste and nomadic tribesmen over 70 km (45 miles) away from the centre of the blast had been lifted into the air and their tents had blown away. The shock waves were felt as far away as Europe and the United States. It was, beyond doubt, the greatest unexplained disaster ever recorded. In the town of Kirensk, survivors told of a pillar of fire (like the mushroom cloud of a nuclear explosion) rising above the devastation, and people described the River Kan as 'foaming and broiling like a tormented sea'.

◆ See Ball Lightning p. 165

▲ *ABOVE: Devastation caused by the Siberian Fireball; the greatest unexplained disaster ever recorded.*

UFOS?

Mineralogist Professor Leonid Kulik of the Soviet Academy of Science claimed that a mega-meteorite must have hit the Earth. Since that time, however, this theory has been discarded. There was no massive crater and little evidence of meteorite dust. Theories about the cause of the blast abound. Some people suggest that a spaceship visiting the Earth blew up and that its nuclear reactor exploded. Although the UFO theory has been widely discounted, there is evidence suggesting that the blast could have been nuclear – before man had mastered the splitting of the atom. The Earth's magnetic field was disturbed after the blast, just as it would be after the nuclear bomb tests that came later. Furthermore, after a nuclear blast, there are tiny green globules of melted dust, called trinites. These were found after the Russian blast, and experts confirmed that the trinites did not come from the Tunguska River valley. This seems to confirm the experts' opinion that it could have been some form of nuclear explosion.

◆ *See* Earth Magnetism p. 30

Other Explanations

A number of other theories have been put forward to explain the occurrence. These include:

- A black hole. Little is known of black-hole phenomena, but their gravitational pull is so strong that no light escapes. According to American physicist John Carlson: 'A massive atom-sized black hole entering the Earth's atmosphere at a typical collision velocity for an interplanetary body would create an atmospheric shock wave with enough force to raze hundreds of square kilometres of Siberian forest, ionise air, produce flash-burning and seismic effects. No major crater or meteoritic residue would result.'

- A meteorite. Some scientists say that the blast could have been caused by a giant meteorite that exploded before hitting the ground. The effect would have been like that of a giant shrapnel shell, burning the area around it but creating no crater.

▶ *RIGHT: One of the theories to explain the Siberian Fireball is that a giant meteorite exploded before hitting the ground.*

- A comet. Similar to the meteorite theory is the comet theory detailed in a 1977 paper. In it, two British university professors say that the energy of a comet would have been too low for a full-scale nuclear explosion, but that it could have created a blast almost the size of an atom bomb. No comets or meteorites were detected in the skies at the time of the explosion, but academics say that this could be due to the comet only becoming visible to the naked eye at dawn, which would have made it indistinguishable from the Sun.
- Despite the plethora of theories, nearly a century of scientific study has failed to come up with a conclusive cause for the Siberian disaster.

▲ *ABOVE: The comet Hale Bopp above Mt Fuji in Japan in April 1997. Was a comet responsible for the devastation of the Tunguska River valley?*

HESSDALEN LIGHTS

In November 1981, the inhabitants of the Hessdalen Valley, stretching across 12 km (7.5 miles) of central Norway, near the Swedish border, began to experience strange luminous phenomena. The lights sometimes appeared as frequently as four times a day, often below the horizon, along mountain tops, or on the roofs of houses. Usually white or yellowish, they were typically cigar-shaped, or like spheres or vortices.

163

Occasionally, a red light maintained a position in front. The lights hovered, sometimes for up to an hour, and then left at great speed.

In 1984, a team of experts calling themselves 'Project Hessdalen' trekked to the valley and with a great deal of technological equipment, set out to either establish the presence of UFOs, or to find another cause for the phenomenon. For several weeks they investigated the area, recording and measuring the lights, some of which were red and blue in colour. On 12 February 1985, the lights seemed to respond when laser beams were flashed at them. One of the objects changed its regular flashing light to a regular double flashing light until the investigators changed the rhythm back again.

The expedition produced excellent photographs and other readings of the structure of these phenomena. Later research suggested that they were witnessing a type of atmospheric plasma somehow generated in the area, but whose origin was unknown.

In 1986, the lights subsided. A University of Oslo physicist, Elvand Thrane, who had participated in the research, later said, 'I'm sure the lights were real. It's a pity we cannot explain them'.

See Earthlights p. 31

INSTANT HEAT WAVE

On the morning of 7 July 1987, the temperature in Greensburg, Kansas, rose 11°C (20°F) in just 10 minutes. At 7.30 a.m. it was 24°C (75°F), and at 7.40 it was 35°C (95°F). John May, National Weather Service meteorologist at Topeka, had never heard of such a phenomenon, but speculated that the layer of cool air that normally develops overnight close to the ground simply switched places with warmer air thousands of metres up. 'We are not sure why this happens,' he said.

See Ice Cold p. 166

BALL LIGHTNING

Ball lightning is a little-understood phenomenon, usually lasting less than five seconds. It is generally spherical, ranging from one to more than 100 cm (0.4 to more than 40 ins) in diameter. The balls are reported to move at a few metres per second and to decay silently or with a small explosion. In January 1984, a Russian passenger plane experienced the phenomenon. The crew saw a glowing light several inches in diameter in front of the cockpit. It suddenly disappeared with a loud roar, and reappeared seconds later – after piercing the fuselage in some odd way – in the passengers' cabin. As the passengers watched in disbelief, the spherical object flew above their heads until it reached the tail of the plane, where it divided into two glowing crescents. The crescents then merged into a single sphere and disappeared. Later, when mechanics examined the aircraft, they found a hole in the front of the fuselage and another in the tail.

Some experts claim that ball lightning does not exist, attributing the phenomenon instead to extra-terrestrial activity.

➧ See Earth Magnetism p. 30

▶ RIGHT: Examples of ball lightning reported by a Swedish magazine.

ICE COLD

On 11 March 1978, at 10.30 a.m., workers in fields at Becquerel, France, heard a loud explosion, followed by the sound of something falling. They rushed to the site and came across a fresh crater containing a 25-kg (11-lb) lump of transparent ice with 'greenish depths'. The lump stayed intact for an hour.

SAINTED SHADOWS

Mountaineers can get a big fright when climbing the Harz Mountains in Germany thanks to a phenomenon known as Sainted Shadows. Under certain conditions, shadowy figures surrounded by a halo of white light stretch out before them over the dew-covered grass on the mountainside. As the mountaineers continue climbing, the apparitions climb with them, duplicating their every move. Understandably, climbers have returned to base badly shaken by the experience. So much so that it has revived ancient tales of witches celebrating a black sabbath on Brocken peak in the Hartz Mountain. The phenomenon, however, is not necessarily a supernatural one. A scientific theory shows that foggy conditions on the mountain peak can enlarge the climbers' shadows, which are then reflected on clouds and fog banks, where they glow, surrounded by 'halos'. As the climbers move, so do their own shadow 'apparitions'.

▶ RIGHT: Mountaineers have told of shadowy apparitions that follow them.

RAINING CATS AND DOGS

Rainfall can bring all sorts of unusual things: showers of corn, peas, nuts, seeds, various fruits and even frogs. Sometimes, it does not even need to be raining for this to happen. In 1951, men working on top of New York's Empire State Building had to run for shelter when they were peppered with millions of grains of barley. In 1977, a shower of hazelnuts fell on a Bristol couple going home from church. The sky was clear and there had only been a light wind. In 1980, a shower of peas fell over the town of Tonna, in South Wales. In 1984, thunderous noises were heard at East Crescent in the UK as thousands of apples rained down for over an hour.

These, though, were not the weirdest 'showers' to occur. Live worm-lizards fell on Memphis, Tennessee in 1877; a turtle came down in a hailstorm at Vicksburg, Massachusetts in 1894; and maggots fell on Acapulco, in Mexico in 1968. Other locations have been peppered with various types of lifeform falling from the sky, including snails on Algiers, in Algeria in 1953.

◈ See Frog Falls p. 168

▲ *ABOVE: There are no reports of the sky actually raining cats and dogs but many other items have apparently fallen from the sky including snails and maggots!*

FROG FALLS

There have been many instances of frogs falling from the sky over the centuries:

- Pliny recorded a strange rain of frogs in AD 77.
- In Sutton Park, Birmingham, UK, hundreds of frogs peppered people's umbrellas during a summer shower in 1954.
- On a golf course in Arkansas, USA, in 1973, players watched as thousands of frogs came down during a rainstorm.
- In 1977, at Canet-Plage in France, frogs the size of peas were seen bouncing off the bonnets of people's cars.
- In 1979, a housewife from Bedford, UK, found not only frogs all over her lawn following a rainstorm, but also frog spawn hanging from the bushes.

TSUNAMIS

In 2001, the geologist Professor David Smith told a conference of the British Association for the Advancement of Science, of a giant tsunami which, he claimed, turned Britain into an instant island some 7,800 years ago. At that time, Britain was still attached to the Netherlands and Denmark by a land bridge now covered by the English Channel. Rising sea levels were already beginning to engulf this bridge when a series of giant waves or tsunamis, over 9 m (26.5 ft) high, finished the job virtually overnight. The tsunamis were apparently set off by a huge landslide on the sea floor across the North Sea, at Storegga in Norway. Sediments on

the sea bed were moved and by the time it had ceased, had covered an area of sea floor as big as Scotland. No one knows what caused the landslide, but according to Professor Smith, the result was dramatic. The landslide caused ripples to run across the North Sea and gradually build up momentum to become giant waves. These waves smashed down on the land bridge, causing it to disintegrate and turn Britain into an island.

◆ See The Lost Continent of Atlantis p. 190

▼ BELOW: According to Professor David Smith, Britain is an island because of a giant tsunami: a destructive wave often caused by an earthquake under the sea.

CROP CIRCLES

The first of numerous crop circles, in which patterns appeared in fields of wheat and other crops, arose in the south of England at Warminster, Wiltshire, on the night of 12 August 1972. Bryce Bond and Arthur Shuttlewood were out in a wheat field when they heard a noise. As they watched in the bright moonlight, an imprint took shape on the wheat, forcing it down flat in a clockwise direction. Since 1972, an estimated 10,000 crop circles in various formations have been reported, some of them over 1 km (0.63 miles) long, others covering areas nearly 19,000 m (62,339 ft) square. Ufologists, devotees of UFO theories, have claimed crop circles as signs left by the exhausts of alien spacecraft either landing or hovering above the fields. Other explanations have also come to light, dividing experts on the subject. The various explanations include:

- Parties of hoaxers who have entered cornfields to craft the crop circles and confound the experts. Many have afterwards confessed.
- The circles are created by hedgehogs or rabbits, hovering helicopters, whirlwinds or ancient Earth power lines or, more fancifully, the Devil or fairies.
- The circles are linked to disturbances in the Earth's magnetic field, an explanation endorsed in August 2000 by Rockefeller Institute researcher Colin Andrews, but only for simple circles. Andrews dismisses complex circles as hoaxes.

◀ *LEFT: An aerial view of the crop circle that mysteriously appeared below the Huish Ridge, north-west of Pewsey in Wiltshire, England.*

- According to Dr Terence Meaden, head of TORRO, the Tornado and Storm Research Association in the UK, unusual air vortices have been behind many simpler circles.
- The circles are 'Landscape Art' created and subsequently photographed by artists.

One of the most puzzling aspects of crop circles is the way in which extensive complex patterns are crafted with perfect symmetry and mathematical precision. If the circles are hoaxes the hoaxers would have to levitate above the field in order to get the right perspective. Another mystery is the lack of trails to mark the apparent entry route of hoaxers into fields where crop circles have been found. By answer, the theory of hoaxers in hot-air balloons has been put forward, but no one has yet worked out how the hoaxers, standing in the balloon's basket, could keep a balloon perfectly still while they hovered a few metres above the ground and carved out the circle.

The more scientific or mundane explanations do not solve the mystery of the catalogue of strange events that have been reported to accompany the creation of some of the most complex crop circles. For instance, dogs in the vicinity start barking between 2 a.m. and

▶ *RIGHT: The intricate patterns formed within crop circles have ruled out many explanations.*

4 a.m., and next morning, another crop circle is noticed nearby. Cattle or sheep that enter crop circles have become sick. Freak winds have been noted occurring on hillsides, orange balls of light are seen and strange rustling noises are heard. Many UFO sightings have also been reported just before the crop circles appear.

◆ *See* Alien Visitations in the Ancient World p. 232; Earth Magnetism p. 30

MARINE MYSTERIES

There is no question that seamen are amongst the most superstitious of us all, but does that explain the inordinate number of mysteries that surround ships and other vessels that travel on or under the sea and the aeroplanes that fly over it?

Despite the fact that almost three-quarters of the globe is covered by water, we have charted just two per cent of the ocean floor. What lies within its depths may never be fully understood, but it would appear that the sea holds a strange power that has not yet been explained by science. One of the most frightening characteristics of the sea is its power to engulf large vessels completely, without any trace. Years-long searches into strange marine disappearances have been undertaken and have come up with nothing but a pocketful of useless and unproved theories. Unexplained vanishings at sea are more numerous and baffling than those on land. Furthermore, we may never fully comprehend this vast unknown.

◆ *See* The Bermuda Triangle p. 175; Amelia Earhart p. 93; Vortexes p. 33

THE POWER OF THE SEA

Even more frightening, perhaps, is the idea that triangles of sea can have a hypnotic or magnetic effect on aircraft and seacraft in its vicinity. The Bermuda Triangle and the Devil's Sea off Japan are two such examples. The huge number of vanishings and other phenomena in their midst have been classified 'natural', but other mysterious circumstances have yet to be explained by natural causes.

There are those who believe that the sea carries a great and almost living power. Can a powerful marine tragedy create ghost ships? Can people really disappear on the sea, with no sign of wreckage, bodies or attempts to flee a sinking ship? Although the likelihood is that one day we will find rational explanations for these occurrences, for now they remain a mystery.

See The Bermuda Triangle p. 175

THE *MARY CELESTE*

In November 1872, Captain Benjamin Spooner Briggs set sail with his wife and two-year-old daughter and a crew of seven aboard the cargo ship *Mary Celeste*. They left New York on their way to Genoa with a cargo of crude (unconsumable) alcohol aboard, and passed through good weather before meeting a 'moderate gale' around the Azores.

Also sailing from New York was the *Dei Gratia*, a British ship heading for Gibraltar. On 5 December, the crew spotted the *Mary Celeste*. It appeared to be in trouble, and upon drawing closer they found that the wheel was unattended. Three seaman were sent aboard to investigate, but they found the ship deserted. The cargo was intact, as were the food supplies, and the crew's clothing was on board. The ship's log had been

◀ LEFT: *The power and mystery of the sea is captured in Francis J. Mortimer's photograph 'Spirit of Storm', taken in 1911.*

filled in regularly until the last entry on 25 November, which suggested that the ship had been empty for up to 10 days. A small sailboat, a chronometer and a sextant were missing, but apart from a little storm damage to the sails and rigging, the ship was in good order and there was so sign of any untoward activity on the boat.

To this day, what happened to the ship is unknown. Various theories have been put forward, including murder of the captain by the crew, voluntary abandonment by the crew, pirates and even an attack by a sea monster, but none has been proved, despite over 100 years of investigation. One of the most widely accepted explanations is based on the work of Dr Richard McIver, who believes that deposits of methane

◄ LEFT: The mystery of what happened to the Mary Celeste on 25 November 1872 has been investigated for over 100 years, but remains unexplained.

gases are held under the oceans. When the gas is released, it bubbles up to the surface. If the boats do not sink before the gas disperses, they ride back up to the surface. Perhaps this occurred on the night of 25 November 1872, causing the crew to panic. They may have abandoned ship and been sucked down by the gas, while the *Mary Celeste* stayed afloat.

◄► See The Vanishing Village p. 101

THE BERMUDA TRIANGLE

The Bermuda Triangle, also called the Devil's Triangle, is an area of the Atlantic Ocean off south-east Florida, where the disappearance of ships and aeroplanes has, on a number of occasions, led to speculation about inexplicable turbulence and other atmospheric disturbances. Violent storms and downward air currents frequently occur there, but studies have failed to reveal any significant peculiarities about the area in question. Today, boundaries of the Bermuda Triangle have been formed by drawing an imaginary line from Melbourne in Florida, to Bermuda, to Puerto Rico, and back to Florida.

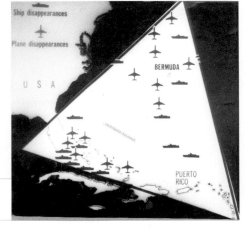

► RIGHT: Map showing the area of the Atlantic Ocean known as the Bermuda Triangle.

Many planes have disappeared or experienced inexplicable navigation equipment failure while in the Bermuda Triangle. Key cases include:

- In 1928, Charles Lindbergh reported both his compasses failing and the presence of a 'heavy haze' obscuring vision, while on a flight from Havana to Florida.
- In 1948, a DC3 private charter plane carrying 32 passengers plus crew disappeared.
- In March 1950, an American Globemaster disappeared on the northern edge of the triangle en route to Ireland.
- In 1954, a Navy Lockheed Super Constellation vanished with 42 people on board.
- In 1962, an Air Force tanker KB150 flying from Virginia to the Azores disappeared.
- In 1965, a C119 flying Boxcar with 10 aboard was lost in the south-east Bahamas.
- In 1968, Jim Blocker reported radio and navigational failure inside a bank of clouds while flying from Nassau to Palm Beach.

 See Vortexes p. 33

▶ RIGHT: The aviator Charles Lindberg.

Flight 19

On 5 December 1945, five Avenger torpedo bombers took off from a US Navy base at Fort Lauderdale, Florida, for target practice off the coast. After the first run they regrouped, but inexplicably failed to recognise their surroundings. Lt Charles Taylor radioed base saying, 'We seem to be lost ... everything is wrong, strange.... We can't be sure of any direction ... even the ocean doesn't look as it should.' Confused scraps of conversation between the crew hinted at malfunctioning compasses, high winds and low fuel. Despite a massive search by nearly 100 ships and several submarines, no wreckage or bodies were ever found.

See Glen Miller p. 92

Eye-Witness Report

On 11 June 1986, Martin Caidin and his crew were flying from Bermuda to Jacksonville Naval Air Station in Florida, equipped with a great deal of navigational equipment. The craft received satellite photographs of the area in which they were flying, and it was a clear, bright day with no sign of poor weather. Without warning, Caidin was unable to see the outer portion of his left wing, and then the right wing. According to their readouts, there should not have been any mist. Around him the blue sky changed to yellow and they were in what he later described as a 'creamy yellow version of a whiteout', with the instruments 'going crazy'. He said 'two million dollars of avionics just up and died'. Caidin was able to see a tunnel-like hole above the plane, where he could see blue sky, and another hole running down to the sea visible below. They stayed calm and managed to guide the plane through the mist for four hours. When they finally reached clear air again, they looked back to see what had caused the problems and saw only clear sky for miles on end. Their equipment began to work again and the plane landed without incident.

See Pilot's Encounter p. 246

NAVAL MYSTERIES

There are more than 30 recorded disappearances relating to sea vessels in the Bermuda Triangle area. Some of these include:

- In 1840, the French ship *Rosalie* was found on course to Havana from Europe in the Triangle area, with sails set, cargo intact and all hands missing.
- In January 1880, the British frigate *Atlanta* left Bermuda for England with 290 aboard. She vanished without trace.
- In 1924, the *Raifuku Maru*, a Japanese freighter, radioed for help between the Bahamas and Cuba before disappearing.
- In 1938, an Anglo-Australian freighter with a crew of 39 disappeared. The last message was received west of Azores. It read 'All well'.
- In 1963, the *Marine Sulphur Queen*, a 130-m (425-ft) freighter, vanished without message, clues or debris en route to Norfolk, Virginia, from Texas.
- In 1970, the freighter *Milton Latrides*, en route from New Orleans to Cape Town, disappeared.
- In 1984, the 27-m (88-ft) brig *Marques* was lost on the northern border of the Triangle. 18 were missing.

There have been many theories surrounding the incidents that have occurred in the Bermuda

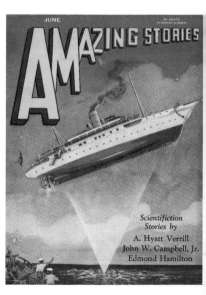

JUNE

AMAZING STORIES

Scientifiction Stories by
A. Hyatt Verrill
John W. Campbell, Jr.
Edmond Hamilton

Triangle. One popular notion is that the Triangle is an ideal place for aliens to abduct humans. Another theory links the Triangle with Atlantis, suggesting that the legendary lost civilisation existed in the area, and that its magnetic or gravitational forces continued to exist long after the city sank beneath the waves.

Others suggest that planes and ships are affected by some type of magnetic-field disturbance which may exist in the Bermuda Triangle. More straightforward is the idea that the ships and planes lost went down for conventional reasons – mechanical failure, pilot error, fuel loss or even blistering heat. However, no wreckage from any of the missing planes or ships has been found, and there is still no explanation for the equipment failure and whiteouts which appear to occur there.

◆ *See* The Bermuda Triangle p. 175; The Lost Continent of Atlantis p. 190

THE *DAWN* AND THE *ISLAND QUEEN*

In the 1930s, a 75-ton schooner named *Dawn* set sail from Alabama heading for Barbados. It was commanded by Captain Reg Mitchell, a very experienced seaman who knew the route and the area well; the ship carried a crew of eight. Despite continuing fair weather, the ship went missing and failed to arrive at its destination. A look-out for it was kept by Captain Mitchell's fellow skippers and by aircraft flying over the area. There was no sign of the ship or its crew. Yet three months later, the ship turned up again, adrift a few miles off the Mexican coast. They found the *Dawn* to be in excellent condition: the sails were neatly furled, the engine was in good running order, and the diesel tanks were more than half full. But there was no sign of Captain Mitchell and his crew.

◀ LEFT: *There are many 'amazing stories' of ships that have been mysteriously lost in the Bermuda Triangle.*

On 5 August 1944, a 75-ton schooner, *Island Queen,* set sail from the port of St George's in Grenada. Aboard the vessel were its crew, consisting of the experienced Captain Salhab and 10 seamen, and 57 passengers. The latter were mainly tourists who were travelling to the island of St Vincent to take part in a holiday festival there. The journey was some 120 km (75 miles) and would take a night to complete. En route, the *Island Queen* was passed by another boat, the *Providence Mark*, and all seemed to be well. When the schooner failed to reach its destination, an air search was begun, and the British Fleet Air Arm and the US Navy department became involved. The search went on for several days without result. No survivors were picked up. No bodies were discovered afloat nor were any washed ashore. No wreckage was found. No oil patches were sighted on the surface of the sea. The ship had vanished completely, with 68 people on board. No clue has since been found to suggest what took place on that clear night.

See The *Mary Celeste* p. 173

THE *TITANIC*

The loss of the *Titanic* was undoubtedly the most tragic accident in marine history, and although conspiracy theories abound, there is no doubt that her sinking was the result of a collision with an iceberg. What is interesting, however, is the fact that the sinking of the Titanic was the subject of numerous prophecies.

Several days into her first voyage, *Titanic* struck an unseen iceberg and sank, taking 1,500 passengers and crew to their deaths. The tragedy of the sinking lay in the fact that the owners of the ship, who had been utterly convinced that she was 'unsinkable', had failed to provide enough lifeboats.

There are at least 20 known cases of people who had premonitions of disaster before the ship sailed. In fact, the theory of precognition (the ability to see things before they happen) gained international credence following the accident. Some passengers refused to board the ship; others had relatives among the passengers and warned them in advance, or sensed disaster.

William Stead, a well-known newspaperman, was warned in writing by a psychic that he would be in great danger during April 1912, and that he should avoid water and

▲ *ABOVE: German artist Willy Stoever's interpretation of the sinking of the* Titanic.

travel at the same time. He ignored the warning and died in the disaster. Ironically, Stead had written an article noting that just such an accident could occur.

Retired seaman Morgan Robertson was a struggling writer when, in 1898, he had a vision in which he saw a huge liner collide with an iceberg. He remembered hearing the words 'April' and 'unsinkable'. Inspired by this vision, he wrote the story *The Wreck of the Titan*, in which a near-identical ship to the *Titanic*, the *SS Titan*, sinks on her maiden voyage after striking an iceberg, with hundreds perishing because of an inadequate number of lifeboats.

▶ *See* The Curse of Princess Amen-Ra p. 113; Extra-Sensory Perception p. 138

MEDICAL CURIOSITIES

SPONTANEOUS HUMAN COMBUSTION

The extraordinary phenomenon of spontaneous human combustion (SHC) has been recorded on some occasions, and has never been satisfactorily explained. It appears to occur when solitary humans have, in some unknown manner, burned up almost entirely, usually in a closed room, without setting fire to their surroundings beyond perhaps a hole in the floor, a chair and some nearby furnishings. Some believe that, as many of the subjects are elderly smokers, often alcoholic and known to take sleeping pills, this combination could lead to a person catching fire.

Interestingly, however, the flames seem to start from inside the person and younger people have also been affected. Whatever the cause, SHC is on the increase. No one knows why. One of the strangest fact about spontaneous human combustion is that, although a reasonably rare occurrence, 10 per cent of all known cases of the phenomenon took place in the year 1980.

See The Candle Effect p. 184

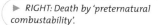

▶ RIGHT: Death by 'preternatural combustability'.

THE CINDER WOMAN

Mary Reeser, a 67-year-old woman from St Petersburg, Florida, is now known as the 'cinder woman'. Sometime during the night of 2 July 1951, Mary went from being a completely healthy woman to nothing but a charred foot in a heap of ash. Nothing around her had been burned, and the plastic tiles that lay beneath her had not melted. Forensic scientists and fire-fighters were completely baffled. The FBI became involved, because of the suspicion of foul play, but this was soon ruled out. She died within three hours, which put paid to the idea that SHC victims burn slowly over the course of many hours, as previous evidence had suggested.

LONDON NIGHTCLUB

Another case of SHC occurred in a London nightclub when a girl, dancing with her boyfriend, suddenly erupted into flames and died on her way to the hospital. There were no other flames in the room. Her boyfriend declared that the flames had burst from her back, chest and shoulders, setting her hair alight.

HENRY THOMAS

In January 1980, the remains of a 73-year-old Welshman, Henry Thomas from Ebbw Vale, were found by his sons-in-law in his home. He had been reduced to ashes, apart from his skull and still-trousered legs below the knee. An orange-red glow had been seen in the room. The window and lightbulb were covered in an orange substance. The television was still on, although its plastic knobs had melted. Yet a settee, only 1 m (3 ft) from the armchair in which Mr Thomas had been sitting, was unscathed.

◆ See The Cinder Woman p. 183

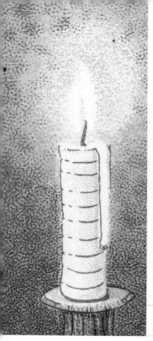

THE CANDLE EFFECT

One possible explanation of SHC has become known as the Candle Effect. This describes how, if a body is ignited and the fire is not put out, a gradual combustion process will take place in which the bones (like a candle wick) will be reduced to ash and the flesh (like the wax) will melt away. This explains why in most cases of SHC, little or no damage is found to the surroundings. Other research has suggested that the phenomenon may be caused by a combination of products in a person's diet, causing a chemical chain reaction resulting in internal ignition; electricity and nuclear energy within the body have also been cited as other rational explanations.

◀ *LEFT: The Candle Effect has been used to explain Spontaneous Human Combustion.*

ANCIENT STRUCTURES

CHICO STONES

On 8 March 1922, stones varying in size from small pebbles to large rocks began cascading down on the roof of a grain warehouse and several surrounding houses near the railway tracks at Chico, California. The 'rain' lasted for seven days and despite a full-scale police operation on the site, no explanation was ever found. The local fire chief and police officer, who were investigating the riddle, had a narrow escape when a large boulder crashed out of the sky on to to a fence beside them, in front of several witnesses.

Charles Fort, a virtual hermit who investigated unexplained phenomena for decades in the US and UK, wrote several books, including *The Book of the Damned* (1919). He had an explanation for falling objects: he believed that these objects come from the Super-Sargasso Sea, which is a 'region somewhere above the Earth's surface in which gravitation is inoperative'. He believed that 'things raised from this Earth's surface to that region have been held there until shaken down by storms'. An imaginative concept, certainly, and one that garnered some following in its day.

▶ *See* Raining Cats and Dogs p. 167

▶ *RIGHT: According to legend the Sargasso Sea is where all the wrecks of the ocean end up.*

STONEHENGE

Stonehenge is the most famous prehistoric megalithic monument in Europe. Excavations and radiocarbon dating have revealed that Stonehenge has an exceptionally long history of use as a ceremonial or religious centre. It was built in four distinct stages, from c. 2800 BC to c. 1100 BC. Among the megalithic monuments of Europe, Stonehenge is unique because of its long period of use, the precision of its plan and its architectural details.

In 1963, Gerald Hawkins, Professor of Astronomy at Boston University, USA, stated that Stonehenge was like a giant computer: a huge observatory capable of extremely complex calculations based on the position of the Sun, Moon and stars. When Hawkins fed all the data he had about the site into a computer, he found that the stones could be used to predict the occurrence of eclipses. His theory was corroborated by the work of C. A. Newman, who said that the highly educated astronomer priests of the time could have stood in the centre of the great circle and determined the position of the Sun or Moon in their orbits by using the stones as a guide.

Sir Fred Hoyle, one of Britain's most famous astronomers, supported the theory that Stonehenge was a giant observatory. He agreed that the megaliths could be used as markers to gauge the moon's activity as it passed through different stages of its cycle. He noted that Stonehenge's construction 'demanded a level of intellectual attainment higher than the standard to be expected from a community of primitive farmers'.

If these academics are right, Stonehenge and other standing-stone sites were designed for making complex astronomical observations at a time when there was no form of written word.

See Ancient Mysteries p. 27; Nazca Lines p. 187

LEY LINES

The word 'Ley' is an old Anglo-Saxon term for 'cleared strips of ground' or 'meadows'. 'Ley lines', which were discovered in 1921 by the Herefordshire businessman, Alfred Watkins, describes tracks laid down across the landscape to form a route from one ancient site or holy place to the next. Watkins surmised that ley lines represented prehistoric trading routes, even though some of them led across extremely steep mountainsides. These routes date back possibly as far as Neolithic, New Stone Age, times almost 3,000 years ago.

Watkins, who died in 1935, took his thinking on ley lines no further than this, but since then, a number of different theories have arisen about their nature and purpose. In 1936, for example, Dion Fortune, an author of occult novels, suggested that the lines were 'lines of power'. Other explanations had it that they indicated the lines of the Earth's cosmic energy, which could be detected by means of dowsing. In 1954,

◀ LEFT: Ley lines in Hereford; which may represent prehistoric trading routes.

when there was an outbreak of alien spacecraft sightings in France, UFO proponents claimed that the lines showed where UFOs hovered or landed. It was also claimed that the UFOs picked up energy from 'magnetic currents' flowing through the Earth. More recently, the idea of ley lines as lines of energy has been taken up by the New Age movement, which has suggested, inter alia, that the ley lines came down from the sky as columns of force and, on landing, ran along the ground.

◆ See Alien Visitations in the Ancient World p. 232

NAZCA LINES

The Pampa Colorada, or Red Plain, which runs for some 60 km (37 miles) along the Pacific coast of South America, is the site of a complex of 'lines' created by the Nazca tribe who inhabited this area around 2,600 years ago. The lines, which took centuries to create, were made by removing the dark red stones and soil on the surface so that the lighter-coloured subsoil showed through as pathways, geometric shapes and stylised 'geoglyphs' depicting humans, animals and plants.

Finding the reason for crafting the lines has attracted many differing theories. In 1955, James W. Moseley

▶ RIGHT: The Nazca lines on the Red Plain along the Pacific coast of South America.

suggested that they formed a landing ground for alien aircraft. This idea has been supported by the author Erich von Däniken, and others who believe the Nazcas were too primitive to have possessed the sophisticated knowledge required to create the lines. As a counter-argument, it has been pointed out that the ground shows no sign of the disturbance that would have occurred had alien spacecraft landed there.

Other theories are more earth-bound. Georg von Breunig has postulated that the lines were used for running races. The anthropologist Paul Kosok once thought they were part of an irrigation system, an idea he later abandoned for another – that the lines were part of a gigantic calendar. The archaeologist Maria Reiche believed the lines demonstrated the Nazca's astronomical knowledge. More recently, it has been suggested that the Red Plains were the site of Nazca religious worship.

◆ See Gods and Aliens p. 233

EASTER ISLAND

The almost 1,000 *maoi* stone head statues with Polynesian features that stand on Easter Island in the Pacific Ocean have been a mystery ever since they were first discovered by Europeans in 1722. Some of the statues, which closely resemble one other, weigh more than 81 tonnes and stand over 10 m (33 ft) high. Most were carved and set up on the island between the eleventh and sixteenth centuries. A few stood on special platforms known as *ahu*, which served as hiding places for the inhabitants of Easter Island in times of danger. It has been reckoned that it took some 150 people to shift a single statue, using trees as sleds and rollers. Several statues suffered damage while being transported and were left where they were. Others were damaged or fell over during the tribal wars that were fought on the island in the seventeenth and eighteenth centuries.

No one, however, has yet formulated a universally accepted explanation for the existence of the statues or their unusual form. One theory is that the statues were religious and political symbols of male dynastic authority. Another has it that the statues were regarded as repositories of divine spirits. These spirits entered the *maoi* statues by means of a magic spiritual essence known as *mana*.

Despite the similarity in carvings to others found in the Polynesian islands, the Easter Island statues remain unique and it has been suggested that the island might be the remnant of a lost continent. Some have even suggested that both the island and its monolithic statues were created by extra-terrestrials.

◼ *See* Stonehenge p. 185

▲ *ABOVE: One of the upright giant statues near the ancient volcanic quarry on Easter Island in the Pacific Ocean.*

THE LOST CONTINENT OF ATLANTIS

According to the Greek philosopher Plato, the continent of Atlantis was once a paradise inhabited by peaceful, noble people. They led an idyllic life, creating wonders of architecture – palaces, temples, harbours, docks and canals as much as 30 m (98 ft) wide. One of the temples, which was dedicated to Poseidon, the Greek god of the sea, was covered with gold and silver pinnacles and had ceilings made of ivory. But tragically, Atlantis was destroyed by an all-consuming flood and sunk beneath and sea, never to be seen again.

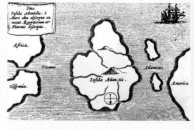

▲ ABOVE: Athanasius Kircher's map of the lost continent of Atlantis, thought to be fictional until remains were found in 1856.

Since Plato's time, the myth of the lost continent of Atlantis has been dismissed as pure fiction, an exaggerated account of a volcanic eruption that destroyed the Minoan civilisation on Crete around 1500 BC. But could it have actually been a true account of a real place that prefigured the earliest civilisations? Crete has, in fact, been named as the location of Atlantis. In 1856, an earthquake convulsed the ground on the nearby island of Thera and revealed the remains of an ancient city thought to be the ruins of Atlantis.

In 1928 American psychic Edgar Cayce pronounced that Atlantis would rise again from the depths of the ocean near Bimini in the Bahamas. Forty years later, in 1968, a pilot flying over Bimini saw what looked to be an ancient temple in the water. Scuba divers have subsequently found flights of steps, monolithic stones and underwater pyramids and walled structures.

➡ See Vortexes p. 33

THE PYRAMIDS OF ANCIENT EGYPT

The three pyramids at Giza near Cairo in Eygpt are sited along a north-south axis. The reasons are not scientific, but religious. The Ancient Egyptians believed that after dying, their pharaohs would go on into another world. This was why they mummified their bodies to preserve them after death, and buried them with worldly possessions deemed necessary for the journey.

The three pyramids at Giza, built in around 2500 BC to house the tombs of the pharaohs Cheops, Khafre and Menkaure, were carefully aligned in accordance with this belief. The pyramids were provided with long narrow shafts that were open to the sky at the entrance, and led deep inside. The entrance to the northern shaft was aimed at the star Kochab which was associated in the Egyptian religion with the immortality of the soul. The southern shafts of each pyramid were aimed at stars in the constellation Orion, which was associated with Osiris, god of resurrection and rebirth. The Great Pyramid of Cheops was aligned with Al Nitak, the brightest of the three stars in Orion's belt, the other two being Al Nilam and Mintaka. The southern shaft of the pyramid of Khafre pointed straight at Al Nilam and in the third pyramid, which housed the tomb of Menkaure, the shaft was directed at Mintaka. In addition, on the ground, the three pyramids were so placed that they matched the positions of the three stars in Orion, all suggesting that the Ancient Egyptians were indeed trying to recreate the heaven of their gods on Earth.

◆ *See* The Curse of King Tutankhamen
p. 105; Stonehenge p. 185

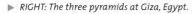

▶ *RIGHT: The three pyramids at Giza, Egypt.*

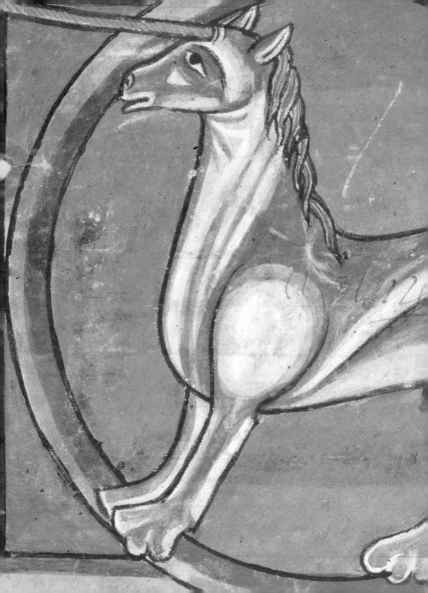

MYTHICAL CREATURES

LITTLE PEOPLE

Fairies are generally believed to be a type of supernatural being, neither ghost, god nor demi-god, which exists on Earth and either helps or harms humankind. Fairy beliefs are widespread and, across many cultures around the world, they are remarkably similar.

THE ORIGINS OF FAIRIES

There is no absolute agreement on the origins of the many varieties of fairies. Some suggest that they are the dispossessed spirits of humans not yet ready for heaven. Others believe that they are a distinct life-form capable of multiplying by means of the usual reproductive process. In Devon, in the UK, one tradition is that they are the spirits of infants who died before baptism. Folklorists and anthropologists have theorised that the original fairies were members of conquered races who took to the hills and whose descendants were sighted on rare occasions.

Besides the speculations of scholars and folk explanations, all that is known with any certainty is that wherever they come from, fairy beliefs exist in every traditional society. And the fact remains that fairies are

sighted and documented by reliable witnesses, even in the twentieth century. Are they an illusion? Like many aspects of the paranormal, fairy sightings remain on the fringes of human experience.

While there is no convincing proof that they exist, neither is there proof that they do not, and many acclaimed and respected individuals, such as Sir Arthur Conan Doyle, have apparently been witness to the phenomenon. Even if we do not understand the underlying basis – be it psychological or paranormal – the stories told of fairy sightings are marvellous, and there to be marvelled at.

◘ See Bright Little People p. 199

THE COTTINGLEY FAIRIES

In 1917, two Yorkshire children, Elsie Wright and Frances Griffiths, claimed that they had met and photographed fairies. The photographs were sent to Sir Arthur Conan Doyle, who was intrigued enough to send a friend to interview them. Upon examining the photographs, Conan Doyle published a book entitled *The Coming of the Fairies* (1922), in which he confirmed that he believed the photographs to be genuine. The photographs were taken to the Kodak laboratory in London, and Doyle later wrote: 'Two experts were unable to find any flaw, but refused to testify to the genuineness of them, in view of some possible trap.'

◘ See Fairy Rings p. 197

◄ *LEFT: An illustration by Arthur Rackham.*
► *RIGHT: Sir Arthur Conan Doyle was a renowned believer in fairies.*

RIGHT: One of the Cottingley photographs entitled 'Fairy offering flowers to Iris'.

Photographing the Fairies

The Cottingley girls claimed that they had seen fairies several times behind their homes at Cottingley in Yorkshire and, unable to convince their parents of the fact, they had undertaken to capture them on film. The first photographs were taken in 1917; further photographs were taken in 1920.

The *Strand* magazine published Doyle's first article with the original two pictures at Christmas the same year, and the following March a follow-up on the latter three. The story received worldwide publicity, and almost everyone considered the photographs to be fakes.

In August 1921, a noted psychic was sent to Cottingley and he saw the fairies along with Frances. No photographs could be taken that day, so apart from the word of the psychic and, once again, the girls, there was no further proof that the fairies existed.

For years afterwards attempts to debunk the photographs failed, and the two girls stood by their story. However, in 1972, Elsie sent the two cameras, along with other material related to the case, to Sotheby's for sale and with them a letter confessing for the first time that they had faked the photographs. Three years later, however, when interviewed by *Woman* magazine, Elsie and Frances gave the impression that the photographs were, after all, real.

See Spiritual Children p. 23

A Hoax?

Finally, shortly before Elsie and Frances died, both finally confessed that four photographs were outright hoaxes. They pointed to the fact that you could see the head of a hat pin that was holding up the gnome. It was sticking out of the figure's chest, although Conan Doyle had thought this to be a psychic umbilical cord. As for the fifth image, it was slightly less two-dimensional and clear. Elsie said that it was also a hoax, but until her death Frances was adamant that it was the only real fairy photograph they ever took.

In 1982, an issue of the *Unexplained* and the *British Journal of Photography* reopened the case, and published extensive investigations by the BJP's editor Geoffrey Crawley. It was revealed that the girls had agreed that the pictures were a practical joke to be continued until after the deaths of everyone involved. Elsie, a gifted artist, had apparently created the figures, using as her models fairies depicted in a popular children's book *Princess Mary's Gift Book*. Elsie and Frances complained that the 'confessions' were unauthorised and untrue.

In the 1980s, Elsie finally showed how she and Frances had taken the fake photographs, using paper cut-out fairies. Despite this, both women – even on their death beds – insisted that regardless of the status of their photographs, there were real fairies and elves in Cottingley Beck and that they, and others, saw them.

◄ *See* The First 'Ghostly' Picture p. 134

FAIRY RINGS

According to folklore, fairies often dance in circles in the grass. The formations left are known as fairy rings and they spell danger for human passers-by. The fairy music can be so enchanting that a person may be led into the ring, where they remain captive forever in the fairy world.

If a human steps into the ring they will become trapped in the wild dancing and may become lost to the sight of their companions, who can hear the music but see nothing. The interlude might seem to last only two minutes, or at most a whole night, but outside of the ring years can elapse.

We now know, however, that the circles are formed by a collection of fungi growing in a ring formation. The fungus is known as the fairy ring champignon (*Marasmius oreades*). The young mycelia spread outward as the fungus gets older and its outer rim produces the fruiting bodies in a ring. Mycelia help the grass absorb nutrients and hence the grass becomes darker in the 'fairy ring'.

See Fairy Playmates p. 199

▶ RIGHT: Arthur Rackham's interpretation of how fairy rings are made.

FAIRY VOICES?

In 1972, while strolling along the shore of a peninsula in the Scottish Highlands, American folk singer Artie Traum heard disembodied voices chanting 'Run, man, run' in a strange harmony to the sound of fiddles and pipes. When Traum fled to a nearby wood, he heard crackling sounds and 'great motion'. He later said, 'my head was swarming with thousands of voices, thousands of words making no sense'. The voices ceased when he found his way back to the open air.

FAMOUS SIGHTINGS

FAIRY PLAYMATES

Edgar Cayce was one of the twentieth century's most famous psychics and he had an extraordinary ability to diagnose health problems by taking psychic readings. His psychic talents first manifested themselves in childhood, when he played in his garden with a host of 'imaginary friends'. These 'nature playmates', as his mother called them, were a secret between mother and son because of the ridicule he received at school when he described them. Many years later Cayce read about the fairy realm and realised that perhaps his playmates had been real.

▲ *ABOVE: Edgar Cayce and his wife.*

 *See* The Cottingley Fairies p. 195

BRIGHT LITTLE PEOPLE

On 30 April 1973, a London woman named Mary Treadgold was travelling by bus through the Scottish Highlands. The bus pulled over to let an oncoming car pass and Treadgold saw, outside her window, a 'small figure, about 45 cm (18 in) high, a young man with his foot on a spade arrested in the act of digging.... He had a thin keen face (which I would know again), tight, brown, curly hair, was dressed in bright blue bib and braces, with a very white shirt with rolled-up sleeves. An open sack, also miniature, stood at his side. He was emphatically not a dwarf nor a child, nor (last desperate suggestion of a sceptic) a plastic garden gnome. He was a perfectly formed living being like any of us, only in miniature.' Treadgold later mentioned the story to a Highland friend, and was told that the area was known for sightings of small people, who lived happily among them. The descriptions were of very 'bright' people. She later said, 'This ... I do recollect in the brightness of the hair and clothes, and the general appearance of energy and alertness'.

See The Origins of Fairies p. 194

ALIEN VISITATION?

Stories of small aliens visiting Earth have inspired the theory that they were the source of stories about fairies, leprechauns and dwarves. Like these creatures, the aliens were unusually small in stature. For example, a young girl called Anna went out into the woods to pick berries near her home on Washington Island. She was about to start picking when a group of tiny *huldrefolk*, or hidden people, appeared and begged her not to deprive them of the berries, which they needed for food. After Anna agreed, they danced with her and taught her a song which she repeated to her mother when she returned home. Anna's mother accused her of making up the story – and the song. Anna's grandmother, however, told the young girl that she knew she had been telling the truth: when she was a child, the grandmother said, she, too, had seen the *huldrefolk*, who taught her the same song.

In the summer of 1919, 13-year-old Harry Anderson encountered a group of 20 diminutive men just outside the town of Barron in Wisconsin, in the US. Harry was walking across a cornfield when he saw the little men walking towards him in single file. Their heads were bald, they were white-skinned and they wore *lederhosen* (leather knee-pants). Harry was terrified and hid behind a maple tree until they had disappeared into the forest.

Later, this experience was classed as a 'close encounter' with alien beings. They aliens were reported to have appeared again over 50 years later, at midnight on 15 October 1973, also in Wisconsin, at Oshkosh. Three humanoids around 1.37 m (4.5 ft) tall with wrinkled skin and pointed ears materialised in the bedroom of a witness who was so frightened that he fainted. When he recovered, he found his visitors were examining his legs with an oval object that revealed the bones beneath the skin.

◆ *See* Encountering the EBEs p. 247; The Green Children p. 235

MONSTERS

Cryptozoology is, according to its founder Belgian biologist Bernard Heuvelmans, 'not an arcane or occult zoology'. It comes from the Greek words *kryptos* ('hidden') and *logos* ('discourse'). Heuvelmans explains that such 'animals' (often deemed monsters) are typically 'known to a local population – at least sufficiently so that we often indirectly know of their existence and certain aspects of their appearance and behaviour. It would be better to call them animals undescribed by science'.

According to the founding meeting of the International Society of Cryptozoology, held in 1982, 'what makes an animal of interest to cryptozoology is that it is unexpected'.

◆ *See* Ogopogo p. 205

WEIRD CREATURES

What falls into the brief of a cryptozoologist? Many would consider it to be the stuff of nightmares – phantom animals, known varieties

◀ LEFT: *A giant squid supposedly encountered by the* Alecton *in 1861. Its arms were said to be 11 m (35 ft) long!*

of animals in unbelievable or impossible locations, sea and lake monsters, ape-men, giant squid, sea serpents and the Yeti.

Many of the most intensive cryptozoological investigations have been unsuccessful, leading many mainstream scientists to dismiss the discipline as illegitimate. But how can we explain the well-documented, amazingly similar accounts of animals or monsters appearing in unexpected places? While science might speculate that these animals simply cannot exist, evidence suggests that they may – outside the imaginations of witnesses, many of whom are unwilling and highly reputable.

The debate is, however, irrelevant in the long term, for first-hand accounts continue to pile up. Some sightings have been captured using the tools of modern-day technology, including photographs and films. In some cases we have to rely on the integrity of the multiple witnesses. But as long as there are witness accounts, the search for the planet's most mysterious and elusive creatures will continue.

THE MONSTER OF CHESAPEAKE BAY

Chessie, as it has come to be known, is the frequently sighted creature of the Chesapeake Bay area in the eastern United States. The creature has been sighted regularly since the nineteenth century, and is described as being a long, dark, serpent-like animal. In 1982, the American Robert Frew filmed Chessie from a house on Kent Island, which overlooks the bay. Frew and his wife spotted the creature in shallow, clear water about 200 m (700 ft) from the house. He videotaped the creature as it moved towards a group of swimmers. It dived beneath them and reappeared on the other side. The creature they caught on film was around 9 m (30 ft) in length, and about 30 cm (1 ft) in diameter. It was dark brown with a humped back.

▲ *ABOVE: Chesapeake Bay, the home of Chessie, a dark serpent-like animal. Sightings of Chessie have remained consistent since the nineteenth century.*

In 1978, a retired CIA employee, Donald Kyker, reported seeing Chessie and three other sea monsters about 70 m (230 ft) offshore. His neighbours also witnessed the animals, and they provided descriptions of 9-m (30-ft) long, sleek, dark-grey creatures swimming at about 10 kph (6 mph).

Sightings of Chessie have remained consistent over the years and occur most frequently between May and September. The area is more heavily populated during this period, which could explain the increased sightings, but it is also possible that the creature migrates during this time. The witness list includes members of the coastguard and naval officers, airline pilots, an ex-CIA official and an FBI agent. The photos and film that exist of Chessie were studied by Smithsonian officials and they concluded that it was a living animal that was pictured, but they could not identify it.

◆ *See* The Loch Ness Monster p. 204

THE LOCH NESS MONSTER

The Loch Ness Monster, or 'Nessie', has an almost mythical status. It is said that in AD 565, when the Irish priest who became St Columba went to Scotland to convert the Picts to Christianity, the monster threatened a follower of St Columba. The priest made the sign of the cross and thwarted the beast. Sightings of Nessie have been reported regularly over the years since that time, although some sightings have proved to be hoaxes or honest mistakes. The likelihood of a creature of that size living in the lake is small, but not impossible. Interesting photographs have been taken and a great deal of supportive data indicates that something does exist in the lake. However, sophisticated sonar

equipment has been used to try and track Nessie and little evidence has been provided to show that a monster really does live in the loch. Numerous separate serious investigations have been conducted, but no physical evidence has been found. However, since the 1930s more than 3,000 separate sightings have been reported and studied by experts.

One of the most detailed sightings occurred in 1933. Mrs John Mackay was being driven along a road which had a perfect view of the lake. She said: 'I couldn't believe what we were seeing. I have never seen such an

◄ LEFT: The much-loved notion of 'Nessie', the Loch Ness Monster, continues to fascinate.

enormous thing. It was just an enormous black body, going up and down. You could not put a name to it. It could have been an elephant or a whale.' Two of the strongest pieces of evidence to support the existence of Nessie were put through stringent scientific analysis. They were two cine films, far more difficult to fake than still photographs, and they seemed to show an animal speeding through the water and then submerging. Experts assessed that the animal was more than 2 m (7 ft) long, and moved at around 15 kph (10 mph). Positive identification, however, has remained impossible.

◇ *See* Ogopogo p. 205

OGOPOGO

The best-known Canadian lake monster is Ogopogo. In 1926, Roy W. Brown, editor of the *Vancouver Sun*, wrote: 'Too many reputable people have seen [the monster] to ignore the seriousness of actual facts.' Archival records of Ogopogo's existence date back to 1872 and sightings continue to be reported to the present day.

Ogopogo is most often described as being approximately 30–60 cm (1–2 ft) in diameter, and 4.5–6 m (15–20 ft) in length. He has been seen repeatedly across the years in Lake Okanagan, and some witnesses claim that they have seen him on land. Unusual footprints have been found by the lake, which give credence to the view that the monster may be partly reptilian. His head has been described variously as horse- or goat-like, and many witnesses claim that the monster is log-shaped.

Cryptozoologist Roy P. Mackal believes that there is a small population of aquatic fish-eating animals residing in Lake Okanagan. Mackal initially assumed that the type of animal in Lake Okanagan was the same creature that he believed was in Loch Ness, but after a careful examination of the available data, he determined that the Canadian creature may be a form of primitive whale: *Basilosaurus cetoides*. He notes that the general appearance of *Basilosaurus* tallies almost exactly with the log-like descriptions of Ogopogo.

While Ogopogo has never attained the fame of the Loch Ness Monster, the creature of Lake Okanagan has regularly caused quite a stir in the international press. Monster hunters from all over the world have been drawn to the area for research purposes, and multiple witness sightings of Ogopogo, so rare with many other controversial phenomena, have occurred on many occasions.

◆ *See* Films from the 1950s p. 300

THE YETI

The Yeti, or the Abominable Snowman, has been regularly sighted in the Himalayan mountains for hundreds of years. According to legend and eyewitness reports, the creature is tall and manlike, covered with shaggy hair. Accounts say that it ranges between 2 and 3 m (6 and 9 ft) in height and has a conical scalp, pointed ears, a hairless chest and a human-like face. The creature is said to be aggressive, and will attack anyone who ventures close enough. The descriptions are quite similar to those of Bigfoot.

In 1832, the British explorer B. H. Hodgson travelled to the Himalayas to record the

▶ *RIGHT: A Lamaist monk displays a reputed Yeti scalp and skeletal hand he found in 1976.*

lifestyle of the Nepalese. In one letter home he told how the tribespeople lived in fear of a mysterious, tall, erect creature covered in thick black hair. Men like Eric Shipton, the Everest pioneer, and Lord Hunt, leader of the first successful assault on Everest, have also been convinced that the Yeti exists. Don Whillans, a famous British climber, was on Annapurna in 1970 when, by the light of the Moon, he watched an ape-like creature cavort in the snow for about 20 minutes. The next day he saw distinctive and inexplicable tracks.

But the most intriguing evidence relating to the Yeti is the photographs of footprints in the snow. There are at least two dozen photographs of footprints taken by mountaineers, but no photographs of the Yeti itself are known to exist. Eric Shipton's 1951 picture of the tracks, taken in the Menlung Basin in Nepal, is clear and precise. When Lord Hunt took his 1978 pictures of tracks 35 m (14 in) long and 17.5 cm (7 in) wide, he noticed that the animal was so heavy that it had broken through snow on which he could safely walk.

◻ *See* Bigfoot p. 207

OTHER MAN-BEASTS

Similar creatures to the Yeti have been spotted all over the world, including Russia, where they are known as 'Almas', Australia, where they are called 'Yowies', and not forgetting the better-known American Bigfoot or Sasquatch and the Chinese Wildman.

BIGFOOT

According to the Native Americans of the United States and Canada, there is a manlike beast of no known species, about 2.5 m (8 ft) tall, with a broad chest and shoulders but virtually no neck. It was known by the Native Americans as Sasquatch, later named 'Bigfoot' by settlers. In the nineteenth century, explorer David Thomas discovered evidence of the strange animal, in the shape of footprints, which were at least 35 cm (14 in) long, near Jasper, Alberta.

Sightings continued across the years, but they gained ultimate credibility in 1903 when President Theodore Roosevelt recounted the story of two trappers in Idaho who were attacked by a mysterious creature. In 1924, Albert Ostman, a lumberman from Langley, British Columbia, claims to have been attacked by a giant Bigfoot. He said the beast was about 2.5m (8 ft) tall. The creature picked up Ostman, still in his sleeping bag, and carried him 'like a sack of potatoes' for three hours.

He was kept in the lair of the Bigfoot, where other males and females also lived, for almost a week. He finally escaped, and his description of the creatures matched exactly the accounts of Bigfoot.

On 20 October 1967, Roger Patterson, a former rancher, was tracking through the forests around Bluff Creek in Northern California with a Native American friend when they emerged into a clearing and came face to face with a Bigfoot. Patterson shot an amazing 9 m (29 ft) of colour film as it loped

◀ *LEFT: A still made by Ivan Marx showing the legendary Bigfoot in California.*

across his field of vision. They also took casts of the footprints left by the creature. The film was shown worldwide and most experts believed it to be genuine.

Leading authority Dr Napier wrote: 'The North American Bigfoot or Sasquatch has a lot going for it. Too many claim to have seen it, or at least to have seen footprints, to dismiss its reality out of hand.'

See The Chinese Wildman p. 209

THE CHINESE WILDMAN

In China, too, there are legends of a wildman, or 'yeren'. Information collected over the years suggests that there are two types of yeren, one of about 1 m (3 ft) in height and another of perhaps 2 m (7 ft), and two types of footprint have been documented, which lend credence to this belief, the larger one bearing similarities to that of a man, only 30 to 40 cm (12 to 16 in) in length, the smaller one more like that of an ape, roughly 20 cm (8 in) long. The yeren share the characteristics of other man-beasts from around the world, with their ape-like features and hairy bodies.

In the 1980s, a party led by Gene Poirier, professor of anthropology at Ohio State University, collected a number of hair samples. These had been found by farmers working in some of the most remote regions of central China. At Ohio, and at Birmingham University in the UK, researchers used special microscopes to establish that the hairs contained 54 times more zinc and iron than human hairs and eight times as much as animal hairs. Professor Poirier, an avowed sceptic of man-beasts, declared: 'We have established that the animal does not fall into any known category. This is the first evidence of the existence of a higher primate.'

See Other Man-Beasts p. 207

MYTHICAL CREATURES AND FABULOUS BEASTS

All over the world, myths and legends have featured fearsome or fanciful creatures such as unicorns, dragons, werewolves or the *golem* of Jewish folklore. *Golem*, meaning 'lump', was supposed to protect the Jews from persecution and was fashioned by a rabbi from clay or mud. One famous rabbi, Judah Loew of Prague animated his *golem* by placing a small tablet underneath its tongue and wrote the word ameth or 'truth' on its forehead in Hebrew letters. *Golems* were big and powerful, but they would die if the tablet were removed from its mouth and the 'a' in *ameth* were rubbed off their foreheads, leaving the word as *meth* or death.

See Monsters p. 201

◄ LEFT: A statue of Rabbi Loew on the New Town Hall in Prague, where Loew lived and where the legend of the golem began.

UNICORNS

Unicorns have appeared in many of the world's mythologies, including Chinese, Greek and Roman. They are even mentioned several times in the King James version of the Bible, although it is possible that 'unicorn' may have been a mistranslation of the Hebrew word for wild ox. In biblical times the Hebrews regarded the unicorn as a fierce beast, able kill an elephant with its horn. Early Christians, on the other hand, came to regard it as a symbol of Jesus Christ. For the Chinese, the sighting of a unicorn was considered a good omen. They believed that one appeared before the mother of the great philosopher Confucius prior to his birth in 551 BC. Confucius himself is supposed to have seen one shortly before his death in 479 BC. The universal prevalence of the unicorn legend is a mystery. Did such a creature really exist? Its appearance in the Bible certainly gave early Christians little need to question its authenticity. But today many people believe that tales of unicorns simply have their origins from early distorted descriptions of the rhinoceros. The first mention of the unicorn appeared in China five thousand years ago, while first written accounts in the West date to around fourth century BC. Exact descriptions of the unicorn varied from culture to culture, but it came to be embraced as a creature symbolizing goodness and virtue.

◄ *LEFT: The unicorn has come to symbolise goodness and virtue.*

DRAGONS

Dragons, fire-breathing monsters, are also mentioned in the Bible and abound in legends and creation myths around the world, usually as a fearsome, destructive monster. The 'great red dragon' mentioned in the book of Revelations was a huge creature with seven heads, which signalled the end of the world. Fafnir, a giant character in Norse mythology, took the form of a dragon while guarding his treasure. In the Anglo-Saxon myth of Beowulf, the hero of the title fought with a dragon that was devastating his

► *RIGHT: Dragons have caught the imaginations of artists for centuries.*

211

kingdom and was killed in the process. Just as dragons are rife in myths and legends, so are dragon-slayers: Sigurd who killed Fafnir, for instance and, perhaps most famously, St George. Like the unicorn, the recurrence of this supposed mythical beast the world over begs the question if such a beast really did, or does, exist. To this day there are legions of dragon believers around the world. Sceptics point out that the idea of dragons could have easily originated from some of the living creatures mentioned in the Bible: great sea monsters, whales and leviathans perilous to anyone who encountered them. Judging from the similarity of early dragon descriptions to birds, alligators, crocodiles, snakes and other reptiles, it is quite possible that dragon myths were simply inspired by distorted accounts of existing animals. Its fire-breathing nature might have been early attempts to explain the phenomenon of lightning.

WEREWOLVES

Stories about the werewolf or lycanthrope, both meaning 'man-wolf', arose from the supposed ability of certain people to transform into wolves, usually at the time of the full Moon. This was thought to be hereditary, although in the first century BC, Roman poet Virgil wrote of a sorcerer who took certain herbs to bring about the transformation. Since Virgil's time, fascination with the werewolf has increased and innumerable legends, stories, and, more recently, films, have featured them and tell of their penchant

for killing and feeding on both humans and animals. In medieval times wolves were prevalent near towns and villages, and their habit of killing people and animals by tearing out their throats struck fear in many. Legends of the werewolf may have arisen from actual cases of individuals suffering delusion and, believing themselves to be werewolves, went around killing people. Today monsters and beasts such as werewolves, dragons and unicorns may seem fanciful, but their presence in the folklore of so many different cultures worldwide is certainly intriguing.

◌ See Vampires p. 213

VAMPIRES

Stories of the vampires and blood-suckers Count Dracula and Elisabeth Bathory, the Blood Countess, both of them based on real people, have created numerous examples of popular horror fiction and films. *Dracula*, popularised in 1897 by the novel of the same name by the Irish writer Bram Stoker, was a creature of the night who perpetuated his existence after death by sinking his fangs into the necks of his victims and siphoning off their blood. In nature, the vampire bats who were, apparently, the model for this method do not, in fact, attack

humans or suck blood directly from animals or birds. Instead, they make small cuts in the skin or hide and suck up the blood that oozes out. The character of Dracula was loosely based on the sadistic fourteenth-century Transylvanian ruler Vlad Dracul, whose nickname 'the Impaler'

◄ LEFT: *Illustration by Frank Kelly Freas to the story* The Werewolf of Ponkert *showing the popular image of a werewolf attacking a human.*
▲ ABOVE: *The fourteenth century Transylvanian ruler Vlad the Impaler.*

◀ LEFT: *Countess Elizabeth Bathory of Transylvania, who delighted in the slow torture and death of girls and bathed in their blood in order to retain her youthful beauty.*

said everything about his method of punishing his enemies. Elizabeth Bathory, born in 1560, was also thought to be a blood-sucking vampire. She retained her youth by bathing in the blood of young girls and was eventually condemned to life imprisonment for killing 600 of them.

Scientific explanations vaunted today claim that so-called vampires were actually individuals afflicted with either rabies or a condition known as porphyria. Porphyria, a rare genetic disorder, includes symptoms in sufferers such as severe sensitivity to light, skin and teeth discolouration, and mental disorder. Early tales of vampires in the Balkans also coincide with recorded outbreaks of rabies epidemics in humans. People suffering from rabies have been noted to react to stimuli such as water, light, mirrors and odours with spasms in the facial and vocal muscles. Such spasms cause them to bare their teeth, emit hoarse sounds and froth at the mouth.

◆ *See* Does Science Hold the Key? p. 29; Horror Movies p. 214

HORROR MOVIES

Tales of Dracula and other vampires have a considerable appeal to atavistic human fears, aided by the fact that bats have been the subject of superstition for many centuries. Many Dracula and other horror movies were remarkable for the frightening, suspenseful, brooding atmosphere they created onscreen and were largely responsible for the enormous and enduring popularity of this cinematic genre.

◆ *See* Films from the 1990s p. 305

BIG CATS

Many reports involving sightings of big cats occur in countries not associated with such animals. In England, where the wild cat is believed to have been extinct for more than 70 years, reports of creatures described as pumas, leopards and panthers are on the increase. Theories proposed to explain reports of big cats include suggestions that they are:

- Escaped zoo or circus animals that have managed to establish a local population, perhaps by cross-breeding with other cats. However, studies show that there is little evidence of such wild-cat populations, particularly in England.
- Survivors of an ancient species, thought to be extinct. This theory has been widely disputed because large cats would require large kills, in the form of deer, sheep or other animals. There seems to be no regular disappearance of such animals.
- Nothing more than misidentification of feral cats, domestic cats, or other animals.
- They may also be big cats living wild – many big cats sighted in the UK are in fact thought to have been former pets which were released into the wild when the laws on keeping dangerous animals were tightened.

All that is definite is that we still do not know why and how these cats appear, and the number of reputable witnesses claiming to have seen them is increasing.

◆ *See* Black Dogs p. 221

▲ *ABOVE: Unexplained sightings of big cats such as the black panther have become increasingly frequent in England.*

PHANTOM ANIMALS

Reports of phantom animals in a wide variety of situations and across the centuries are as common as those involving humans. Many pet owners claim to be aware of the spirits of dead pets, and often the hauntings cease when the pet's owner dies, leading experts to speculate that the animals remained on earth as an act of profound loyalty. Not all animal sightings involve pets – wild animals such as tigers and even an octopus have been sighted.

See Pet Apparitions p. 222

SPECTRAL CREATURES

Folklore abounds with stories of animals appearing and then vanishing. Throughout history many spectral animals have been considered as bad omens, or manifestations of evil or the devil. Cats, for example, were traditionally viewed as being a witch's familiar spirit and sightings brought great fear to a community. Spectral dogs are often seen sweeping through the countryside as packs of demon dogs, threatening death or misfortune to anyone who sees them.

Although many animal sightings appear to have natural explanations, ordinary animals have been credited with supernatural powers. There is little doubt that some animals appear to have a sensitivity to ghosts, often being the first in a household to confirm the appearance of something otherworldly. This sensitivity, along with a powerful loyalty to a particular person, family or place, may explain why so many animals return as ghosts after death.

See Devil's Dandy Dogs p. 222

▶ *RIGHT: Blickling Hall in Norwich, Norfolk, is said to be haunted by a phantom coach, which appears every year on the anniversary of Anne Boleyn's death.*

ANIMAL APPORTS

An apport is an object that appears in the presence of a medium, as though it has been formed from thin air. Apports were once common in spiritualist séances, with mediums producing many items such as flowers, books and precious stones. Most peculiarly, some mediums were able to produce live birds and animals, including lions, hawks, buzzards, eels and lobsters. While some mediums may have hidden these animals on their persons, many of the cases defy explanation.

◆ *See* Mediums p. 266

HORSES AND COACHES

THE COACH AND HORSES OF BORLEY RECTORY

The sound of a coach and horses was regularly heard outside Borley Rectory. Indeed, the house came to the attention of the *Daily Mail* in June 1929 when Reverend G. E. Smith and his wife claimed to experience a variety of paranormal events, including hearing a phantom coach and horses. Harry Bull, the son of the original owner, Reverend Henry Bull, alleged that he had once seen the coaches driven by two headless horsemen.

BLICKLING HALL, NORFOLK

Anne Boleyn spent several years of her childhood at Blickling Hall, a place of which she had many fond memories. She was executed at the Tower of London on 19 May 1536, and on the anniversary of her death every year, a phantom coach is said to convey her ghost, carrying her head on her knees,

217

towards Blickling Hall. The coach and horses are seen to drive very slowly to the front door and then vanish. It is also said locally that the ghost of her father is doomed to drive his coach over 40 bridges in the county every year before returning to Blickling.

◆ See The Tower of London p. 74

BLYTHBURGH, SUFFOLK

Tobias Gill, known as Black Toby, a black drummer with the Fourth Hussars, was stationed in the village of Blythburgh in Suffolk, in the middle of the eighteenth century. He allegedly raped and strangled a local girl called Ann Blakemore on 26 June 1750.

The following morning, three farm labourers found him in a drunken sleep beside the cold, lifeless body. He was tried for Ann's murder, found guilty and sentenced to death. Despite a plea that he should be allowed to die by being dragged at the end of a rope by a stagecoach, he was hanged near the scene of his crime. The ghost of Black Toby has been seen many times, even recently, in the area now known as Toby's Walk, but only ever during the month of June. The phantom still bemoans the fact that he was hanged. He has been seen thundering over the common on a hearse pulled by four black chargers, with Toby urging the horses forward at even greater speed.

◆ See Devil's Dandy Dogs p. 222

OULTON HOUSE, SUFFOLK

A phantom black carriage, drawn by a team of horses, is regularly seen driving up to Oulton House in Suffolk, which was the scene of two murders. In the eighteenth century, the squire of the house returned home after a day's hunting to find his wife in bed with an army officer. In a duel, the officer killed the squire and then fled, taking the squire's wife with him and leaving her young daughter behind. The daughter grew up and planned to marry a local farmer. On the night before the wedding, a strange coach pulled up at the house, and out of it stepped a veiled woman carrying a bottle. The following morning the girl was found dead and it was locally believed that the veiled woman was the girl's mother, who had returned to prevent her daughter from revealing the identity of the man who had killed her father.

◆ *See* Spectral Creatures p. 216

▲ *ABOVE: A sighting of a phantom coach and horses suggests that a tragic event took place in that location and is being re-enacted.*

DO COACHES HAVE SPIRITS?

There have been many sightings of phantom coaches, including one that haunts Thorpe Hall in Lincolnshire, where two children claimed to have seen it on several occasions. Experts believe that it is impossible for a coach to have a spirit, but suggest that these types of phantoms are re-enactments of a tragic event that has somehow imprinted itself on a particular place.

◆ *See* The Souls of Intelligent Species p. 213; What Causes Hauntings? p. 63

DOGS

RETURNING AS A DOG

In Ballechin House, Scotland, a bizarre haunting occurred. The army major owner of the house expressed a wish to return to life in the body of one of his dogs. His family were horrified by this wish, and upon his death arranged for his dogs to be shot. The major was buried next to his wife, but almost immediately after his death, strange occurrences began, including rappings and knockings, explosive noises and the sound of quarrelling. His nephew's wife was in the study one day and she experienced an overwhelming smell of dogs. She also felt herself being nudged by an invisible dog. These and other events frightened the staff so much that they refused to stay in the house. Such hauntings were reported at the house for more than two decades.

See Reincarnations and Past Lives p. 151

Bute's Proof

Lord Bute, an avid ghost-hunter, agreed to sponsor an investigation into the Ballechin House hauntings. He and his colleagues invited 35 guests to stay, all of whom were unaware of the house's history. The guests reported numerous supernatural activities, including the apparition of a black spaniel and phantom dogs' tails heard striking doors and other objects. One of the investigators had brought her own dog and was wakened in the night by its whimpering. Following its gaze, she saw two disembodied dog's paws on the table beside the bed. An account of the investigation was published in *The Times*, and the explanation offered was that the owner of the house had been forced to remain as a disembodied spirit, and with his dogs he haunted the house in protest.

See Ghost-Hunters p. 20

BLACK DOGS

There is an old superstition that the first soul buried in a new graveyard has to guard it for eternity. For centuries it was common practice to kill a large dog and bury it in a new graveyard, where it would protect the dead. The Black Dog, as it became known, is fiercely territorial and will even protect the living. In the early 1900s, a woman was walking home one night in the Midlands when she was approached by a black dog. At first she felt alarmed, but when a group of labourers passed her, saying 'what they'd like to do with her' if the dog was not there, gratitude replaced fear. As soon as the men were out of sight, the dog disappeared.

Not all black dogs are greeted with enthusiasm around the world. In some countries they are considered to be guardians of the underworld or manifestations of the Devil. Folklore insists that mischievous spirits take the form of black dogs. In 1577, a black dog supposedly appeared in a church in Bungay, Suffolk, and ran down the aisle. Two people who were praying died when he ran between them.

THE HOUND OF THE BASKERVILLES

Sir Arthur Conan Doyle based his novel *The Hound of the Baskervilles* on a true story. In the seventeenth century, Richard Cabell pursued his wife to a moor in Devon and stabbed her to death. Her loyal hound leapt for his throat and killed him as he stabbed it. This dog is said to haunt the Cabell family to this day.

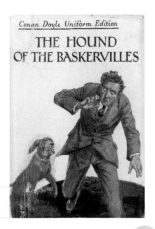

◆ *See* Ghosts in Literature p. 306

▶ *RIGHT:* The Hound of the Baskervilles *is based on a true story.*

DEVIL'S DANDY DOGS

According to local folklore in Cornwall, a pack of spectral hounds that runs along the ground or just above it, is hunting for human souls. A twelfth-century account describes a hunt numbering 20 to 30 riders astride black horses and accompanied by black hounds with hideous, staring eyes. Monks between Peterborough and Stamford, UK, claimed to hear the haunting throughout the night, with hounds baying and horns blowing. Sightings or hearings of these events have been reported as recently as the 1940s.

◆ *See* The Souls of Intelligent Species p. 223

PET APPARITIONS

Many pet owners have had experiences involving their pets returning after death. A significant number of these experiences do not involve visual apparitions of their pets. It is common for old toys, balls of twine and bones to appear, even though there is no longer an animal in the house. Similarly, many people claim that they have felt something

rubbing up against their leg, or have heard the sound of barking, mewing or howling in the night. Some experts speculate that the trauma of losing a pet can 'will' a loyal pet back from death. When the pet's owner has recovered sufficiently, many cases of pet hauntings stop.

◆ *See* Pet Dogs p. 223

◀ *LEFT: Pet hauntings can be caused by the grief of losi*
much-loved pet.

THE SOULS OF INTELLIGENT SPECIES

Dale Kaczmarek of the Ghost Researcher's Society claims that the most common reports involve dogs, cats and horses, in that order, and he suggests that only intelligent animals are able to return. He writes: 'There aren't, to my knowledge, any reports of phantom mosquitoes or flies, etc. Perhaps only the intelligent species have souls? Those and other questions remain unanswered. Man is the only species that some day realises that he or she will terminate and leave this world. All other species simply exist from day to day and die without being able to communicate to us the possibility that they in fact are dying.' He goes on to say that the scenario for most human ghosts is usually one of a violent or tragic death, when they were not given warning of impending loss of life. Perhaps the same thing works here.

See What Causes Hauntings? p. 63

PET DOGS

In Hollywood Cemetery in Richmond, Virginia, USA, the grave of the author Ellen Glasgow is believed to be haunted by her pet dogs. When she died, she stipulated in her will that her two pet dogs (who had died prior to her own death) should be exhumed from her garden and buried beside her. There are literally dozens of reports of sightings and sounds of the dogs, scampering near the grave late at night.

See Returning as a Dog p. 220

ANIMAL CEMETERY

At Hinsdale Animal Cemetery, south-west of Chicago, witnesses claim to have seen the dark forms of dogs and other creatures flicker by in their car headlights, often causing them to brake suddenly. When they stop and look for the animals however, they find nothing there.

See Cemetery Traffic p. 42

LONDON ROAD, BRIGHTON

A visitor to a house in London Road, Brighton in 1975 claimed that he saw the ghost of a dog run through two rooms and then disappear. The description he gave resembled that of Kylin, the pet of former resident Lady Thomas-Stanford. A lady in white has been seen by many visitors, one of whom went upstairs to change her shoes after a game of tennis and saw the figure of a woman standing on the stairway. She did not recognise her as one of the players but assumed that she was another guest. She greeted the stranger, but received no reply. As she offered her hand and wished the woman 'good afternoon' the figure vanished. There is also said to be 'an unpleasant atmosphere' in the corner of one bedroom.

ATHELHAMPTON, DORSET

One of the finest medieval houses in England, and the site of Thomas Hardy's 'Athel Hall', this property was owned by Robert Cooke, an MP. In 1957 he claimed that he had experienced ghostly activity. While working in his study he had heard his cat padding down the stairway. Wondering where the animal was off to, he spent half an hour looking for it. The following morning he was told that the family pet had died the previous week while he was away, and had been buried in the garden.

See Pet Apparitions p. 222

HORSES, CATS AND OTHER ANIMALS

PIT PONIES

In 1919, a coal miner named Gibbon saw the ghost of a pit pony in a Durham coal mine, echoing a disaster that had occurred there years before. Gibbon was checking the pumps

when he heard the sound of hooves and the jangle of a harness and chains. He looked up to see a pony, and then an arm grabbing at it from the darkness. He later found out that a young miner had been killed at that spot while trying to stop a runaway pony.

PHANTOM HORSES

Dale Kaczmarek of the Ghost Researcher's Society describes a regular series of ghostly horses that appear near Chicago. A busy intersection marks the border of the Cook County Forest Preserve. There are stables nearby and horse-riding trails wind their way through the flora. One of the trails crosses the busy and dangerous intersection. Until recently there was no traffic-control device in place to allow those on horseback to cross safely. At least seven people had been killed – and some horses as well – not to mention many injuries sustained. Kaczmarek reports numerous incidents – usually at night or near dusk – where motorists have seen what appears to be a horse and rider in silhouette, attempting to cross from one side to another. As the drivers slow down, they simply disappear. They are best described as smoke grey silhouettes seen from afar, with no distinguishable features.

See The Souls of Intelligent Species p. 223

DEMON PIGS?

According to folklore, pigs are vulnerable to the Evil Eye and have a tendency to become demons after death. At the notorious house in Amityville, the youngest child of the Lutz family, Melissa (Missy), communicated with a devilish spirit

LEFT: *The ghost of a pit pony was seen by a coal miner in Durham.*
RIGHT: *Associated with the Evil Eye, pig spirits can be devilish.*

225

pig who haunted her room. She came to know the pig by the name 'Jodie'. Although many plausible explanations for the many alleged paranormal experiences in the house were put forward, the phantom pig was never explained.

◆ See Amityville p. 68

BLACK CAT OF KILLAKEE

In 1968, a ghostly cat was seen at Killakee in Ireland. The Dower House in Killakee had a heavy front door that would not stay shut unless bolted. Tom McAssey locked it, only to hear a strange voice calling out: 'Leave it open'. McAssey fled the scene, but when he looked back he saw a large black cat with fiery eyes.

◆ See Spectral Creatures p. 216

WINGED MESSENGERS

Many families have experienced a ghostly white bird that appears to foretell death. In fact, a white bird is believed to be an omen of death, as it represents the soul. Many gravestones are carved with the figure of a bird. The Oxenham family in Devon claim that since the head of the family died in 1618, a white bird arrives to let the family know when one of its members is near death.

◆ See Black Dogs p. 221

▶ RIGHT: A white bird represents the soul and is therefore an omen of death.

ARUNDEL CASTLE

The ancestral home of the Dukes of Norfolk in Sussex, Arundel Castle is haunted by several ghosts, one of which is a bird. Considered to be the family 'death omen', a phantom white bird flutters against the windows to warn of the impending death of a member of the Howard family (the family of Catherine Howard, Henry VIII's fifth wife). The ghostly bird was said to have appeared just before the death of the last Duke of Norfolk in 1917.

◈ See Hampton Court Palace p. 78

▲ ABOVE: The Library at Arundel Castle is haunted by a phantom white bird.

EGYPTIAN TIGER

The medium Rosemary Brown was often visited by phantom animals. She described one particularly moving sighting, when her husband was ill. She lay beside him in bed and felt a weight on her legs. Looking down, she saw a tiger cub. When she described the tiger to her husband, he recognised it as being Sabrina, a pet tiger owned by his family when they had lived in Egypt.

SIGHTINGS FROM THE SEA

The *Fortean Times* describes the sighting of an octopus in an old priory in Wales. A vicar woke up in the middle of a summer's night feeling very cold. He saw a slimy, writhing shape in the fireplace. Looking more closely, he saw that it was an octopus, with pale, watery eyes. He felt paralysed by this creature's gaze, and he spent the night praying and trying to release himself. As morning came, the creature disappeared and was never seen again.

227

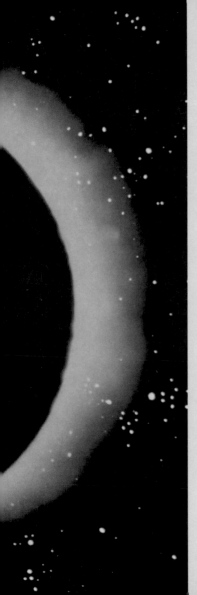

UFOs AND ALIEN SIGHTINGS

THE UFO AGE DAWNS

It is generally accepted that the modern age of UFOs began when Kenneth Arnold sighted nine strange objects over the Cascade Mountains, Washington, on 24 June 1947. Arnold, a businessman from Boise, Idaho, was flying his personal aircraft from Chehalis to Yakima in Washington state at an altitude of 2,700 m (8,858 ft) when he saw a flash of light near Mount Rainier, a 4,392-m (14,410-ft) dormant volcano. Suddenly, to the north of Mount Rainier, nine strange-looking aircraft came in sight, flying around 150 m (492 ft) above him. Arnold noticed that the aircraft, which were spread out over a distance of 8 km (5 miles), were about the size of DC-4 airliners. They were shaped like discs and were coloured silver on top and black underneath. They left no trails across the sky normally associated with aeroplanes.

Arnold later recalled that they reminded him of a formation of geese, or the tail of a Chinese kite blowing in the wind. He also likened the aircraft to saucers travelling in the same way as small objects skipping across the water in a pond. He assumed they were some kind of experimental government planes. The craft were flying at extremely high speed, which Arnold timed at over 2,700 kph (1,668 mph): this was more than twice as fast as the speed of sound, a pace as yet unknown to aviation at the time.

Arnold's experience set off tremendous worldwide interest in Unidentified Flying

◀ LEFT: Kenneth Arnold, who claims he saw nine round objects skimming through the air in 1947.

Objects (UFOs), as the military came to call them, although the popular description became 'Flying Saucers'. In the half-century and more since the Mount Rainier sightings, hundreds of thousands of reports have come in from all parts of the world about strange objects and lights seen in the sky. A new 'science' was born – Ufology – which captured the popular imagination with stories of showers of UFOs, sightings of their alien crews and abduction of humans for the apparent purpose of medical examinations.

◆ See Roswell, 1947 p. 236

STRANGE SIGHTINGS

At least 90 per cent of sightings of supposed UFOs have nothing to do with aliens or outer space: the other 10 per cent, though, is not so easily explicable. In this context, interest in UFOs has been increased by the seeming unwillingness of governments or the military to provide – or even attempt to provide – a believable scientific explanation. As a result, when UFOs were dismissed as 'weather balloons' or natural emanations of light from Earth,

▲ *ABOVE: Photograph of a UFO taken by Ralph Ditter in Zansville, Ohio 1966.*

the suspicion arose that the authorities were trying to hide something. This was, and still is, greatly fuelled when blankets of secrecy and security have smothered several well-documented instances of what observers believed to be alien landings and the capture of alien crews. One of these, the most famous, was the Roswell incident in New Mexico in 1947. Another was the Varginha episode in Brazil in 1996.

◆ See UFO at Varghina, Brazil p. 247

ALIEN VISITATIONS IN THE ANCIENT WORLD

Aliens from outer space have not been a purely modern preoccupation. The folklore and legends of many cultures worldwide have shown striking correlations between ancient and modern accounts. Theorists such as Eric von Däniken, the Swiss author of *Chariots of Fire*, published in 1968, have long claimed that Earth was visited by interstellar travellers between 40,000 BC and 500 BC. Their activities, according to von Däniken, include supervising the construction of the pyramids at Giza in Ancient Egypt. Since 1968, von Däniken has promoted the theory of the involvement of spacecraft and aliens from outer space in a large number of apparently inexplicable happenings, such as the appearance of crop circles in fields.

◆ *See* The Nazca Lines p. 187; The Pyramids of Ancient Egypt p. 191

▲ *ABOVE: Eric von Däniken believed that interstellar travellers visited Earth and during their time here supervised the construction of the pyramids at Giza.*

BIBLICAL CONNECTIONS?

The involvement of aliens and alien spacecraft in human history has also been traced through certain incidents detailed in the Bible. For example, the pillar of smoke by day and the pillar of fire by night that guided the children of Israel across the Sinai desert have been likened to the exhaust of a spaceship. The Bible recounts how a cloud surrounded the prophet Elijah as he was taken up to Heaven in a fiery chariot. That, too, has been taken to mean Elijah encountered aliens and their craft. The fashion in which he left Earth may have been one of the first alien abductions.

GODS AND ALIENS

Gods who descend to Earth from the sky and teach humans the skills they need to survive are common in pagan folklore from all over the world. A variant on this idea is that the One God of monotheistic faiths – Judaism, Christianity and Islam – was a spaceman – according to the theorist Eric von Däniken, God the spacemen communicated with Moses by means of an electrical transmitter. As a visitor from outer space, God made such an impression on primitive peoples

▲ *ABOVE: Native American pictographs depicting spaceman-like animal-gods.*

thousands of years ago that they depicted his image in their rock art. Ancient paintings from pre-Hispanic America (particularly Peru), France, North Africa, Italy and Australia appear to depict humanoid figures with their heads inside space helmets. Nazca rock art, from the east of South America, goes further and shows a man in a complete 'space suit'.

◆ *See* Ley Lines p. 186

PREDICTING THE FUTURE

Involvement by aliens in the distant past has also been suggested as one of the explanations for a code which, it is claimed, has been found in the Bible. This code, derived from an arrangement of letters in biblical texts, predicts certain important events, such as the terrorist attack on the World Trade Center in New York on 11 September 2001. In his two books analysing the Bible, American journalist Michael Drosnin claims to have deciphered that, unless the governments of the world mend their aggressive ways, World War III will ensue and the end of the world will occur in 2006. The cause, Drosnin suggests, will be through weapons of mass destruction.

Aliens from outer space, it would appear, are not only present-day visitors. According to many theories, they have always been with us.

See Nostradamus p. 260

◄ LEFT: It has been claimed that a code found in the Bible predicted the terrorist attack on New York in September 2001.

ALIEN SIGHTINGS

THE GREEN CHILDREN

A story dating from the middle of the twelfth century revolves around two green children who were found weeping and wandering in a field. They were taken to the nearest village, Woolpit, in Suffolk, and held in captivity at the home of Sir Richard de Calne.

According to William of Newburgh, the children were dressed in 'garments of strange colour and unknown materials'. They spoke no English and refused all food offered to them, apart from green beans. The children were baptised and the boy sickened and died. The girl learned to eat other foods and soon lost her green colouring. Over time, she was able to communicate in English and she 'asserted that the inhabitants, and all that they had in that country, were of a green colour; and that they saw no sun, but enjoyed a degree of light like what is after sunset. Being asked how she came into this country with the aforesaid boy, she replied that as they were following their flocks they came to a certain cavern, until they came to its mouth. When they came out of it, they were struck senseless by the excessive light of the sun, and the unusual temperature of the air; and they thus lay for a long time. Being terrified by the noise of those who came on them, they wished to fly, but could not find the entrance of the cavern before they were caught'.

Were these children really beings from another time and place, or could there be a rational explanation for their existence? The simplest answer is that they strayed to Woolpit from their own home, far away. Researchers have made suggestions based on the information provided by the children. It is probable that the story grew with re-telling, so that today it is part fact, part fairy tale, and the mystery is unlikely to be solved.

◆ *See* A Fourth Dimension? p. 31

ROSWELL, 1947

The incident that occurred near Roswell in New Mexico in 1947 has become the most famous, and also the most infamous, episode in the history of unidentified flying objects. More than 50 years after the event, Roswell is still controversial and what happened there has become the subject of numerous books, documentaries, hoaxes and, most recently, a fictional series of television dramas.

According to ufologists, the facts appeared to be straightforward. On the night of 3 July 1947 an alien spacecraft crashed in the desert of New Mexico near the secret Roswell air-force base. A number of alien bodies were recovered from the debris. Half a century and more later, the belief remains that bodies and debris are still being kept hidden at Area 51, a semi-secret US government base that logs paranormal events. After the incident, many ufologists became convinced that a cover-up ensued in which the government denied the crash had happened at all,

▶ *RIGHT: A flying saucer in the Californian desert.*

or that any alien bodies were found. The official version of the incident was that the supposed alien spacecraft was a weather balloon. This explanation was released only a few hours after the crash at Roswell, and official denial of the UFO story has continued ever since.

◘ *See* UFOs in Soviet Russia p. 248

Background to the Incident

The Roswell incident occurred at a sensitive time. Only nine days had passed since the first sighting of massed UFOs at Mount Rainier by Kenneth Arnold. World War II had ended less than two years earlier, and was at once followed by the Cold War (1945–90) against an erstwhile ally, the communist Soviet Union. Soviet Russia had long been feared as subversive and dangerous in the United States. The Cold War presented Americans with a sinister new enemy, ostensibly armed with missiles and atom bombs, which could attack and destroy them on their home territory. The somewhat hysterical atmosphere this created made the nervous public susceptible to stories about visitations from outer space and rumours proliferated that aliens were arriving on Earth in large – and possibly threatening – numbers. Mount Rainier and Roswell, it seemed, were only the beginning.

◘ *See* Russian Sightings p. 250

'Flying Saucer' Falls to Earth?

The fears were fuelled by newspapers like the *Roswell Daily Record*, which headlined the story on 8 July with the title 'RAAF [Roswell Army Air Field] Captures Flying Saucer on Ranch in Roswell Region'. A cryptic sub-heading added: 'No details of the flying disk are revealed'. The facts, as they later emerged, appeared to fill the gaps left by the newspaper and the government's blanket of secrecy. Two days before the reported

▲ ABOVE: Silver foil material found in Roswell and believed to be part of an alien craft that landed there in 1947.

crash, on 1 July, a strange object was seen on radar: it moved at enormous speed with erratic motion, suggesting that it was neither an aircraft nor a meteor. On 4 July, the object disappeared from the radar screens and the same day, Mac Brazel and other local farmers reported hearing a tremendous explosion. At the same time, a flaming object was seen falling to Earth. Mac Brazel later found one of his fields covered in the debris.

◆ *See* The Siberian Fireball p. 160

Beginning of a Cover-Up

On 4 July, military personnel arrived from Washington to search for, and retrieve, the wreckage. They were followed by a team of archaeologists. The crash site was located on 5 July. Civilian eyewitnesses were escorted from the scene and were later ordered to forget they had seen anything: they were also threatened that if they talked about it, they and their families would 'go missing'. The site was made secure within a few hours and five bodies were removed from the crash wreckage. Melvin Brown, one of the guards on the truck taking the bodies away, later claimed that the 'aliens' were small in stature, with large heads and orange-yellow skin. Subsequently, a journalist, Lydia Sleppy, who tried to send reports about the Roswell crash by teletype had her transmission intercepted by the FBI: she was forbidden to send any more. Similarly, the KGFL radio station, which conducted an interview with farmer Mac Brazel, was told not to broadcast it. Later, Brazel spent several days being questioned by the military. When they had finished with him, Brazel was placed under military guard for a week.

In addition, Major Jesse Marcel, an intelligence officer involved in the recovery of the debris, was ordered to Fort Worth by Brigadier-General Roger Ramey, commander of the US Eighth Air Force. Marcel took some the crash debris with him to show Ramey, but it disappeared and was replaced by pieces of an old weather balloon.

Precisely what was going on at this juncture was not clear and quite possibly, neither the government nor the military meant it to be clear. Either a cover-up was underway to conceal the alien visitation from the general public or officials were behaving in a secretive manner because of highly classified, more Earth-bound, experiments that were being conducted at Roswell. Whichever version was true, neither explanation sufficed for why officials were being so furtive and so unwilling to give anything away.

Alien Debris

Even so, there still appeared to be an element of the inexplicable about the whole Roswell affair. For example, claims that the bodies removed from the Roswell site were alien rested partly on 'evidence' that the debris of the 'spacecraft' could not have been the remains of a crashed weather balloon. Witnesses noticed that there were strange flower designs or hieroglyphics on some of the debris. The debris itself seemed to be made of strange and unknown materials: a foil-like substance, beams that looked like balsa wood and some sort of narrow binding tape resembling string. Pieces of the debris seemed impervious to fire. It was impossible to make scratch-marks on them and the debris appeared to be weightless. The strangest of these supposedly alien materials was the foil: after being crumpled into a ball, it quickly resumed its original shape when released.

The evidence was cleared away and the area was thoroughly cleaned. By 9 July, all debris that had fallen on Mac Brazel's field had been carted off. Six days later, on 15 July, Brazel was released from military custody but was told to deny all that he had seen and heard – or his family would suffer. By the end of 1947, the Roswell incident was officially closed. Everyone who had witnessed anything had been silenced and, it was widely believed, the crash site had been ploughed over and buried so that no evidence remained.

◆ *See* Strange Sightings p. 231

Hoax Autopsy

Ufologists, of course, had never been convinced that the official weather-balloon story was true, but there was little that they could do apart from stick to their own claim that aliens had visited Earth in 1947 and died in the attempt. The secrecy and uncertainty also opened the door to

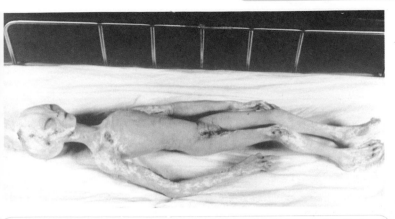

▲ *ABOVE: The alien puppet created for the* Showtime *telefilm on the Roswell incident.*

hoaxes. The most elaborate emerged in 1995, when a film was released by British ufologists that purported to show autopsies being carried out on the alien corpses. It was immediately labelled a fake and medical evidence was brought to bear in order to prove it. When one part of a body was moved, the rest did not move with it, as would ordinarily happen. In fact, the alien body was not moved at all during the entire autopsy. This pointed to the corpse being a specially made dummy. Also, the tool used to cut the corpse's skin was not held in the normal way employed by pathologists, and the skin itself did not automatically retract after cutting. The thigh muscles on the alien body were particularly suspicious: they were rounded and tensed, as they might be when alive rather than relaxed and sagging as they should be after death. This would suggest that the body was a plaster body-cast made from a living subject who had been standing up at the time.

◆ *See* Encountering the EBEs p. 247

Project Mogul

At around the same time the hoax film was released, a once top-secret project entitled Mogul was revealed as an explanation for the Roswell incident. Professor Charles B. Moore, one of the scientists who had worked on Project Mogul, revealed that the official explanation had been truthful: the crashed UFO was, indeed, a constant-level balloon being developed for meteorological purposes. That, though, had been its unclassified purpose. Heavily classified, and so sectionalised that even the scientists working on it did not realise the full truth, Project Mogul's real purpose was to monitor Soviet nuclear testings with acoustic microphones placed at high altitude.

Several balloons were used in the experiments. One of them was NYU Flight 4, which Professor Moore helped launch on 4 June 1947. A month later, Flight 4 crashed and scattered debris over Mac Brazel's field. Part of the top secret element of Project Mogul was the use of new, unusual materials in the construction of the balloons and it was these materials that were found at the crash site in New Mexico. Professor Moore also explained that he had himself used reinforcing tape on the NYU balloons which was patterned in stylised flower designs: these could easily have been mistaken for the 'hieroglyphics' observed at the site of the crash in 1947.

Doubtless, Professor Moore intended to lay the Roswell episode to

◀ LEFT: Parking sign in Roswell, New Mexico, alien capital of the world since the 1947 landing.

242

rest, but many ufologists refused to accept this new explanation. As a result, after more than 50 years of claim, counter-claim, speculation, media scare-mongering and sensational publicity, it seems unlikely that the Roswell story will go away or that the full truth about it will ever be known.

▶ *See* Alien Debris p. 240

UFOS IN MEXICO

After 1991, when a total eclipse of the Sun was observed above it, the Valley of Mexico became the world centre for UFO visitations. A total eclipse is the most awesome sight the sky affords, provoking an extraordinary spiritual and emotional response in anyone who observes it. However, the eclipse that took place over the Valley of Mexico on 11 July 1991 and lasting nearly seven minutes afforded an extra and fascinating excitement. As the Moon intruded over the solar disk, seemingly 'eating away' an

▲ *ABOVE: During the total eclipse of the Sun in Mexico in 1991, a UFO was seen beneath the Sun.*

arc-shaped segment, a round silvery object was seen hovering beneath the Sun. It was a UFO and it appeared over Mexico at exactly the time predicted twelve centuries earlier by ancient Mexican astronomer-priests as the start of the era of the Sixth Sun.

▶ *See* Nostradamus p. 260

The Sixth Sun

The Aztecs, whose vast empire dominated Mexico before the Spanish conquistadors arrived in 1519, believed that the Earth and the Sun had been created, destroyed and created again several times. The Sixth Sun was therefore the next 'creation' and, as an Aztec prophesy had it 'the sons of the Sixth Sun will be the first to journey to new worlds in the stars'. The appearance of the UFO at the eclipse of 1991 was therefore regarded by ufologists not as a coincidence but as a sign that the Aztec prediction was about to come true. After all, the Space Age had begun 30 years earlier and the time to break out of the Solar System and explore the universe beyond appeared imminent.

See Alien Visitations in the Ancient World? p. 232

Alien Invasion

The eclipse of 1991 was only the beginning. Afterwards, Mexico City, which lies in the Valley of Mexico, witnessed wave after wave of UFOs. They came on a daily basis and became one of the regular sights in the Mexican capital. The first reports of mass UFO visitations occurred in the spring of 1992, when they began to come in from the volcanic regions to the south-east of Mexico City. Observations, reports and eyewitness accounts became regular fare for newspaper front pages and headlines, radio stations and television programmes, some of which lasted up to seven hours at a time. Later, it was reckoned that at least 90 per cent of the capital's inhabitants had seen a UFO, many of them more than once. One UFO intruded on a night-time stake-out in which the police hoped to catch drug runners. Two police officers took a photograph of what they thought was a cargo plane carrying narcotics: when the picture was developed, it turned out to be a photo of a round, orange-coloured object with lights showing from apertures around its rim.

In May 1992, a triangular-shaped UFO, shining brightly, 'performed' for an enthusiastic crowd gathered round a small knoll known as Casita Blana. The UFO flew above the desert floor, banked, flew over the nearby volcano, then vanished. Much to their excitement, a Japanese crew from Nippon Television managed to film the whole event.

▲ *ABOVE: An early sighting of a UFO in New Mexico. This picture was taken by a government worker in October 1957.*

This, though, was nothing compared to the spectacular appearance of massed UFOs which appeared over Mexico city on New Year's Day 1993, and remained visible in the sky for more than six hours. The Mexican capital came to a virtual standstill as pedestrians crowded the streets and stationary cars blocked the roads; everyone who could, watched the show going on overhead. UFOs made further appearances throughout the year but in 1994, the phenomenon moved on to a new stage.

◆ *See* Films from the 1990s p. 305; Hessdalen Lights p. 163

Pilot's Encounter

In August 1994, a routine commercial flight was approaching Mexico City at the end of a trip from Acapulco on the Pacific coast. The aircraft was on approach at 3,650 m (11,975 ft) when an object flashed across its path. The captain of the aircraft, Fernando Mezquita, described the object as 'oval or round and very fast. It made a manoeuvre that was very difficult, coming straight for us. It banked and went under us, very, very close

▲ *ABOVE: A plane flying over the Mojavi Desert has a close encounter with a UFO in 1987.*

to the aircraft.' Mezquita later learned that there were no other flights in the area and that no object had been spotted on radar.

In the following week, UFOs appeared on both sides and above, below and in front of incoming aircraft, and before long the inevitable occurred: a DC9 airliner lurched forward as it was coming in to land and it was afterwards discovered that a strut had been cut in half. The captain, Raimundo Ruano had seen nothing that could have accounted for the damage, and the conclusion was that his DC9 had collided with a UFO. Later investigation showed that the UFOs were solid, reflective and that their flight patterns were totally unlike those of ordinary aircraft or balloons.

Mexico's pilots, like Mexico's people have since learned to live with the UFOs which still provoke intense curiosity and interest more than a decade after the first of them heralded the era of the Sixth Sun.

◘ *See* Flight 19 p. 177

UFO AT VARGINHA, BRAZIL

Over three days in January 1996, the city of Varginha in the Brazilian state of Minas Gerais was reportedly the site of an alien landing. Several Extraterrestrial Biological Entities (EBE) were retrieved from a crashed spacecraft and were later examined by Brazilian doctors.

The alien visitation began at midnight on 19 January 1996, when the North American Air Defense Command (NORAD) warned the Brazilian air defence authority that a UFO was heading towards the southern area of Minas Gerais. Ninety minutes later, a farmer, Enrico Rodrigues, and his wife Augusta saw a UFO hovering in the sky above. It showed no lights. The craft was shaped like a submarine and was giving off smoke as it came down to within 5 m (16 ft) of the ground. Later, it was reported that the UFO had crashed. Several EBEs survived and escaped from the wreckage to take shelter in nearby Jardim Andere park. One of the EBEs was spotted and was, apparently, shot as it crawled out of the spacecraft.

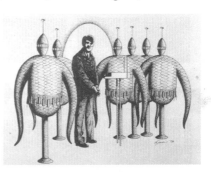

▲ ABOVE: A visual interpretation of the robot-like entities who allegedly abducted Antonia La Rubia, a bus driver from Paciencia near Rio de Janeiro in Brazil.

◆ See Films from the 1970s p. 302

Encountering the EBE

Shortly afterwards, the Varginha fire department and the Brazilian military received several calls about strange animals wandering about in the Jardim Andere. They investigated and eventually apprehended one injured EBE and another five unhurt; two other EBEs were found dead.

Later the same day, two young housemaids, Lilliane and Valquiria Silva and their friend Katia Xavier were returning home through the park when they saw a strange creature squatting by the wall of an old garage with its long arms between its legs. The creature had dark, greasy skin, three protuberances on its head and enormous red eyes. A smell of ammonia hung about it. Terrified, the three girls ran away and later told relatives that the creature seemed to be neither animal nor human. Another observer described the creature as having 'very small hands with three extremely long fingers, like a starfish. It was a little over one metre in height and had neither hair nor clothing.'

The EBEs were taken to the General Hospital in Varginha, where nursing and other staff were warned not to talk to the press. Already, though, the word at the hospital was that extra-terrestrials were on the premises, though one of the doctors, named Rogerio, hotly denied it. One dead EBE was taken to the Humanitas Hospital at 6 p.m. on 22 January, where several witnesses saw it unloaded. Next day, when the corpse was removed from the hospital to Campinas University, three trucks were used in convoy so that no one would know which one contained the EBE. An autopsy was performed, though this was denied by the pathologist Dr Palhares. The body was then frozen to preserve it. According to later reports, the dead EBE may still be at Campinas today. The six live EBEs were put on board a US Air Force C-17 transport plane and were taken to the Albrook base in Panama. After that, no more was heard of them and to this day, no-one has discovered their fate.

See Beginning of a Cover-Up p. 239; Films from the 1980s p. 304

UFOs in Soviet Russia

Over a period of some 13 years, from 1978 to 1990, two Russian investigators, Dr Yule Platov of the Academy of Sciences and Colonel

Boris Sokolov of the Ministry of Defence conducted secret research into UFO incidents over Russia and eastern Europe. This project was prompted by a cosmic event that occurred on 20 September 1977 over the city of Petrozavodsk in north-west Russia. Several explanations were given for the cause of this spectacular event. Nikolay Milov, who was a correspondent of TASS, the Soviet news agency, described it as 'a huge star' which 'suddenly flared up ... sending shafts of light to the Earth. The star spread out over Petrozavodsk in the shape of a jellyfish, showering the city with a multitude of very fine rays which created the image of pouring rain.' However, Aleksandr Kazantsev, science-fiction writer and expert on UFOs, identified this as an alien vessel from outer space that was engaged in reconnoitring the Earth and came to grief while doing so. On the other hand, Aleksei Zolotov was in no doubt that UFOs were the answer: Zolotov was an expert on the destruction and fire at Tunguska in Siberia in 1908, in which one of the causes was named as the crash of a spaceship of alien origin. Other explanations featured an impacting meteorite or a small asteroid.

See The Siberian Fireball p. 160

LEFT: Colonel Boris Sokolov of the Russian Ministry of Defence.

RUSSIAN SIGHTINGS

UFOs were nothing new in Soviet Russia in 1977. As far back as 1946, the Russians had published details of more than 50 sightings: it was believed, though, that this was nothing compared to the real figure for, in the highly secretive Russian communist society, news of most UFO incidents was suppressed. Like the US government, the Russian authorities tended to dismiss the possibility that

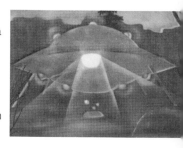

▲ *ABOVE: Artist's impression of a landed UFO.*

UFO sightings involved the paranormal but they had their own way of silencing those who talked too much about unusual objects in the sky.

APRAKSIN'S ENCOUNTERS

On 16 June 1948, an experienced and highly decorated Soviet air-force pilot, Arkadii Ivanovich Apraksin, was testing a new jet aircraft, when he saw an object shaped like a cucumber crossing his flight path. The object also appeared on radar at Apraksin's base at Kapustin Yar which instructed Apraksin to investigate, get close with the flying object and order it to land. Failing that, Apraksin should open fire. He never got the chance. His plane came within 10 km (6 miles) of the object when light beams shot out in a fan-shaped blast, scoring several direct hits. At once, Apraksin was in deep trouble. His engine and all technical systems failed and Apraksin's aircraft began plummeting to Earth. As it did so, Apraksin saw the mysterious object disappear behind the clouds. Thanks to his considerable flying skills, he managed to glide his aircraft in to land safely.

Afterwards, Apraksin was closely interrogated and his plane was examined by aviation experts specially sent to Kapustin Yar from

Moscow. Then, less than a year later, it happened again. On 6 May 1949, Apraksin was testing another aircraft when another mysterious object, similar to the first, appeared at a height of 15,000 m (49,215 ft). Once again, Apraksin's plane was showered with beams and again it was forced to land with its engine and all technical systems inoperative.

This time, Apraksin was taken to hospital. After he reported the second encounter, he had to appear in front of a special medical board in Moscow. Their verdict was that Apraksin was mentally unstable, He was sent to a psycho-neurological institute for shock treatment and other similarly drastic therapy. He never flew again.

◆ See Pilot's Encounter p. 246

MASS UFO SIGHTINGS

Sightings of UFOs over Russia proliferated during the late 1950s and '60s – there were 60 fully documented between 1958 and 1966 alone – until the pyrotechnic display over the city of Petrozavodsk in 1977 provoked the authorities to investigate officially. This was not, however, an investigation in the true scientific sense. From the start, it was assumed that UFOs and any other unusual sightings were due to military or technical activity, especially activity connected with rocket launchings. Between 1980 and 1990, Platov, Sokolov and their teams analysed some 400 individual events. Mass UFOs seen at night were routinely identified as effects from rocket launches or the testing of aerospace equipment. Most of these centred around the secret rocket base at Plesetsk, north of Moscow. There were, however, no recorded reports of alien abductions or any other kind of contact with aliens.

This led Platov and Sokolov to conclude: 'Either the territory of the USSR was ... closed for alien visitations during, at least, 13 years, or the hypothesis of an extraterrestrial origins of UFOs is inconsistent.'

ALIEN FORMS

Face-to-face encounters with aliens have produced several accounts of different types of visitor from outer space. The most familiar is of a spindly humanoid with an oversized head, large slanting eyes, greyish skin, no hair and no discernible nose or mouth. At a certain stage in human gestation, this is exactly what a foetus looks like, suggesting that the standard extra-terrestrial may be a pre-birth memory.

However other described forms have included 'animal entities' with features resembling those of fish, reptiles or, more commonly, apes. They have pointed ears, snouts for noses, extra large teeth, fur and claws, but their eyes are not human. Most are bipeds.

Robot-type aliens have also been reported. They jerk along on stiff legs or have the ability to float: glowing eyes have often been named as a distinctive feature. Some reports seem to combine characteristics to suggest more exotic forms: robots with human arms and humanoid bodies topped by animal heads. Non-corporeal aliens are less commonly reported, and supposedly resemble ghosts or columns of light. They 'shape-shift', appear, disappear or move objects by telekinesis. Telepathy seems a frequent means of alien communication, even for robots, who may also speak with metallic voices.

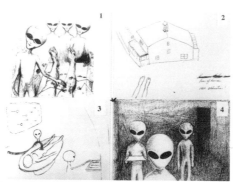

See Films from the 1980s p. 304; Telekinesis p. 150

◀ LEFT: Pictures drawn by people allegedly kidnapped by aliens.

▲ *ABOVE: A klingon, a character from the popular sci-fi series* Star Trek.

SCIENCE FICTION AND FANTASY

Several of these alien forms closely resemble fantasy figures out of folklore, such as giants, gnomes, pixies, or the animal-like kelpies. More recently, science fiction has impressed certain forms on the mind: the variety of alien characters seen, for instance, in *Star Trek* provides a wide choice of images. The conclusion could be that while those who believe they have encountered aliens and also believe that what they saw of them was genuine, the original model may already be stored in the human brain. Extra-terrestrials could be less alien and more human than previously supposed.

◆ *See* Alien Visitation? p. 200; Little People p. 194

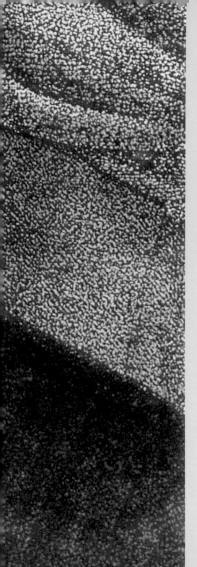

MAGICIANS AND MEDIUMS

MAGICAL TRADITIONS

Thousands of years ago, magicians, sorcerers, witches, wizards, augurers, seers, soothsayers, shamans and others who specialised in prophecy held privileged positions in pagan society. They were valued because of their special line to the gods, who revealed to them truths that were hidden from ordinary people. This, of course, gave them enormous power. Magicians and other prophets had special skills, enabling them to see into the future. Kings consulted them to learn the outcome of wars against their enemies. Farmers relied on them to make rain where there was drought. Ordinary people asked for their help to ensure a good annual harvest.

With the advent of the monotheistic religions – Judaism, Christianity and Islam – the magicians and others lost their exalted status. They were seen as the evil rivals of the One God, whose powers encompassed Heaven, Earth and everything and everyone on Earth. Instead, demoted magicians were labelled agents of the Devil and practitioners of the

◀ *LEFT: A Tibetan magician who, in the shamanistic tradition, deals with unfriendly ghosts and demons.*

'dark arts'. The burning of witches in medieval Europe was one result of this fall in reputation, but even after that persecution was over, in the late eighteenth century, magicians never regained their previous high standing. They were marginalised as 'oddities' or, worse still, as charlatans. Even alchemists, whose attempts to turn base metal into gold significantly failed, were regarded as dangerous dabblers in forbidden magic.

Nevertheless, the tradition of magic has lived on in modern mediums, the séances they conduct and their predictions of future events. Personalities such as Grigori Rasputin, the Russian peasant who became adviser to the last Tsar and Tsarina of Russia, or Aleister Crowley, the so-called 'Beast' and 'most dangerous man in the world', have forged reputations for extraordinary prescience and their connection with the 'dark forces' that are thought to lurk behind the civilised façade of everyday life.

◪ See Evil Spirits in History p. 129 Ghosts in Primitive Cultures p. 282; Mediums p. 266

CROWLEY, ALEISTER, THE 'GREAT BEAST'

In 1898, when he was 23, Aleister Crowley embarked on his pursuit of magic power. He joined the Hermetic Order of the Golden Dawn, which dabbled in alchemy, tarot, astrology, divination, numerology, Masonic symbolism and ritual magic. Crowley, however, was a practising bi-sexual and this shocked the leaders of the Order so greatly that they refused to create him Adeptus Minor, even though he had completed the necessary studies. Crowley asserted that in the fierce dispute that ensued, astral attack methods were used on him, causing his rubber raincoat to burst into flames. Crowley was expelled from the Golden Dawn in 1900.

For many years, Crowley had been trying to contact his Holy Guardian angel and in March 1904, he encountered him at last, in the form of an entity known as Aiwass. For three days, Crowley took down the text of his most famous book, *The Book of the Law*, at Aiwass' dictation. During his youth, Crowley had adopted 666, the number of the Beast in the Bible, as his personal number. This helped to account for his reputation as 'The Great Beast', a reputation he furthered by his passions for drugs and orgiastic womanising.

In 1920, Crowley set up his Abbey of Thelema on the Mediterranean island of Sicily. However, reports of black magic and other occult rituals performed at the abbey soon reached British newspapers, and resulted in Crowley being expelled from Sicily in 1923. By this time, Crowley was regarded as 'the wickedest man in the world' and he had difficulty in finding a publisher for his writings. Addicted to heroine, Crowley died alone on 1 December 1947.

◼ *See* Contacting the Dead p. 264; Spiritualism p. 264

▶ *RIGHT: Aleister Crowley at his altar.*

DEE, DR JOHN

Mathematician, philosopher and astrologer Dr John Dee lived at a very dangerous time for a man of his occult talents. Fear of the supernatural was common in sixteenth-century England and anyone demonstrating occult or prophetic abilities was regarded with deep suspicion. Dr Dee was fortunate, however, in finding favour with Queen Elizabeth I, who ascended to the English throne in 1558 and immediately asked him to use astrology to discover the most propitious date for her coronation.

Protected by his royal patron, Dee began to delve into the spirit world. He became convinced that spirits and angels were sending him messages, which he received through a crystal ball handled by his assistant, the necromancer and alchemist, Edward Talbot. In 1583, Dee and Talbot produced *Liber Logaeth* or *Book of Enoch* which was dictated to them in 'angel language': this took the form of a series of squares containing numbers and letters. When complete, the angels assured Dee, the book would offer the 'perfect truth' from God.

▲ *ABOVE: Portrait of the sixteenth-century astrologer, occultist and Rosicrucian, Dr John Dee.*

Unfortunately, the angels never delivered the final language key and with the death of his patron, Elizabeth I, in 1603, Dee's influence at court faded. He died in poverty at Mortlake in 1608.

◆ *See* Spirit Messages p. 263

HOME, DANIEL DOUGLAS

The Victorian spiritualist Daniel Douglas Home, a relative of the Earls of Home, first demonstrated his occult powers when he claimed that he was warned, telepathically, of his mother's death. Home's family, however, did not take kindly to the rappings that occurred during his séances, and his aunt threw him out of her house. The séances proved a great deal more popular with Americans, however, and Home's clientele included several highly respected figures, including a judge. In 1852, aged 19, Douglas Home gave a demonstration of levitation, the first of many he eventually performed. In 1868, for instance, he was seen levitating out of a third-storey window, then re-entering the building through another window. While levitating, Home said he felt 'an electric fullness' in his feet.

Home returned to England from the United States in 1855 and held séances which were attended by Robert and Elizabeth Barrett Browning, the famous poets. His occult powers, including his ability to levitate, were attested to by the Earl of Dunraven, among others, but he did not find favour in Italy, where the authorities deported him as a sorcerer in 1864. Daniel Douglas Home died at Auteil in France, in 1886.

◆ See The Fox Sisters p. 271; Séances p. 274

◀ *LEFT: The poet Elizabeth Barrett Browning, one of the many convinced by the psychic powers of Daniel Douglas Home.*

NOSTRADAMUS

Michel de Nostredame, better known as Nostradamus, became Europe's most renowned astrologer during his time, and still is to this day – so much so that his predictions were avidly consulted by Americans after the terrorist attack on the World Trade Center in New York in 2001. Supposedly, they found what they were looking for – references made to the disaster over four centuries ago.

Like Nostradamus's other prophecies – said to predict the Great Fire of London in 1666, the French Revolution of 1789, the rise of Napoleon in France, the advent of Hitler in Nazi Germany or the two World Wars – the wording was vague and was open to almost any interpretation.

Nostradamus was born in 1503, in France, of Jewish parents who were forced by persecution to convert to Catholicism. Initially, he worked as a physician, specialising in cures for the Bubonic Plague, but in 1555, he turned to astrology and wrote his first collection of prophecies: consisting of 100 quatrains, they were named *Centuries*. Eventually, Nostradamus completed 10 *Centuries*. Some interpreters say the verses can be applied to anything, or nothing, whereas others claim that various verses foretold the Great Fire of London in 1666, the deaths of several monarchs, details of the French Revolution, the rise of both Napoleon and Hitler, and World War II. On 1 July 1566, Nostradamus predicted his own death, telling a priest who bade him farewell 'until tomorrow', that he would not be alive at sunrise. Nostradamus died that same night.

◆ *See* Predicting the Future p. 234

◀ *LEFT: The Great Fire of London in 1666 was amongst Nostradamus's predictions.*

RASPUTIN, GRIGORI

Born in 1875, Grigori Rasputin was a *starets*, a peasant mystic of the sort employed in Russian noble households as seers and soothsayers. Rasputin was still a boy when he acquired a reputation for prophecy: he correctly identified a horse-thief without venturing outside his parents' house. Later, Rasputin added to this an aptitude for healing and this eventually brought him to the attention of the Russian Tsarina, Alexandra.

Alexandra's only son, the Tsarevich Alexei, suffered from haemophilia, a disease in which the blood fails to clot normally. Rasputin showed a remarkable ability to cure attacks of haemophilia by prayer. The *starets* could even cure from a distance. In 1912, the Tsarevich fell seriously ill while the royal family was on holiday in Poland. The desperate Tsarina

contacted Rasputin, who telegraphed back his reply that 'the little one' would not die. Alexei recovered almost at once.

Alexei's parents regarded Rasputin as a miracle-worker and refused to believe rumours that he was a drunkard, a rapist and worse. As a result, Rasputin gained such influence over the royal couple that he was able to interfere in Russian government policy. On 16 December 1916, a group of young noblemen

◄ *LEFT: Grigori Rasputin, shown here with two Russian Generals.*

attempted to kill him, but despite poisoning him with cyanide, shooting and beating him, Rasputin refused to die. His horrified assassins eventually disposed of him by drowning him in the River Neva in St Petersburg.

Rasputin had predicted that the Romanov dynasty would not last long after his death. The prophecy came true. Ten weeks after Rasputin died, the Tsar was overthrown by revolution. Eighteen months later, on 16 July 1918, the royal family was murdered by a firing squad.

⬥ See Nostradamus p. 260

SPIRIT MESSAGES

The ancient belief that the world is full of unseen spirits is still extant in the twenty-first century and its practitioners can have large, enthusiastic followings. One of them, the former football star turned New Age mythologist David Icke, promotes the concept of a Hidden Brotherhood: these disembodied creatures, Icke believes, have been present throughout human history and exist to keep a benign watch on human progress.

There is little doubt that many people have found ways to communicate with the dead, and a variety of techniques through which messages from the spirit world are received have been employed by both serious mediums and amateurs. The Ouija board, for example, has become a party game, although serious spiritualists warn that people play at their peril.

⬥ See Evil Spirits p. 273; Ouija Boards p. 273

▶ RIGHT: David Icke believes he is 'guided by souls from other dimensions'.

CONTACTING THE DEAD

Attempts to communicate with the dead are fed by the desperation of those who wish to receive a message from their loved ones. This demand spawned an industry many years ago that attracted its fair share of fraudsters. In an attempt to eliminate the charlatans from their ranks, serious researchers developed sophisticated experiments and technology in order to ensure that communications were logged and accurate. Numerous hoaxes were uncovered, but a number of cases still remain in which spirit communication has been uncannily accurate and, in some cases, proved.

◆ See Clever Hoaxers p. 276

THE PSYCHOLOGIST'S GHOST

William James and J. H. Hyslop were two famous psychologists with an interest in spiritualism. They made a pact with each other that the first to die would attempt to make contact from the spirit world. James died in 1910, and Hyslop waited for years to hear from him. He had nearly given up hope, when he received a call from Ireland. A couple claimed that in their séances, they had been pestered by messages from someone called William James, who repeatedly asked them to contact a Professor Hyslop. It had taken months, but they had eventually succeeded in tracking him down.

SPIRITUALISM

Spiritualism achieved particularly widespread popular appeal during the 1850s and 1860s and later after World War I, although support diminished when many nineteenth-century mediums (someone who 'channelled' communications between the earthly and spirit worlds, now also called channellers) were proved to be fakes. Along with other New

Age beliefs, spiritualism again became popular during the 1980s, particularly in the United States.

The repertory of the early mediums included table levitations, extra-sensory perception (ESP), speaking in a spirit's voice during trances, automatic writing, and the manifestation of apparitions and ectoplasmic matter. All these phenomena were attributed by the mediums to the agency of spirits. Spiritualism in its modern sense traces its origins to the activities of Margaret Fox and her two sisters. Early supporters of spiritualistic phenomena included American journalist Horace Greeley, British author Sir Arthur Conan Doyle, and British scientists A. R. Wallace and Sir William Crookes.

◆ *See* Extra-Sensory Perception p. 138; The Fox Sisters p. 271; Spiritualism p. 264

▲ *ABOVE: Two photographs taken simultaneously by two cameras to show the levitation in a séance held in October 1923.*

MEDIUMS

The term 'medium' became popular with the advent of spiritualism, when subjects who were magnetised or hypnotised fell under the control of spirits and were able to deliver messages from the dead.

Mediums were not the product of spiritualism alone, however. Throughout history, and all over the world, man has attempted to communicate – with varying degrees of success – with the spirits of the dead. The people, or mediums, through which this communication takes place have been known by various names, including oracle, witch, shaman, fortune teller, witch doctor, mystic, channeller and soothsayer.

▲ ABOVE: A selection of wares used to help contact the spirit world.

There are numerous different types of medium, each with a particular gift for contacting the dead:

- Physical mediums are able to turn spirits into solid form by producing a jelly-like substance called ectoplasm from their bodies. The ectoplasm takes the form of the spirit with whom they are in contact.
- Clairvoyant mediums hear messages from the spirit world. Some hear the voices inside their heads, and transmit the message in their own voice. Others hear the voices externally, and occasionally others are able to hear them, too.
- Transfiguration mediums allow spirits to enter their bodies and talk through them. They adopt the physical and verbal mannerisms of the spirit.

◆ See Clairvoyance p. 141; Ectoplasm p. 276

Who Becomes a Medium?

Many people appear to have been born with the ability to receive information not available through the five senses. Experts claim that the ability to act as a medium begins early in life – normally in childhood. These children exhibit signs of seeing and hearing things that others do not, although this is often suppressed by the pressure of parental and societal expectations. The ability can, however, begin at any age, and numerous cases have been recorded of mediumship evolving following a head injury, a trauma, a near-death

▲ ABOVE: Baron von Schrenk-Notzing with medium Eva C. during a series of experiments during which she produced ectoplasm.

experience, emotional shock or profound grief. Whether these triggers awaken an instinct or talent already present, or create a new ability to read or see what others do not is unclear. What we do know is that mediums are not brain damaged or mentally ill. Mediums are considered to have a psychic gift that they are able to control, while the mentally ill, including schizophrenics, have no control over voices they hear and visions they see or encompass into their own personalities.

Some mediums have the ability to create physical phenomena, including moving objects, levitation and controlling weather. Many mediums use their spiritual powers, or energies, for healing others. Many of today's spiritual healers have a learned or intrinsic gift for channelling external spiritual energy in order to heal.

◆ See Spiritual Children p. 23; Spiritual Healing p. 148

GARRETT, EILEEN

Eileen Garrett was an Irish medium and the founder of the Parapsychology Foundation in New York City. Her mediumship began after World War I, when she joined a group of women who wanted to contact the dead through séances. She went into a trance and began relaying information about spirits, which she saw around the table. A spirit called Uvani became her first guide, and although she resisted his efforts to convince her that there was life after death, he became her control. She went on to become one of the most successful and well-respected mediums of her day, encouraging organised scientific research through grants.

◀ LEFT: Eileen Garrett, the trance medium and founder of the Parapsychology Foundation in New York City.

MANNING, MATTHEW

The British psychic Matthew Manning has become increasingly well known for his extraordinary powers, which include writing and drawing automatically, communicating with spirits, bending metals, starting and stopping mechanical devices, apporting objects, psychic healing and communicating telepathically. In 1974, Manning was extensively tested by doctors and scientists in Toronto. Using an EEG, doctors traced the source of Manning's brain waves during psychic demonstrations to a part of the brain believed to be non-functional – although some experts believe that this part of the brain can be activated with electric-shock treatment. No plausible scientific explanation was found.

See Moving Objects p. 40; Automatic Writing p. 271

INCREDIBLE KNOWLEDGE

Some mediums appeared to have remarkable abilities. The British medium Doris Stokes, for example, helped to solve murder cases with her intuitive advice to the police and was noted for her astonishing accuracy in spiritualist demonstrations. During World War I, another British medium, Estelle Roberts told Mary Cartland, the mother of romantic novelist Barbara Cartland, that her sons, Ronald and Tony, had been killed one day apart. At the time, Tony was thought to be a prisoner of war. A year later, however, Mrs Cartland was informed that he was dead, killed in action, one day before his elder brother Ronald, just as Estelle Roberts had told her.

▶ *RIGHT: Estelle Roberts was considered to be one of the world's greatest mediums.*

PIPER, LEONORA

Leonora Piper was a celebrated medium investigated by experts on both sides of the Atlantic. All claimed that she was the genuine article. From the age of eight, she appeared to have an extraordinary ability to communicate with the dead. On a trip to England between November 1889 and February 1890, she held 83 sittings under the supervision of SPR investigators, including Frederic Myers. She performed perfectly, leading the SPR to claim that she was an undoubtedly gifted woman. Piper believed she received her information by ESP. After being especially harshly treated by investigators in 1909, she temporarily lost her powers, but when they returned, they took the form of automatic writing, rather than ESP as before. She died in 1950, having provided what many consider to be the first real evidence of life after death.

See Extra-Sensory Perception p. 138; Ghost-Hunters p. 20

Dr Phinuit

Leonora Piper's guide, Dr Phinuit, claimed to be a French doctor, although he apparently knew little French and even less about medicine. He was also unable to provide verifiable details of his life before death. Although experts were suspicious about his role, there was no doubt that Leonora, through Phinuit, was able to reveal things about other people that she otherwise had no way of knowing. It was determined that the spirit guide was a secondary personality with considerable psychic ability.

See Leonora Piper p. 269

SPIRIT GUIDES

Many mediums use particular spirits as 'guides' to provide a link between the medium and spirits that need to be contacted. Leonora Piper worked through a spirit guide named Dr Phinuit, and Eileen Garrett's spirit guide was known as Uvani, although she had others as her career progressed. Some experts believe that the spirit guide is actually a sub-personality of the medium's own mind. Others believe that everyone possesses a spirit guide who understands the ways of the world and can draw on experience to help people through life. Spirit guides and pure spirits, it is believed, are reached through 'channelling'. This is a technique involving intense mental concentration. Once the connection is made, the spirit advises and guides on problems and difficulties.

See Leonora Piper p. 269; Eileen Garrett p. 268

THE FOX SISTERS

Beginning in 1848 at their parents' farmhouse near Hydesville, New York, the Fox sisters were able to produce spirit 'rappings' in answer to questions put to them. They claimed that their home was haunted by the ghost of a peddler, and they seemed able to control his poltergeist-like activity.

After moving to Rochester, New York, and receiving a wider audience, their fame spread to both sides of the Atlantic. By the mid-1850s they had inspired a host of imitators, and the birth of the spiritualist movement. Margaret Fox later claimed to have manipulated her joints in order to create the rapping sounds, but after her death, when the farmhouse where she had grown up collapsed (1904), the body of a peddler was found sandwiched between two walls.

◆ *See* Spiritualism p. 264; Spiritual Children p. 23

▶ *RIGHT: The Fox sisters levitate a table during a seance in Rochester, New York, in 1850.*

AUTOMATIC WRITING

Automatic writing is writing produced while a person is unconscious or semi-conscious of the act. In the nineteenth century the phenomenon was used by practitioners of spiritualism, and was later adopted by workers in parapsychology. A medium enters a trance-like state, lightly holding a pen, which then moves spontaneously across a page. The message tends to be written in the hand of the person transmitting the message, and appears in their style of expression. Matthew Manning received messages in many languages, including French, German, Italian, Greek, Latin, Russian and Arabic, and sometimes in medieval forms. Many of the messages were incoherent, but others were accurate and predictive. He later went on to draw automatically in a similar way, producing pictures in the style of many famous artists, including Picasso, da Vinci, Rackham, Matisse and Beatrix Potter.

See Matthew Manning p. 268; Ouija Boards p. 278

◄ *LEFT: A right-handed woman holds a pen in her open left hand and writes automatically.*

ELECTRONIC VOICE PHENOMENON

In 1947, Russian-born film producer Friedrich Jurgenson was listening to a recording of birdsong when he heard a man's voice. He believed it was a coincidence, but when he made further recordings, having ensured there were no humans present, he found that they contained messages. He had stumbled on one of the most successful forms of contact with the dead: Electronic Voice Production (EVP). Many experiments into the authenticity of EVP have been undertaken, including some by Matthew Manning. He tried to contact Hitler with a tape running, and wrote the following: 'It began with distant bumbling gunfire, which soon gave way to regimented marching. Behind this noise a sound like a brass band could be heard playing a marching tune ... later identified as one of the German Nazi songs ... gunfire could be heard more clearly in the background. Still the music kept playing over it all and incoherent shouting was audible.' When the tapes were later assessed by experts there was no evidence of tampering.

◆ *See* Automatic Writing p. 271

EVIL SPIRITS

There is a continuing belief in demons and other evil spirits and their power to disrupt human life. Exorcism, in which prayers and commands offered in the name of God are thought to drive troublesome spirits away, has a very long history, dating back to ancient Babylonia and Egypt. However, spiritualism in which the basic tenet is contact and conversation with the dead in the 'next' world', is a fairly recent development. It first arose in the mid-nineteenth century as a response to the rapid social changes brought about by advancing technology and scientific discoveries which, like Darwin's theory of evolution, disturbed belief in the old religious certainties. The first demonstration by a spiritualist 'medium' was given at the Corinthian Hall in New York in 1849. In 1852, the first public demonstration of the medium's skills was given in Britain. Spiritualism attracted some very high profile adherents, including Queen Victoria, Empress Eugenie of France, Sir Arthur Conan Doyle, creator of the famous detective Sherlock Holmes, Robert Owen, co-founder of the co operative movement, and Mary Todd Lincoln, wife of the US President Abraham Lincoln.

◆ *See* Séances p. 274; Spiritualism p. 264; Queen Victoria p. 275

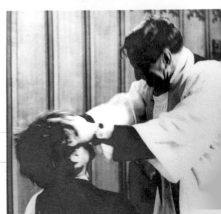

▶ RIGHT: The exorcising of evil spirits dates back to ancient Babylonia and Egypt.

SÉANCES

A séance is a sitting organised for the purpose of receiving communications from the dead or a physical manifestation of a spirit. Séances normally involve a medium, although many are undertaken by laymen in the hopes that they will be visited.

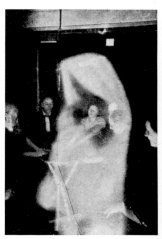

The first recorded séance occurred in 1659, but there was little documentation or widespread interest until the Fox sisters introduced spiritualism in the 1800s. After that, séances were conducted regularly around the world, and they have remained popular ever since. There are many codes of etiquette involved in holding a séance. These include admitting few strangers, ensuring that they last no more than two hours, arranging chairs around a circular table with no more than eight sitters, avoiding touching the medium, and beginning with the Lord's prayer in order to prevent unwanted spiritual activity.

The first indication of spiritual activity can be experienced as a cold rush of air. If the medium is transfigural or clairvoyant she or he may begin automatically writing, or announce the arrival of a spirit.

Experts recommend that séances are not undertaken without a medium, who can sense if any danger is present and close off communication. Séances are considered to be 'uncontrolled' forms of communications and therefore susceptible to potential dangers.

See Clairvoyance p. 141; Mediums p. 266; Spiritualism p. 264

◀ *LEFT: Flash photograph taken during the Warrick Deane series on 23 June 1924. In the foreground, a materialised form is just about to dematerialise.*

QUEEN VICTORIA

Queen Victoria conducted her own séances at Osborne House on the Isle of Wight and was a firm believer in second sight, psychic phenomena and the power of magnetism. The queen was certain that in the afterlife, she would meet those 'dear ones waiting', in particular her adored husband Prince Albert who died in 1861, nearly 40 years before her own death.

Victoria's attachment to spiritualism encouraged Mary Todd Lincoln who longed to contact her two lost sons, Eddie and Willie. Willie died in 1862 and on 23 April 1863, a séance was held at the White House in Washington. The president was there. Two years later, he was assassinated. Subsequently, Mrs Lincoln had her picture taken by William

Mumler, the 'spirit photographer'. He produced a photograph showing Mrs Lincoln with her dead husband standing behind her, his hands on her shoulders. Mary Lincoln took great comfort from the thought that the murdered president was watching over her. Mumler, however, was known to fake his photographs by using double exposures.

◨ *See* Abraham Lincoln p. 81; Séances p. 274; Spiritualism p. 264

▶ *RIGHT: Queen Victoria was sure that she would meet her husband Albert in the afterlife.*

CLEVER HOAXERS

The horrific slaughter in the trenches of World War I, in which millions of young men died, created an upsurge of interest in spiritualism. Bereaved parents, fiancées, wives and other relatives were desperate to have some contact with the loved ones who had been so brutally taken from them, and attended séances in the hope of speaking to them again. Unfortunately, this was a great opportunity for hoaxers. The séance was the stage on which the medium performed and it was all too easy to fake. A séance was usually conducted in a darkened room and featured table 'rappings' and movements, disembodied voices and in some cases the appearance of a substance called ectoplasm. Ectoplasm purported to be a liquid that flowed from the mouth, nose and ears of mediums while they were in contact with 'the other side'. Hoaxers used a combination of cheesecloth and netting covered in luminous paint.

See Ectoplasm p. 276; Mediums p. 266

ECTOPLASM

Ectoplasm is a substance that resembles a fine, delicate fabric, but with the consistency of egg white or light jelly. It often shapes itself into human faces, hands or even bodies. Many mediums produce ectoplasm from their nose or mouth (occasionally also from the navels, nipples, eyes, ears or vagina) when they are in a trance. Some mediums use the ectoplasm that is produced to mould the face and body of the spirit who has communicated with them. Ectoplasm can also appear spontaneously; in this case, it is a product of psychic energy that usually forms as a fog-like mist, solid white mass or vortexes.

The term ectoplasm was first coined by French physiologist Charles Richet in 1894, and since then many studies have been undertaken to analyse this substance. The structure varies from formless clouds to spider-web-like tendrils. It disappears in white light, and is evident only in red incandescent light and darkness. If a bright light appears, it snaps back into the medium's body.

In experiments in the early 1900s, medium Marthe Beraud produced a large amount of ectoplasm. She was thoroughly examined before and after the sittings, often wearing tight clothing. No evidence of anything concealed could be found. When the ectoplasm was touched by someone else's hands, it writhed back into Beraud's body. After forming, the ectoplasm took on the faces or shapes of historical figures. Gustave Geley, head of the Institute Metapsychique in Paris, described ectoplasm as an externalisation of decentralised energy in solid, liquid or vapour form. Medium Robert Chaney's description was that ectoplasm is the spiritual counterpart of protoplasm. He believed that the ectoplasmic body exists in the inter-cellular spaces of a medium's physical body, halfway between psychical and spiritual forms.

However, sceptics say that ectoplasm does not exist and is produced through tricks of the light or that it is really fabric, such as cheesecloth.

◆ *See* Clever Hoaxers p. 276; Mediums p. 266

▶ *RIGHT: A medium extruding ectoplasm, the substance that forms spirits during séances.*

TRANCES

A transfiguration or trance medium loses consciousness, either partly or altogether, and is usually not aware of what is going on during a séance or reading. Often, while in this state, the medium's body is taken over, controlled, or possessed by a spirit entity who may speak or act through the medium's physical self.

Trances are not, however, the exclusive domain of mediums. The term 'trance' is applied to a state of inwardly focused attention during which a person, although not asleep, shows little awareness of the immediate environment and exhibits a minimal response to stimuli. The body of the entranced individual is thought of as being suspended between life and death, while the mind is free to explore higher realms.

🔷 *See* Contacting the Dead p. 264; Séances p. 274

▶ *RIGHT: Photograph taken of Bromson Murray in a trance with the spirit of Madame Bonner behind him.*

OUIJA BOARDS

The Ouija board has been used by thousands of people for spirit communication and is very similar to automatic writing. It should not be used as a party game, say experts, who claim that this form of communication with the spirit world is extremely dangerous.

A Ouija board is simply a piece of compressed wood and is widely available. Ouija is a combination of the two words *oui* and *ja* which mean 'yes' in French and German respectively. In itself, the Ouija board

▶ *RIGHT: Communicating with spirits using a Ouija board can be extremely dangerous.*

is not dangerous, but the form of communication is. Numbers and letters and usually the words 'yes' and 'no' are arranged in a circle on the board. In the centre, there is an object called a planchette, although an upturned glass can be used instead. Each sitter rests a finger on the planchette and when a spirit is asked a question, it responds by moving the planchette around the board. Because of their contact with the planchette, the sitters can easily influence the outcome by moving the planchette themselves.

Dale Kaczmarek says that the spirits most often contacted through a Ouija board are those who reside on a lower astral plane: 'These spirits are often very confused and may have died a violent or sudden death; murder, suicide, etc. Therefore, many violent, negative and potentially dangerous conditions are present to those using the board.'

A US case involving two couples who played with the Ouija board for fun had an unexpected outcome. Previous owners of the property had left the board behind. Unexplained disturbances had already occurred, but these increased after the couples played with the Ouija. Eventually, the activity became so overwhelming, the residents took refuge with a relative, leaving most of their belongings behind. Investigations by a psychical research organisation showed that there was undoubtedly paranormal activity in the building.

↪ *See* Automatic Writing p. 271

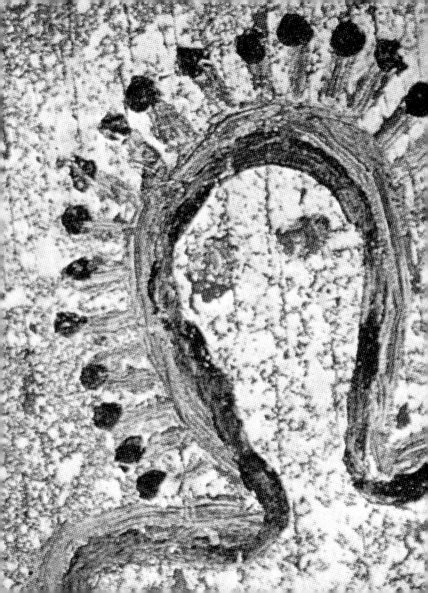

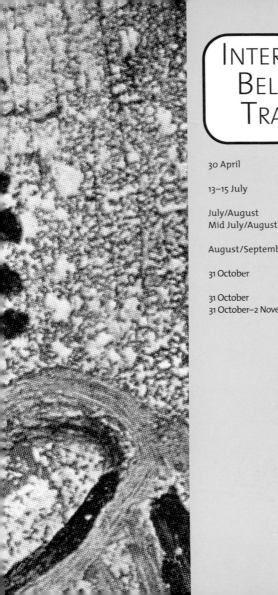

INTERNATIONAL BELIEFS AND TRADITIONS

30 April	Walpurgis Night (Europe)
13–15 July	Feast of Lanterns (Japan)
July/August	Ghost Month (Taiwan)
Mid July/August	Obon: The Festival of the Dead (Japan)
August/September	The Hungry Ghost Festival (China)
31 October	Halloween (Canada, US and UK)
31 October	Samhain (Ireland)
31 October–2 November	Day of the Day (Mexico)

GHOSTS IN PRIMITIVE CULTURES

The ancient belief in demons, ghosts and spirits inspired many colourful rituals that are still practised today in both primitive and more advanced societies. Although our understanding and practise of religion and science have changed dramatically over the centuries, the idea that some souls remain on Earth after their living bodies have expired has survived relatively intact. In the West, the belief in ghosts is still strong, and a variety of festivals around this belief continue to be celebrated, albeit watered down and without their original purposes. Elsewhere, ancient beliefs in ghosts remain strong, forming a key part of religion, mythology and rites of passage.

Many cultures worship deceased ancestors as if they were deities. Ancestor worship is also a characteristic of animism, a system of beliefs about souls and spirits typically found in tribal societies in Africa, Asia, the Americas and Australia. Ancestors are not considered to be gods as such, but their spirits are believed to be enormously powerful, capable of causing great destruction and unhappiness if they are not appeased regularly. In some cases, food or drink is simply laid out for the deceased in the belief that they will then bring good luck and ward off evil.

Elsewhere in the world, an overwhelming belief system holds the spirits of the dead in much higher regard than we do in the West. These spirits of the dead may return in the form of ghosts, as animals, be born again as children (reincarnation), or have their energy manifested in nature (trees, rocks, etc.).

◆ *See* Ghost Worship p. 283

FESTIVALS

In tribal societies around the world, celebrations continue to focus on the dead and the afterlife. Ghosts and spirits play an important role in daily life, and festivals, feasts and other celebrations are held in order to appease spirits who have gone over to the other side, or to help them on their journey to the afterlife. Many of these traditions have found their way to the Western World, either in the form of superstitions or as part of religious belief. For example, many Christian religions view ghosts as something demonic, hence the need for exorcism, a fundamental ritual of the Catholic Church. Halloween, a pagan Celtic festival, is celebrated by many people, but it is still viewed with concern by religious figures who suggest that by celebrating the dead we are encouraging an unhealthy interest in the occult and the devil.

◆ *See* International Ghost Festivals and Beliefs p. 284

GHOST WORSHIP

In many parts of the world, the dead and their disembodied spirits are a source of great joy and their worship is encouraged. In Mexico, for example, relatives are invited to meet with their dead in an annual festival, in which ghosts return to be with much-loved family members.

◀ *LEFT: A feast honouring the ancestors on the Mexican Day of the Dead, which is celebrated between 31 October and 2 November.*

In other countries, ghosts are viewed as being very wise, and are called upon to help out in times of trouble. All over the world, ghosts are used to guide the living, and whether from fear or genuine reverence, their existence is feted and encouraged.

◆ *See* Mexican Day of the Dead p. 288; Spirit Guides p. 270

▶ RIGHT: *Tibetans praying for the dead.*

INTERNATIONAL GHOST FESTIVALS AND BELIEFS

Africa: Dogon Mourning Rites; Day of the Dead
China: Hungry Ghost Festival
Mexico: Day of the Dead
Canada, US and UK: Halloween
Ireland: Samhain
Japan: Feast of Lanterns
South America, Siberia, Northern Asia: Shamanism
Tibet: Bardo Thodol (Tibetan Book of the Dead)
Europe: Walpurgis Night
India: Bhuta Worship; Hindu Sraddhas
Australia and New Zealand: Aboriginal Festivals

DOGON MOURNING RITES

The Dogon people from Mali in West Africa have a unique form of ancestor worship. When a member of the tribe dies, the men of the tribe mark the end of the mourning with a dama – a rite that aims to settle the troubled souls of the dead and send them safely on their way to the afterlife. Dancers wear intricately coloured and carved masks and perform elaborate movements, mock battles and rites that can last for up to six days, depending on the seniority and importance of the person who has died.

See Ghost Dances p. 294

GHOSTLY SHADES

Certain tribal Africans believe that the 'shades' of the deceased remain with their families and intercede on their behalf with the divine spirits. To keep them happy, living relatives hold a feast with food and drink, and often sacrifice animals. Every member of the deceased's family attends the meal, as it marks a communion among the living and the dead. Any disagreements are resolved at the feast to ward off witchcraft and dangerous spirits.

▶ RIGHT: A ritual of the Ethiopian Galla people to wash away the sins of the deceased.

UKUBUYISA

In central and southern Africa, the forces of good and evil are constantly at work to help or harm people. If a person is exceptionally kind, helpful and generous, the Swahili call him or her *malaika*, 'an angel'. Parents and children help one another and when parents and grandparents die, they do not cease to exist. Their spirits remain alive and stay near their loved ones, anxious to help fulfil their needs and ease their worries. Some spirits are stronger than others, but all spirits can work magic. The Zulu say that a man of strong character has a 'large shadow', meaning much power. After his death, they perform a special ceremony, *ukubuyisa*, to bring his spirit back into the compound so that he may continue to help his family. They believe that many spirits of the dead wander the Earth as ghosts, either because they have a task to perform, a message to convey to the living, or because they want to avenge themselves on an evil-doer.

▶ *RIGHT: An extravagant send-off on the death of an eminent Zulu.*

CHINESE GHOSTS

Chinese culture believes each person has two spirits, a good spirit known as *Shin*, and a bad known as *Kuei*. If a body does not have a proper burial the *Kuei* is left to wander. As in India and Egypt, the Chinese would make offerings to the ghosts to prevent them from bothering the family. Today it is believed that one part of the spirit of a deceased person passes into

▲ *ABOVE: The Chinese believe that their ancestors protect their households and communities. Here they show respect for the dead by crouching beneath a coffin.*

a special tablet after death. The tablets are placed in a ceremonial room where they are treated as though they are living people. The purpose of this is the same as in tribal societies: to ensure the ancestors look out for the household and community.

▶ *See* Ukubuyisa p. 286

CHINESE HUNGRY GHOST FESTIVAL

The Chinese perform special ceremonies in spring, summer and autumn to ease the 'two souls' of humankind (spiritual and animal). The spiritual soul is petitioned to consider the departed's descendants and the animal soul is discouraged from rousing the corpse and disturbing the living. The Hungry Ghost Festival takes place in the autumn during the Seventh Moon, and food is left for ghosts who have no living descendants to take care of them.

MEXICAN DAY OF THE DEAD

On 2 November, Mexico's Day of the Dead, *El Dia de los Muertes*, ghosts of the dead are believed to revisit the living, and their return is celebrated with feasts, parties, songs and parades.

When the Spanish conquistadors invaded Mexico, they were shocked by the native cannibalistic practices and human sacrifices, and attempted to convert the Mexicans to Catholicism. The Mexicans did not distinguish between life and death, seeing each as part of an eternal cycle. They felt that the main function of life was death, which provided the food for future life. Missionaries suggested the date of 2 November (All Souls' Day) and since that time great festivities around this date have continued as part of the Mexican tradition.

On 31 October, the house is prepared for the celebration, and great quantities of food are cooked, including special bread shaped as animals. Small clay altars are built, on which they place offerings of food and toys

for the angelitos (the children in the family who have died). At midnight the family pray and watch the angelitos arrive to enjoy their gifts.

The following day, a greater feast is produced for the older deceased, who arrive the following morning. Larger altars are built, with decorated marzipan skulls and breads. The names of the departed are written on the foreheads of the skulls, with messages for their owners. Tiny candy coffins are eaten, and great quantities of food and alcohol are consumed as parades and bands play music to celebrate the ghosts of the nation. Local priests visit the home altars and offer prayers and blessings.

By the following morning, All Souls' Day, the festivities have ceased and the Mexicans attend mass. The ghosts of the departed return to their graves. That evening, families visit cemeteries, where they share a meal in honour of their loved ones.

◆ See Halloween p. 289

HALLOWEEN

Now predominantly a children's celebration, Halloween was originally a Celtic festival for the dead, celebrated on the last day of the Celtic year, 31 October. Elements of that festival were incorporated into the Christian holiday of All Hallows Eve, the night preceding All Saints' Day (1 November). Until recent times in some parts of Europe, it was believed that on this night witches and warlocks flew abroad; and huge bonfires were built to ward off these malevolent spirits.

◆ See Witches p. 146

◀ *LEFT: Day of the Dead observances in Tzintuntan near Patzcuaro, Mexico.*
▲ *ABOVE: Halloween pumpkins on a front porch in Berkeley, California.*

SAMHAIN

The ancient Celts celebrated the festival Samhain, and observed it to celebrate the onset of winter and the beginning of the new year. Samhain was a solar festival, with sacred and fire rituals. All fires were extinguished, apart from those of the Druids, and in ancient Ireland the Druids offered sacrifices to the deities in the form of burning victims in wicker cages. The veil between the worlds of the living and the dead was believed to be at its thinnest point in the year, making communication between the two worlds easier. On the eve of the holiday, the souls of the dead freely roamed the land.

Children's pranks replaced witches' tricks in the nineteenth century, but most of the other Halloween customs are probably survivals from the Celtic festival. Many people still believe that witches and the devil have free rein to exercise their powers on this night.

◆ See Halloween p. 289

JAPANESE GHOSTS

Virtually all Japanese people believe in ghosts, caring for their dead relatives almost as if they were alive. The *shojo* are a class of Japanese ghosts believed to haunt the seas. Sailors claim these ghosts mean no harm, and enjoy offerings of sake. Less friendly to the Japanese in the Pacific was the *umi bozu*, a giant black sea phantom.

FEAST OF LANTERNS

The Japanese Feast of Lanterns (13–15 July) is a ghost festival. People offer food to dead relatives and tea is poured for the invisible guests every hour. At night, homes are decorated with beautiful lanterns fringed with paper streamers. It is believed that the spirits of the dead come home during this time, and household services are conducted for them, with special lights (lanterns) placed at the gates to guide the spirits in.

See Ghostly Shades p. 285

◀ *LEFT: The Japanese Feast of Lanterns, a ghost festival.*

SHINTO OFFERINGS

Shinto, the state religion in Japan, worships ancestral spirits of clan chieftains and venerated humans who achieved great spiritual awareness during life, or who exhibited great heroism or even great evil. The remains of such persons are enshrined, and people around the country petition them for favours and guidance.

In Shinto homes, small altars called *kamidama* ('godshelf') are kept in a prominently displayed closet. Family members pay homage to *kami* with daily offerings of rice, salt, water and food. The *kami* represent the spirits or gods of the country.

See Indian Ghostly Traditions p. 296

▶ *RIGHT: A Shinto priestess dancing at the Maple Tree Festival.*

KAMI

In the Shinto religion, gods and godlike figures, or *kami*, can be the spirits of great men. These divinised souls of deceased people (often great writers, scholars or national leaders, but also ancestral spirits of families) are regularly worshipped at shrines known as *jinja*, which contain the sacred objects where the *kami* are believed to reside. Special times for worship include important moments in the life cycle of individuals (birth, marriage, etc.) and festivals or *matsuris* that reflect the rhythm of the year: New Year, the advent of spring, rice planting, midsummer, harvesting, and so on. Each shrine will usually have its own special *matsuri* particular to its own history. On any of these occasions the shrine will be crowded with worshippers, many wanting to have their fortunes told or to receive special blessings or purifications.

◆ *See* Chinese Ghosts p. 286

NATIVE AMERICAN TRADITIONS

The traditional Native American way of life was characterised by beliefs and practices stemming from an acceptance of a universe controlled by supernatural beings and forces, with humans as junior partners. All cultures had beliefs in souls, in animistic spirits that occupied natural objects (rocks, trees, unusual land forms, bodies of water, or lightning) and in powerful, distant, usually diffuse creator beings.

In most tribes the supernaturals of greatest importance were the good and evil spirits capable of influencing aspects of human life. These spirits might inhabit caves, forests, canyons, mountains, beasts, or even other people. For a Native American to succeed in life, a constant balance had to be maintained between spirit forces and human needs, a balance made more difficult by the presence of evil spirits. The souls of the dead (ghosts) were often believed to be the most malignant of spirits.

A number of Native American cultures possessed beliefs in a diffuse supernatural power anthropologists call *mana*. This power was sought through ceremonies, vision quests, self-privation or mutilation, drugged states or dreams, control of powerful natural entities who could then lend power, or by taking medicine. Most Native Americans believed that many animals and natural objects possessed this power and if violated by humans might cause pimples, ill health, painful menstruation, accidents, bad luck, or even death.

See Aboriginal Belief in Ghosts p. 297; Ghost Sickness p. 294

THE SHAMAN

All Native Americans employed supernatural techniques with which to face most of life's unpredictable events. Part-time religious leaders known as shamans were usually consulted to effect cures. With the aid of spirit helpers, they massaged, danced, sang, smoked tobacco or took drugs to determine the cause of an ailment, generally considered to be the result of either the loss of the soul or the intrusion of a foreign object.

See Shamanic Healing p. 147

▶ RIGHT: A shaman in traditional costume.

293

DEATH CEREMONIES

After a death in some cultures, the possessions of the deceased were given away or destroyed, names forgotten, and all verbal references to the person's existence terminated. By contrast, in middle America and some adjoining areas, ceremonies accompanying death were aimed at maintaining ties with the now-powerful departed. Although much diluted, many of these beliefs and ceremonies still form part of the Native American culture.

See Ghost Dances p. 294

GHOST SICKNESS

In many tribal societies around the world, the spirit of a dead person is believed to remain close to the corpse for a few days. During this period it is particularly dangerous to the living, causing illness and death. Children are particularly susceptible to 'ghost sickness', because their souls are less strong. Among the Kwakiutl Indians of British Columbia in Canada, children are sometimes disguised or referred to as adults, in order to confuse the ghosts into thinking that they are older than they are.

See Spiritual Children p. 23

GHOST DANCES

The ghost dance refers to a type of Messianic movement that grew up among the Native American Indians. The dance evolved to express a desperate longing for the restoration of the past – a return to a life free of hunger, epidemic disease, and the bitter warring and divisiveness that accompanied the Indians' subjugation by whites. Prophets 'died', visited God, and returned with the message that the dead would soon join the living in a world where game was plentiful and all lived happily together in the old way.

▶ RIGHT: *Sioux Indians performing the Ghost Dance.*

The ghost dance belief began among the Native Nevada Indians with the revelations of the shaman Tavibo in 1870. Between 1887 and 1889 the prophet Wovoka died and returned with a ritual dance to hasten the renewal of the world and return of the ancestors. News of Wovoka's prophecies quickly reached the plains and attracted numerous followers. Ghost-dance teachings excited the Sioux at Pine Ridge, South Dakota, in particular as they were increasingly angry about reduced rations and in despair from diseases and from natural disasters that caused crops to fail and cattle to die. During the battle at Wounded Knee (1890), in which about 200 Sioux warriors, women and children were massacred, many wore 'ghost shirts' emblazoned with eagle, buffalo, and morning-star decorations. They believed that these symbols of powerful spirits would protect them from the soldiers' bullets.

The tragedy at Wounded Knee effectively put an end to the ghost dance, although some Plains tribes performed it until 1895 or incorporated aspects of the ritual into their culture.

◈ *See* Return of the Dead p. 295

RETURN OF THE DEAD

An early prophetic tradition centred in eastern British Columbia and Washington. It emphasised the imminent destruction of the world, return of the dead and change to more righteous ways, and it may have been the ultimate source of the later Messianic movement.

THE TIBETAN BOOK OF THE DEAD

In Tibetan thought, the process of dying is as important as the process of living, and the *Bardo Thodol*, the Tibetan handbook on dying, the afterlife and rebirth, involves taking a physical body through the course of dying so that it can truly perceive the spiritual world. A spiritual meditation has been developed to speed the ghosts of the dead to their afterlife. When the journey is unsuccessful, ghosts can return to haunt the body. The ghosts of the dead are celebrated throughout the dying and funerary process.

WALPURGIS NIGHT

Walpurgis Night falls on 30 April. Although it was named after St Walpurga, a lifelong crusader against evil magic, Walpurgis Night is known for witch ceremonies and heightened ghost activity. It is celebrated in Europe.

See Witches p. 146

INDIAN GHOSTLY TRADITIONS

India was believed to be populated with four types of ghosts: the *bauta*, the *paisachi*, the *virika* and the *mumiai*. It was said that seeing one of these ghosts foretold your impending death. Hindus have erected shrines throughout their country for giving gifts to these ghosts, and to Rudra, their god. Wise men were also called upon to dispel these wretched spirits. A famous spirit is the *djinn*, also known as the *jinnee* or *genie*. While not necessarily the spirit of the departed, the *djinn* is known for pranks (often done at the bidding of its master). These spirits are supposedly born from fire, or created by a crafty magician.

See Belief in Ghosts p. 16

▲ *ABOVE: A scene from a witch ceremony on Walpurgis Night.*
▶ *RIGHT: A cave painting of the aboriginal spirit Wandjina.*

HINDU SRADDHAS

These rituals for the ancestors last for 10 days. During that time the departed spirit receives food to help to survive trips through 10 different hells. On the first night of the new autumn Moon, the head of each Hindu family holds ceremonies venerating the dead of the last three generations.

ABORIGINAL BELIEF IN GHOSTS

In the traditional religious system of the Australian Aborigines, humans were believed to be a part of nature, intimately associated with other living things. This relationship underlined The Dreaming, which refers to the period when mythic spirits were believed to have shaped the land and established life. These beings were thought to live forever in spirit form and to have left tangible evidence of their presence in certain prominent land forms, which are considered sacred. Religious ritual, presided over by males but involving all members of the community, was pervasive in traditional Aboriginal life. Rituals such as elaborate funeral customs and initiation rites served to renew the participants' ties with The Dreaming, continuing the stream from which life came.

See Ancient Mysteries p. 27

THE UNEXPLAINED IN THE ARTS

GHOSTS AND THE UNEXPLAINED IN FILM

Ghosts and unexplained phenomena provide the perfect vehicle for film, which can re-create the fantastic and make it believable. Has the growth of the film industry sparked imaginations and led to our current fascination with the unknown? Are we more able to imagine and therefore see ghosts, unexplained and unexpected phenomena when we have this point of reference? Many of these films also have other themes, including gods or goddesses, spirits, miracles, and other similar ideas or depictions of extraordinary incidents. They may be combined with other genres, including comedy or horror. Interestingly, however, supernatural films are usually presented in a comical, whimsical or romantic fashion, and are often not designed to frighten the audience.

▶ RIGHT: Bela Lugosi played the lead role in the 1930 film classic Dracula.

FILMS FROM THE 1950S

Subtle, violent and magical, the Japanese classic *Ugetsu* (1953) is a superb ghost story set during a civil war in the sixteenth century. The story blends a unique mixture of action, comedy and the supernatural.

The quintessential 1950s' monster movie, *The Creature from the Black Lagoon* (1954) deals with one of the most popular of all unexplained phenomena – monsters from the deep. In this film, the creature (half man, half fish), is a vicious, woman-stealing beast. In reality, many people look rather affectionately on creatures such as the Loch Ness Monster or Ogopogo, but the idea of such life-forms existing in the dark recesses of the ocean is one that has captured the imagination of film-makers for many years.

Other recommended films:
20,000 Leagues Under the Sea (1954)
Beast From 20,000 Fathoms, The (1953)
Blob, The (1958)
Curse of Frankenstein, The (1957)
Curse of the Demon (1957)
Day the Earth Stood Still, The (1951)
Destination Moon (1950)
Donovan's Brain (1953)
Forbidden Planet (1956)
House of Wax (1953)
House on Haunted Hill (1958)
Invaders from Mars (1953)
It Came from Beneath the Sea (1955)
It Came from Outer Space (1953)
Journey to the Center of the Earth (1959)
This Island Earth (1955)
When Worlds Collide (1951)

◣ *See* Weird Creatures p. 201

▶ *RIGHT: A still from the 1954 film* The Creature from the Black Lagoon.

FILMS FROM THE 1960S

In *The Watcher in the Woods* (1962), a young girl experiences repeated sightings of another child who went missing in the woods nearly 30 years earlier (the 'watcher' in the film title).

Alfred Hitchcock's dark and brooding suspense movie *The Birds* (1963) takes nature and gives it human characteristics (and evil ones at that). A flock of birds make unexplained attacks on human beings. They are organised, tactical and inescapable. Like many of Hitchcock's films, *The Birds* is uncomfortable – an unlikely situation that somehow seems possible.

Other recommended titles:
2001: A Space Odyssey (1968)
Burn Witch, Burn! (1962)
Carnival of Souls (1962)
Damned, The (1963)
Failsafe (1964)
Fantastic Voyage (1966)
First Men in the Moon (1964)
Mysterious Island (1964)
Night of the Living Dead (1968)
Planet of the Apes (1968)
Quatermass and the Pit (1967)
Repulsion (1965)
Seconds (1966)
Village of the Damned (1960)
Voyage to the Bottom of the Sea (1961)

▲ ABOVE: The film poster from Hitchcock's terrify suspense movie The Birds.

◗ See Evil Spirits p. 273

FILMS FROM THE 1970S

Steven Spielberg's classic film *Close Encounters of the Third Kind* (1977) was a landmark in the development of science-fiction movies. Spielberg worked with a team of UFO experts in order to come up with a story that was realistic. He based many of the incidents in the film on actual case-studies of UFO sightings. The title of the film reflects a UFO classification: encounters of the third kind cover sightings of UFOs and alien beings.

A ground-breaking 1970s cinematic milestone, William H. Blatty's *The Exorcist* (1973), recounts the harrowing case of Regan, a 12-year-old girl, mentally and physically possessed and abused by a demonic spirit. The haunting, in this case, is internalised and requires religious intervention for its demise.

Other recommended titles:

Alien (1979)
Amityville Horror, The (1979)
Andromeda Strain, The (1971)
Carrie (1976)
Changeling, The (1979)
Colossus – The Forbin Project (1970)
Dark Star (1974)
Dawn of the Dead (1978)
Death Race 2000 (1975)
Deliverance (1972)
Don't Look Now (1973)
Halloween (1978)
It's Alive (1974)
Nosferatu the Vampyre (1979)
Phantasm (1979)
Silent Running (1971)
Sisters (1973)
Soylent Green (1973)
Suspiria (1977)
THX 1138 (1971)
Westworld (1973)

▲ ABOVE: The scariest film ever?
▼ BELOW: A character from *Alien*.

◆ See The Real Exorcist p. 130; Strange Sightings p. 231

FILMS FROM THE 1980S

Stephen Spielberg's project, *Poltergeist* (1982), explores the haunting of an idyllic, suburban, family home invaded by a nefarious alien force emanating from the living-room television.

Another foray into the world of the unknown by Spielberg was a fantasy adventure about a young boy who befriends an alien being who has been left behind after his spaceship has returned to his own planet. *ET: the Extra-Terrestrial* (1982) is still a popular classic – a vision of what we hope alien life forms are really like....

Other recommended titles:
2010: The Year We Make Contact (1984)
Abyss, The (1989)
Aliens (1986)
Altered States (1980)
Back to the Future (1985)
Communion (1989)
Day of the Dead (1985)
Dead Ringers (1988)
Dead Zone, The (1983)
Dressed to Kill (1980)
Dune (1984)
Field of Dreams (1989)
Ghost Story (1981)
Ghostbusters (1984)
Gremlins (1984)
Hangar 18 (1980)
Innerspace (1987)
Legend (1985)

▲ *ABOVE: ET: everybody's favourite extra-terrestrial.*

Nightmare on Elm Street, A (1984)
Poltergeist (1982)
Scanners (1981)
Somewhere in Time (1981)
Time Bandits (1981)
◨ *See* Alien Forms p. 252; Demonic Possessions p. 128

FILMS FROM THE 1990S

The Blair Witch Project (Daniel Myrich and Eduardo Sanchez, 1999, US) generated mass-hysteria with the gripping tale of three Maryland university friends who set out to film a documentary on the Blair Witch, a sinister figure reputed to have provoked horrific killings in woodlands on the town's outskirts. The film's minimalistic approach to horror makes for compelling viewing.

The Sixth Sense (1999), is one of a new generation of films about the unexplained. The film wove movie magic with the story of a child psychologist who tries to help a terrorised young boy with a macabre talent: the ability to see and communicate with ghosts. The twist in the tale made this film an instant classic.

Other recommended titles:
Blair Witch Project, The (1999)
Bram Stoker's Dracula (1992)
Contact (1997)
Dark City (1998)
Fairy Tale (1999)
Fire in the Sky (1993)
Flatliners (1990)
Gattaca (1997)
Ghost (1990)
Independence Day (1996)
Interview with the Vampire (1994)
Mars Attacks! (1996)
Men in Black (1997)
Midsummer Night's Dream, A (1999)
Outbreak (1995)

▲ *ABOVE: Pierce Brosnan in the 1996 film* Mars Attacks!.

Roswell: The UFO Coverup (1994)
Species (1995)
Starship Troopers (1997)
Timecop (1994)
◖ *See* Spiritual Children p. 23; Vampires p. 213

FILMS FROM THE 2000S

The Others (2001) is the spooky tale of a mother and her two children who live in musty manor house on a fog-enshrouded island. The mystery of the story is enhanced by its ominous setting and the understated way in which it is filmed. The twist at the end extends the story's reach from beyond the grave.

Other recommended titles:
A.I. Artificial Intelligence (2001)
Ghost Ship (2002)
Hamlet (2001)
Lighthouse (2001)
Mothman Prophecies, The (2002)
My Little Eye (2002)
Others, The (2001)
Ring, The (2002)
Shadow of the Vampire (2000)
Thirteen Ghosts (2001)
What Lies Beneath (2000)
◆ See Haunted Buildings p. 62

▲ *ABOVE: Nicole Kidman stars as Grace in* The Others.

GHOSTS IN LITERATURE

The quintessential ghost story is Charles Dickens' *A Christmas Carol*, published in 1843. Ebenezer Scrooge is haunted by the ghosts of the past, with the ghostly figures of Ignorance and Want attending the present Christmas.

Edgar Allen Poe was the master of the ghost story, and many of his works are based around local legend and ghost sightings. *The Black Cat and Other Stories* was the basis for a number of films. One of his most

◀ LEFT: *Charles Dickens'* A Christmas Carol.

famous works, *The Fall of the House of Usher* (1839), concerns sentient materiality, spiritual listlessness, possible incest and vampirism, premature burial and revenge – all common focuses of ghost activities on Earth.

Rebecca, by Daphne du Maurier, is a Gothic ghost story, published in 1938. In the novel the new Mrs de Winter is haunted by her own imagination and the ghost of her husband's former wife, the deceased Rebecca de Winter. Other ghostly titles by du Maurier include *Don't Look Now*, *The Winding Stair*, *Echoes of the Macabre*, *The Haunted Heiress (Personal Takes)* and *The House on the Strand*.

Henry James's *The Turn of the Screw* is a sinister tale of two children haunted by the ghost of a woman who feeds off their youth, bewitching and seducing them and filling their minds with evil. The tension is subtle yet inescapable, building to a dramatic and surprising climax epitomised in the age-old battle between the forces of good and evil and the power of the human mind.

A more modern but nonetheless masterful novel is Peter Straub's *Ghost Story*. It is the tale of four old gentlemen who amuse themselves by telling ghost stories. Their accounts are enough to bring the spirits back to life.

William Shakespeare incorporated ghosts into many of his plays, the most compelling of which was *Hamlet*. The ghost of Hamlet's father charges his son to avenge his death, but Hamlet is in doubt as to whether the ghost is 'an honest spirit' or a fiend sent to tempt him. In *Macbeth*, the ghost of the murdered Banquo haunts Macbeth, king of Scotland.

▲ *ABOVE: The famous ghost scene in the Shakespeare play* Hamlet.

Wuthering Heights, Emily Brontë's only novel was published in 1847, and is one of the most successful and compelling romantic ghost stories.

Sir Arthur Conan Doyle's *The Hound of the Baskervilles* was published in 1902 and spawned seven films. More gothic in tone than some of Sherlock Holmes's cases, this story includes both an apparition and a family curse. Doyle was inspired to write the story when he heard details of a West Country legend.

Theophile Gautier, one of the finest and most versatile French Romantic writers, penned a ghost story of incomparable skill in *The Dead Lover* (1836).

Best known for the novel *Robinson Crusoe* (1719), English writer Daniel Defoe was also author of *The True Relation of the Apparition of One Mrs Veal* (1706), a ghost story that he had investigated himself.

◨ *See* The Hound of the Baskervilles p. 221; Spiritual Activity p. 46; Vengeful Ghosts p. 77

▶ *RIGHT: An engraving by Holbein showing the Dance of Death.*

GHOSTS IN DANCE

The Dance of Death, also called *Danse Macabre*, *Danse des Morts* or *Totentanz*, emerged in medieval movement, theatre, art and literature as a spontaneous reaction to the hardships of the feudal system and the horrors of the Bubonic Plague, which in the years from 1347 to 1350 killed a quarter of Europe's population. Victims of plague, war, famine and poverty danced with desperate gaiety in graveyards – surrounded by skeletons, crosses, dead animals, and black draperies – as if enacting the superstition that the dead danced on their graves to lure the living. Although Death was personified in paintings, poetry and pageant as a dancer, the living dancers, originally only men, represented emperors, bishops, and peasants – equal when facing death as nowhere else. Through their macabre celebrations they confronted their mortality and championed death as the avenger over their masters and their hardships. Whatever physical form the allegorical dance assumed, it dealt consistently with death's universal inevitability, the equality of all people facing it, and the vanity of wealth and rank.

Filippo Taglioni's *La Sylphide* (1832) was a ballet for his daughter, Marie Taglioni. The supernatural subject embraced sylphs and all other ghostly spirits or folkloric apparitions.

◆ *See* Ghost Dances p. 294

GHOSTS IN THE THEATRE

Shakespeare's works have some of the best interpretations and dramatic re-enactments of ghosts. In Shakespeare's *Richard III*, the ghosts of the alleged victims of Richard III, appear to the king and his enemy Richmond on the eve of the Battle of Bosworth Field to deliver brief messages, insisting that Richard shall 'despair and die' and assuring Richmond of victory. In *Julius Caesar*, as Brutus rests in his tent near Sardis, the spirit of the assassinated Caesar appears to him, identifies itself as Brutus's 'evil spirit' and warns 'thou shalt see me at Philippi'.

Zeami Motokiyo, the foremost theorist and a principal playwright and actor of the Japanese Noh drama, wrote the now-famous ghost drama *Aoi-no-ue*.

Gothic theatre was the perfect vehicle for ghosts – apparitions, dark-robed figures in shadow and threateningly grandiose settings could be effectively depicted with ingenious stagecraft, yet the danger always remained that the physical representation of these horrors would lessen the effect that textual description could have upon the imagination of a reader. Some of the best plays include: *The Count of Narbonne* based on Horace Walpole's *The Castle of Otranto*, and *The Italian Monk* based on Ann Radcliffe's *The Italian*. Two others are plays written by well-known authors of classic gothic novels: *The Castle Spectre* was written by Matthew G. Lewis, author of *The Monk*, and *Bertram* was written by Charles Robert Maturin, author of *Melmoth the Wanderer*.

The Ghost Sonata was the third of four chamber plays that August Strindberg wrote in 1907 for his Intimate Theatre in Stockholm.

The Tragical History of the Life and Death of Doctor Faustus, written in about 1588 by Christopher Marlowe, is one of the best-known plays of the

English Renaissance and dramatises the damnation of Dr John Faustus, who sells his soul to the devil in exchange for unlimited knowledge and power.

English stage director Peter Brook's nine-and-a-half-hour production of the Indian epic *The Mahabharata* focused heavily on the ghost culture of India.

Henrik Ibsen's *Ghosts* (1881) is not specifically about ghostly hauntings, but it revolves around the emotional and physical ghosts of the past. The tragic murders of some of the characters evolve into the more traditional form of apparition.

◳ *See* Ghosts in Literature p. 306; Indian Ghostly Traditions p. 296; Vengeful Ghosts p. 77

◀ *LEFT: Dr Faustus raising the Devil.*
▶ *RIGHT:* Der Freischütz.

GHOSTS IN MUSIC

The German composer Carl Maria von Weber is best known for his romantic operas, in particular, *Der Freischütz* 'The Freeshooter', whose libretto (by Friedrich Kind), was based on a book of ghost stories. The resulting musical and dramatic mixture of mystery, love and suspense, all heightened by Weber's skilful and imaginative use of the orchestra, captivated the public at the first performance (1821) in Berlin and established romantic opera in Germany.

Boris Godunov, completed in 1869 by Russian composer Modest Musorgsky, was based on a

BIBLIOGRAPHY

Andrews, Colin and Delgado, Pat, *Circular Evidence*, Bloomsbury, 1989

Auerback, Loyd, *ESP, Hauntings and Poltergeists: A Parapsychologist's Handbook*, Warner Books, 1986

Baker, Alan, *The Encyclopaedia of Alien Encounters*, Virgin, 1999

Begg, Paul, *Into Thin Air*, David & Charles, 1979

Berlitz, Charles, *The Bermuda Triangle*, Doubleday, 1974

Bord, Janet, *Fairies: Real Encounters with Little People*, Michael O'Mara Books 1997; Dell Publishing Co., 1998

Bord, Janet and Colin, *Alien Animals*, Grafton, 1981

Bord, Janet and Colin, *Modern Mysteries of Britain*, Grafton, 1987

Bord, Janet and Colin, *Modern Mysteries of the World*, Grafton, 1989

Bord, Janet and Colin, *The World of the Unexplained*, Blandford, 1998

Brown, Slater, *The Heyday of Spiritualism*, Hawthorn Books, 1970

Clark, David, *Vanished!*, Michael O'Mara Books, 1994

Clark, Jerome, *The UFO Encyclopaedia*, Omnigraphics, 1994

Denning, Hazel M., *True Hauntings*, Llewellyn, 1996

Devereux, Paul, *Earthlights Revelation*, Blandford, 1989

Doyle, Arthur Conan, *The Coming of the Fairies*, Doran, 1922

Gauld, Alan and Tony Cornell, *Poltergeist*, Routledge and Kegan Paul, 1979

Green, Celia and Charles McCreery, *Apparitions*, Hamish Hamilton, 1975

Guiley, Rosemary Ellen, *The Guinness Encyclopaedia of Ghosts and Spirits*, Guinness, 1992

Hauck, Dennis William, *Haunted Places: The National Directory*, Penguin, 1996

Hough, Peter and Randles, Jenny, *Spontaneous Human Combustion*, Robert Hale, 1992

MacKenzie, Andrew, *Hauntings and Apparitions*, Heinemann, 1982

Moore, Bill and Berlitz, Charles, *The Philadelphia Experiment*, Grafton, 1979

Nickell, Joe and Fischer, John, *Secrets of the Supernatural*, Prometheus, 1988

Price, Harry, *Poltergeist Over England*, Country Life Limited, 1945

Randles, Jenny, *Paranormal Source Book*, Piatkus, 1996

Randles, Jenny, *The Complete Book of Aliens and Abductions*, Piatkus, 1999

Randles, Jenny, *UFOs and How to See Them*, Anaya, 1992

Spencer, John and Anne, *The Encyclopaedia of the World's Greatest Mysteries*, Headline, 1995

Tyrell, G. N. M., *Apparitions*, The Society for Psychical Research, 1973

Underwood, Peter, *Peter Underwood's Guide to Ghosts & Haunted Places*, Piatkus, 1999

Watson, Lyall, *Supernature*, Hodder & Stoughton, 1975

Watson, Lyall, *The True Life X-Files*, Eddison Sadd, 1991

Welfare, Simon and Fairley, John, *Arthur C. Clarke's A–Z of Mysteries*, HarperCollins, 1994

Wilson, Ian, *Mind Out of Time*, Gollancz, 1981

Witchell, Nicholas, *The Loch Ness Story*, Penguin, 1991

Wolman, Benjamin B., Ed. *Handbook of Parapsychology*, Van Nostrand Reinhold Company, 1977

BIOGRAPHIES & CREDITS

INTRODUCTION

Brendan Kilmartin grew up in the shadow of Stonehenge, so it was probably inevitable that he would develop an interest in the paranormal. Now, living in York, and with many years' research and study in to all kinds of unexplained phenomena, his interest has continued to grow in to a healthy obsession. He recently launched a web site, *The Supernatural World*, which is dedicated to reporting and investigating unexplained phenomena from all over the globe – and beyond.

AUTHORS

Brenda Ralph Lewis has been writing on historical and paranormal subjects for 35 years. She has written and contributed to over 100 books, including *The Unexplained Mysteries of World War II* and *Ritual Sacrifice, an Illustrated History*.

Karen Hurrell has long been fascinated by all aspects of unexplained phenomena, in particular ghosts sightings. She has written a number of books inlcuding *Natural Remedies, The Collins Gem Ghosts* and *Collins Gem Unexplained*

PICTURE CREDITS

The Bridgeman Art Library: 91

Fortean Picture Library: 45, 55, 60, 61, 103, 267, 268, 271, 272, 308, 310

Foundry Arts: 222, 225

Impact Photos: Peter Menzel: 282; Dave Young: 284; Mark Henley: 287; Nigel Amies: 290-291; Tadashi Kajiyama: 291

The Kobal Collection: Universal: 301, 302; Miramax/Canal+/Sogecine / Isasi, Teresa:306

Mary Evans Picture Library: 49, 56, 59, 72, 94, 95, 101, 113, 120, 138, 145, 151, 165, 167, 178, 184, 185, 219, 221, 224, 227, 247, 250, 285, 286, 295, 298-299, 307, 309, 311, 312; Gill Stoker: 44; Harry Price: 134; Arthur Rackham: 198, 226

Still Pictures: 104

All other pictures courtesy of **Topham Picturepoint**, and collections from Associated Press, The British Library/HIP, The British Museum/HIP, Charles Walker, English Heritage/HIP, The Image Works, Jack Kurtz/The Image Works, Keystone, Museum of London/HIP, NMPFT, Bradford/HIP, Press Association, PressNet, Public Record Office/HIP, RPS/HIP, UPPA Ltd.

GLOSSARY

Abacomancy
Predicting the future by using patterns made by dust, or by the ashes of a recently dead person.

Abduction by Aliens
Incidents reported from all over the world in which individuals allege that they have been captured by aliens from outer space and then subjected to a medical examinations.

Albasty (also known as Alma, Almasty)
Mysterious ape-like creature resembling Neanderthal Man found in the Caucasus Mountains of Kazakhstan and other Asian countries. The most recent sighting was in Mongolia in 1992.

Aeromancy
Predicting the future by studying storms, clouds, winds and other weather phenomena.

Alençon spaceman
Humanoid, reportedly from outer space, who emerged from a metal sphere said to have landed at Alençon, France, on 12 June 1790. It ran off into nearby woods and a later search failed to find it.

Apparition
The term used to describe all kinds of ghosts, whether human, animal or objects.

Area 51
Alleged secret US military base in Nevada where paranormal and alien activity is observed and logged.

Atlantis
'Lost Continent' or island which supposedly sank beneath the ocean in ancient times. First mentioned by the Greek philosopher Plato in the fourth century BC. Locations for Atlantis have included the Atlantic, the Caribbean islands and the west of North America. Often depicted as an ideal civilisation with advanced technology, including the ability to travel in space. No authenticated traces of Atlantis have ever been found.

Aura
An invisible emanation produced by a person or object.

Bennington, Vermont
City in the north-eastern United States where unexplained disappearances occurred between 1920 and 1950. One explanation, offered by local native Americans, was that this was due to evil spirits present in the area.

Bermuda Triangle
Area in the west Atlantic Ocean where thousands of ships and aircraft have reportedly disappeared without trace or explanation. First noted by Christopher Columbus during his voyage in 1492. Columbus found his compass was not acting normally and that 'dancing lights' could be seen. One possible explanation is that the irregular compass readings have placed ships or aircraft within the

Bermuda Triangle when, in reality, they were many miles away.

Borley Rectory
Reputedly the most haunted house in Britain. Located near the River Stour in Essex, reports of poltergeist and other paranormal activity became common after the Reverend Lionel Foyster and his family took up residence in 1930. By 1935, the Foysters had reported some 2,000 accounts of unexplained happenings.

Brown Lady
Eyeless elderly woman wearing a brown satin dress who was photographed floating down the stairs at Raynham Hall, Norfolk in 1936. First sighted in 1835. The Brown Lady is also said to haunt Sandringham, the Norfolk home of Queen Elizabeth II.

Clairvoyance
The ability to see into the future and make predictions of future happenings. Taken from two French words, meaning clear (*clair*) and seeing (*voyance*).

Close Encounters
Various types of encounters with aliens fall into five categories:
1) Seeing a UFO in the sky.
2) Seeing a UFO landing or hovering close by.
3) Meeting an alien.
4) Personal contact with alien forms who may communicate with humans telepathically.
6) Abduction by aliens.

Crop Circles
Circles that mysteriously appear in fields where crops such as wheat are flattened in a circular pattern.

Cryptozoology
Search for animals whose existence is unsubstantiated.

Doppelgänger
Also known as a 'fetch'. A *doppelgänger* is supposed to be the double of a living person. If people see their own *doppelgänger*, it can be an omen that they will die in the near future.

Dowsing
The search for underground water using a forked rod or stick.

Ectoplasm
Semi-liquid material that is said to flow from the nose, mouth and ears of mediums during séances.

Exorcism
Driving away spirits that have possessed human beings, by means of prayers, rituals and incantations. An exorcism is usually performed in the name of God.

Extra-Sensory Perception (ESP)
The alleged ability to obtain information about the environment without using the five senses.

Flying Saucer
Popular name for Unidentified Flying Objects.

Folklore
The fairy tales, legends, beliefs and superstitions in

which people over the ages have believed, many of which are still believed in.

Gallipoli, Turkey
Site from which an entire British Army company, the Royal Sandringham Company, disappeared in a cloud during World War I, on 12 August 1915.

Greys
The most common type of alien, as reported by abductees. Grey-skinned, up to 1.5 m (5 ft) tall, they have large heads and slanted black eyes. They resemble human foetuses at a certain stage of development.

Hauntings
A situation in which a particular place is visited over and over again by the same ghost. Hauntings may happen anywhere, from castles and houses, to ships and shops, motorways and airports. The ghost is a visible memory of the event – usually tragic, such as a death – that occurred at the place where the ghost exists.

Hallucination
An image that seems real, even though it does not physically exist.

Highway of Death
Stretch of autobahn (motorway) in Germany, built in 1930, where over 100 cars crashed when driving close to Kilometre Marker No. 239. Presuming the marker to be jinxed, it was removed and holy water was sprinkled over the spot. After this, the accidents ceased.

Lake Anijikuni
Location in northern Canada of an Eskimo village from which 2,000 inhabitants inexplicably vanished in 1930.

Medium
A person used as a spiritual intermediary between the living and the dead.

Mount Rainier
Dormant volcano, Washington State. Scene of first mass sighting of UFOs in 1947.

Nostradamus
Michel de Nostredame (1503–66), known as Nostradamus, was author of 10 *Centuries*, containing verses in which he prophesied important world events in the future e.g. the two World Wars of the twentieth century.

Out-of-body Experience
One in which a person experiences the sensation of floating outside of their own body.

Paranormal
Things that are beyond 'normal' explanations.

Parapsychology
The study of mental phenomena that have no scientific explanation.

Poltergeist
A German word meaning 'noisy ghost'. They can move objects, form cold spots in a room and produce strange sounds among other paranormal activities. Some poltergeists can be dangerous, pushing people downstairs or otherwise injuring them.

Possession
Spirits which enter individuals are deemed to 'possess' them and make them speak with strange voices or, sometimes, levitate. It is thought that these spirits are dead people and that possession is their attempt to communicate with the living world.

Precognition
The alleged ability to forsee future events.

Premonition
An intuitive feeling or vision of a future event.

Prophecy
A message of truth about the future, usually religious.

Psychic
Someone or something that is sensitive to parapsychological forces or influences not recognised by natural laws.

Psychokinesis
The alteration of an object through the power of the mind alone (also called PK).

Reincarnation
The belief that on physical death of the body the soul is born again in another body.

Remote Viewing
Technique used by 'psychic spies' in the USA to 'see' events far away and out of sight and to peruse secret documents without being caught. Remote viewing was used by both the USA and the USSR during the Cold War of 1945 to 1990.

Roswell
Town in New Mexico that was the scene of alleged alien landings in 1947.

Séance
Session during which a medium calls up the spirits of the dead so that they may speak to relatives or friends. A central event in Spiritualism.

Soul
The spirit of a person. It is not part of the physical body, and cannot be touched or seen. It is believed that

the soul is immortal, surviving after the body dies. It used to be thought that a soul that could not pass into the afterlife remained to haunt the Earth as a ghost.

Spiritualism
The belief that it is possible to make contact with the dead in the 'next world'. This is normally done through mediums who are specially gifted with paranormal skills. Spiritualism began in America in 1848.

Supernatural
Events which seem to defy the laws of nature and are, at present, impossible to explain scientifically. Telepathy, PK and ghosts all fall under this realm.

Telekinesis
The movement of an object caused by thought.

Telepathy
The communication between people of thoughts or emotions through the mind alone.

Teleportation
Movement by means of telekinesis.

Tomb, Pharaoh Tutankhamen
After discovery of the 3,300-year old tomb in 1922, numerous deaths among those involved in the excavations gave rise to talk of a 'curse' placed there by Ancient Egyptian priests to ward off grave-robbers.

UFO
Unidentified Flying Object, assumed to be a spaceship.

Vortex
A swirling mass or motion of solid, liquid or gas that has the potential to be all-engulfing.

INDEX